W9-AMW-005

The Invisible Wounds of War

ALSO BY MARGUERITE GUZMÁN BOUVARD

Healing: A Life with Chronic Illness

The Path Through Grief: A Compassionate Guide

Women Reshaping Human Rights:
How Extraordinary Activists Are Changing the World

Revolutionizing Motherhood: The Mothers of the Plaza de Mayo

The Unpredictability of Light
(winner of the Massbook Poetry Award, 2010)

Mothers in All but Name: Grandmothers, Aunts, Sisters, Friends, Strangers

Prayers for Comfort in Difficult Times

38212002967112
Main Adult
362.86 B782
Bouvard, Marguerite Guzman, 1937-
The invisible wounds of war

Marguerite
Guzmán Bouvard, 1937

The Invisible
Wounds of War

Coming Home from
Iraq and Afghanistan

WITHDRAWN
FROM THE RODMAN PUBLIC LIBRARY

 Prometheus Books

59 John Glenn Drive
Amherst, New York 14228-2119

RODMAN PUBLIC LIBRARY

Published 2012 by Prometheus Books

The Invisible Wounds of War: Coming Home from Iraq and Afghanistan. Copyright © 2012 by Marguerite Guzmán Bouvard. All rights reserved. No part of this publication may be reproduced, stored in a retrieval system, or transmitted in any form or by any means, digital, electronic, mechanical, photocopying, recording, or otherwise, or conveyed via the Internet or a website without prior written permission of the publisher, except in the case of brief quotations embodied in critical articles and reviews.

Top cover image AP Photo/Marko Drobnjakovic
Bottom cover image © 2012 Media Bakery
Cover design by Grace M. Conti-Zilsberger

Trademarks: In an effort to acknowledge the names of products mentioned in this work, we have placed ® or ™ after the product name in the first instance of its use. Subsequent mentions of the name appear without the symbol.

Inquiries should be addressed to
Prometheus Books
59 John Glenn Drive
Amherst, New York 14228–2119
VOICE: 716–691–0133
FAX: 716–691–0137
WWW.PROMETHEUSBOOKS.COM

16 15 14 13 12   5 4 3 2 1

Library of Congress Cataloging-in-Publication Data

Bouvard, Marguerite Guzmán
    The Invisible wounds of war : coming home from Iraq and Afghanistan / by Marguerite Guzmán Bouvard.
        p. cm.
    Includes bibliographical references and index.
    ISBN 987–1–61614–553–8 (pbk. : alk. paper)
    ISBN 987–1–61614–554–5 (ebook)
    1. Veterans—United States. 2. Afghan War, 2003– —Psychological aspects. 3. Iraq War, 2003–2011—Psychological aspects. 4. Afghan War, 2001– —Veterans–United States. 5. Iraq War, 2003–2011—Veterans—United States. 6. Families of military personnel—United States. 7. Veterans—United States—Services for. 8. Post-tramatic stress disorder—United States. 9. United States—Armed Forces—Military life. I. Title. II. Title Coming home from Iraq and Afghanistan.

UB357.B68 2012
362.2'5—dc22

2012013459

Printed in the United States of America

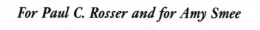

For Paul C. Rosser and for Amy Smee

CONTENTS

ACKNOWLEDGMENTS   11

INTRODUCTION   13

CHAPTER 1: THE WARS IN IRAQ AND AFGHANISTAN:
            OPERATION IRAQI FREEDOM AND
            OPERATION ENDURING FREEDOM   15
A Volunteer Army   17
Iraq   19
Afghanistan   24
Drawdown in Iraq   37
Drawdown in Afghanistan   40
The Media   44

CHAPTER 2: HOMECOMING AND PARALLEL LIVES   47
Women Warriors   62
Family Trauma   64
Taking Space   69

CHAPTER 3: MOTHERS OF SERVICEMEN
            AND SERVICEWOMEN   73

CHAPTER 4. SPOUSES AND CHILDREN OF
            SERVICEMEN AND SERVICEWOMEN   101

CHAPTER 5: THE HIGH RATE OF SUICIDES   123
The Facts   125
The Suicide of Spouses   130
People, Not Statistics   131
Noah Charles Pierce   134

Jeff Lucey   140
The Suffering of Families   149

CHAPTER 6: HEALTHCARE   153
Women Warriors   158
Walter Reed Army Medical Center in Washington, DC   160
Home Base at the Massachusetts General Hospital   165
Project Share   170
Burgeoning Charities   170
Criminal Behavior   171

CHAPTER 7: HIDDEN GRIEF   177
Why We Grieve Alone   178
Minimizing the Losses Servicemen and
    Servicewomen Experience   180
Anger and Grief   183
The Grief of Returning with Mental and
    Physical Disabilities   184
Grief of the Parents   185
Grief of a Spouse   186
Children of Servicemen and Servicewomen   188
The Healing Power of Understanding   188

CHAPTER 8: BRIDGING THE CHASM   191
Social Reintegration   192
Writing   193
Speaking the Unspeakable   194
Photography   196
Theater of War   198
The Soldiers Project   199
Give an Hour   203
Always Lost: A Meditation on War   204

EPILOGUE   211

NOTES   215

BIBLIOGRAPHY   235

INDEX   239

ACKNOWLEDGMENTS

Many thanks to my husband, Jacques, and my niece, Professor Michèle Cloonan, who provided me endless support; to Professor Kathleen O'Neill; Renée LaCasse; Samantha Powers of Military Families Speak Out; Maureen Serrecchia of the Massachusetts National Guard; Brad Saul; Dr. Isaac Schiff of the Massachusetts General Hospital; Professor Marilee Swirczek, who was one of the creators of a powerful memorial to our soldiers; and to all the wonderful servicemen and servicewomen, and their families, who have shared their stories with me.

INTRODUCTION

This book does not take a position for or against the wars in Iraq and Afghanistan. Instead, it explores the lives of US servicemen and servicewomen that have remained invisible during these wars, revealing how these wars affected them and wounded their psyches for years to come. Warriors don't just come home and reenter the life they had left behind as if they hadn't changed. They return with a war that keeps haunting their dreams, their memories, and their behavior.

It's important to realize that it's not just our troops who sacrifice their lives. It's also their entire families, parents, spouses, children, and siblings. The soldiers' homecoming is fraught with unique challenges of social reintegration and the reestablishment of family ties. Many servicemen and servicewomen return from war with psychological and emotional problems due to combat stress that may alienate them from their loved ones or cause them to become reclusive. Their families experience great anxiety while the soldiers are gone, and they have to rebuild their relationships when they return. Many wives and parents spend a great deal of their time caring for their returned family members. And the children of returning soldiers often mourn a closeness that eludes them.

Adequate healthcare for combat stress is seldom available. Returning veterans must deal with a bureaucracy that causes too many of them to wait for months or even years to be treated. During the wars in Iraq and Afghanistan, more soldiers have died from suicide than from combat. Every day, eighteen veterans from all the wars the United States has been engaged in commit suicide.[1]

Returning soldiers harbor a grief that is not widely understood. Their battalions, companies, and units felt closer to them than their own families, and many warriors have watched their buddies die from explosive devices or rocket-propelled grenades. While in combat, they did not have time to grieve because theirs was a 24-7 job. And so many soldiers return feeling numb with pain and grief.

Since our army is a volunteer one, there is a chasm between the military and civilian cultures. Few people are aware of warriors' sacrifices, of their accomplishments and their bravery. Soldiers return to a country where people are preoccupied with what may seem to them to be trivial issues and where the political debate is focused on elections, jobs, and the economy rather than on their needs.

Unlike in previous wars, there is little media coverage about combat in Iraq and Afghanistan, and especially about the needs of our warriors. To respond to this lack, a number of organizations and caring people have created innovative ways of providing returning veterans free counseling and assistance with legal matters and homelessness, and they spread the word by informing the groups that are part of those veterans' lives, such as schools, clergy, and coaches.

As a society, we need to listen to the warriors' stories and have them become part of our lives. Caring groups have created exhibits of photographs of servicemen and servicewomen that serve both as memorials and as a way of helping the civilian world relate to soldiers. Our returning troops have earned our gratitude and our respect. They deserve to be honored.

Chapter 1

THE WARS IN IRAQ AND AFGHANISTAN:
Operation Iraqi Freedom and Operation Enduring Freedom

Fig. 1.1 US unit in Afghanistan leaving with a wounded member to elude Taliban attack. *Prize-winning "C-17 at Sunrise," photo courtesy of Stacy Pearsall.*

WHAT EVERY SOLDIER SHOULD KNOW

To yield to force is an act of necessity not of will;
It is at best an act of prudence.

—Jean-Jacques Rousseau

If you hear gunfire on a Thursday afternoon,
It could be for a wedding, or it could be for you.

Always enter a home with your right foot;
the left is for cemeteries and unclean places.

O-guf! Tera armeek is rarely useful.
It means Stop! Or I'll Shoot.

Sabah el Khair is effective.
It means Good Morning.

Inshallah means Allah be willing.
Listen well when it is spoken.

You will hear the RPG coming for you.
Not so the roadside bomb.

There are bombs under the overpasses,
in trashpiles, in bricks, in cars.

There are shopping carts with clothes soaked
in foogas, a sticky gel made of homemade napalm.

Parachute bombs and artillery shells
sewn into the carcasses of dead farm animals.

Graffiti sprayed onto the overpasses:
I will kill you, American.

Men wearing vests rigged with explosives
walk up, raise their arms and say Inshallah.

There are men who earn eight dollars
to attack you, five thousand to kill.

Small children who will play with you,
Old men with their talk, women who offer chai—

and any one of them
may dance over your body tomorrow.[1]

—Brian Turner

A VOLUNTEER ARMY

In the United States, the army is a volunteer army. It is carrying the burden and experiencing the dreadful consequences of two long wars, the longest in American history: Operation Iraqi Freedom (OIF) and Operation Enduring Freedom (OEF) in Afghanistan. Most of the soldiers have been redeployed many times to make up for the low number of troops. One marine was redeployed six times despite having sustained injuries. Because these wars are fought by a volunteer army, few Americans have any personal stake in them or even know about what is happening in Iraq or in Afghanistan. Previous wars were covered extensively by the media, but only in the past few years have the efforts of US soldiers on the ground been made public. Returning soldiers should be honored and respected for their sacrifices. Learning about the hidden wounds they carry home with them is a matter of human rights, not only because their suffering is unseen but also because so many of them receive neither adequate mental healthcare nor the support they need to regain social trust and to become reintegrated into society.

People enlist in the army for a number of reasons. For example, one woman wanted to get a job and thus get away from an abusive husband. Another woman was dissatisfied with her work and thought the army might be a good place for her. For yet another young man, becoming a soldier was a way out of a dangerous neighborhood; he hoped to build a better life.

Many young people enlist for socioeconomic reasons. They are promised that they will be able to retire after twenty years. They see the military giving them money or college opportunities that once only seemed like distant possibilities. Some young men and women enlist because their parents asked them to leave home and get a job. Many who just graduated from high school are looking for a purpose in life. A number of young people enlist to get away from dysfunctional families and seek a better life.

Among those who enlisted were many young men, like Noah Charles Pierce and Alexander Hohl, who had dreamed of joining the army since they were very young because they wanted to serve their country. A young man, a classics major at Dartmouth College, decided to join the Marines in 1998. It never occurred to him that he would end up in a combat situation. He felt he should join because he was privileged. There were young men who wanted to become heroes, and many of them did, but in ways that they never expected.

The impact of 9/11 was a major factor in increasing the number of volunteers, although, contrary to the claims of the Bush administration, there was no connection between 9/11 and Saddam Hussein's regime in Iraq. Though many of those who joined the military had high hopes and a sense of purpose, a large proportion of those who came back were disillusioned and suffering from severe trauma.

National Guard units and reserve forces called up to active duty have drawn heavily on first responders. Those who volunteered often wanted to benefit from the education recruiters had promised them and that they couldn't afford otherwise. The use of the United States National Guard for overseas combat is a new role for this branch of the military. It has traditionally been used as a civil-defense branch of the armed forces, helping in domestic crises or national disasters. Yet more than 50 percent of US troops in Iraq and Afghanistan have been drawn from the National Guard forces.[2] These weekend warriors generally had full-time jobs, families, and ties to civilian communities. They were older and had a stable income before leaving for battle. But at the same time they may have lacked the intensive combat training, unit camaraderie, and strong leadership from nonactive-duty commanders. Also, in comparison with active-duty soldiers, a greater percentage have suffered from combat trauma when they returned from Iraq and Afghanistan.

For some soldiers, being in the military is a career. Perhaps over time, during the Iraqi war, some lost the sense of national purpose or sacrifice that might have helped them mitigate the hardships they experienced. But many of them were proud of what they accomplished even though the justification for the war shifted over time from hunting for weapons of mass destruction to overthrowing Saddam Hussein. In the end, they helped establish a supposedly democratic government, but one in which there is still a struggle for power among opposing Shiite groups, Sunnis, and Kurds. The prime minister of Iraq, Nour Kamel al-Maliki, is a Shiite, and the parliament does include Sunnis and Kurds, but Iraq is still suffering from recurring terrorist bombings because these factions remain at odds. Also, American influence is waning, as the military withdrew by the end of 2011, even as units of the highly secret Special Operations Forces were brought in[3] and the American embassy is being rebuilt and protected by security forces. Meanwhile, the Iraqi prime minister has expanded his power and undermined the fragile democracy America tried to help create.[4] These developments have affected the attitudes of some of the soldiers who served in Iraq in the final years of the war.

But for others, like the author-soldier Shannon Meehan, what prompted service in Iraq was a desire to put their officer training into practice and exercise leadership. Meehan's father had been in the military in several conflicts and had instilled in him a yearning for honor ever since he was a child. For a professional soldier like Paul C. Rosser, it was his duty to defend his country. And for the noted writer Brian Turner, who came from a military family, it was the desire to be part of that endeavor.

IRAQ

Saddam Hussein's Iraq was dominated by elite security units of the army, such as the Republican Guard, the Special Republican Guard, Fedayeen Saddam, and a paramilitary force, all of which were part of the huge Baath Party. The soldiers were well trained, well armed, and politically loyal, and few of them died in the war.[5] At the beginning of the US occupation, L. Paul Bremer, the president's executive director of the Coalition Provisional Authority, fired all the Baathists and disbanded the Sunni-led soldiers. That left them jobless, and it helped foment a Sunni insurgency that continues today. In so doing, Bremer helped empower the deeply religious Shiite parties that eventually came to power. He paid no attention to the intelligence reports warning that the Iranian secret police were working in Iraq. He didn't appreciate that the open border with Iran was a problem, either.[6] Yet, Sadr City, on the outskirts of Bagdhad, became one of the most dangerous places for US troops. It was named after Muktar el-Sadr's father, the Shiite leader who was killed in 1999 by Saddam Hussein's regime. There were many unemployed young men there who were placing explosive devices on the roads that US soldiers traveled. The city had a huge population that was oppressed under the Sunni regime, as well as many Iranian fighters who crossed the border to join in the battles. And there were many Shiite death squads.

Fallujah was another hostile place. Jaysh-al-Mahdi (JAM) is one of the major terrorist groups that operated there and in Diyala. It has close ties to Iran and is affiliated with the radical cleric Muktada al-Sadr. It infiltrated the local government and rose to positions of power. The mainstream media never covered it, while al Qaeda in Iraq, which was responsible for open, violent attacks, received substantial press coverage.[7] Although there were other, smaller, groups, JAM and al Qaeda were responsible for the killing of thousands of civilians and Iraqi government officials.

There was yet another terrorist group the US Army had to deal with, the People's Mujahadin of Iran (Mujahadin-e Khaliq or MEK). They were Iranian ex-patriots who fought with Saddam Hussein during the Iran-Iraq War to bring down the ayatollah of Iran.[8] Although the MEK is Shia, its main objective is to control Iran. Thus its enemy is JAM because of its connections to the Iranian military. As a consequence, it aligned itself with al Qaeda to limit Iran's influence in Iraq, which helped to destabilize both countries.

From the start of the occupation, the US Army was confronted with the country's dire need for basic services, including water and electricity. But it had insufficient troops available even to prevent the widespread looting that occurred everywhere. Soldiers looked on as people emptied hospitals, homes, museums, libraries, and universities of anything they could carry away, including ammunition and even copper wires and electrical wiring ripped from the walls. The capital city was plagued by weeks of utter lawlessness while American soldiers stood by and watched helplessly because they were stretched too thin to intervene.

There were significant barriers between the US troops and the Iraqi culture. Few soldiers, diplomats, or reporters could speak more than a few words of Arabic, and there were few translators on the ground. That meant that for many Iraqis, young US soldiers did not appear as benevolent people carrying out their country's good intentions, but rather as a terrifying combination of firepower and ignorance.[9]

As a result, there were countless instances of tragic misunderstandings. After finding a cache of weapons that was hidden under a truck belonging to suicide bombers, soldiers were under orders to stop every car approaching a checkpoint. When a car carrying a large family failed to stop as ordered because they didn't understand the word *stop*, the car was gunned down. After lifting out the dead bodies of a mother and her children from that family, one of the soldiers broke down and wept.[10] This kind of incident happened over and over again. Once a woman passed a convoy and raised a white scarf as a gesture of peace. But that gesture was misinterpreted and she was gunned down. Sometimes the reverse happened. What seemed like an innocent child playing on the side of the road turned out to be a terrorist who threw a grenade at a passing Humvee.[11]

Former Defense secretary Robert Gates, who liked to refer to himself as the Soldiers' Chief, admitted that US troops were not prepared for the Iraq and Afghanistan wars. For servicemen and servicewomen, leadership and organizational support are essential to creating stability in their lives, especially when they are deployed in combat situations. One soldier recalls being a gunner in an armored truck that had a high center of gravity.[12] It was nerve-racking because if the truck turned too quickly, it could easily turn over. He knew that IEDs (improvised explosive devices) were going off on the road and that there were frequent small-arms attacks on the street they traveled. Sometimes he would realize that he escaped death time and time again. He was given two weeks of superficial instruction, basic refresher training, and then he was sent to a base where he received more advanced training. He was originally in air defense artillery with Patriot missiles and studied air defense for a month. After that, he went to Fort Benning for three weeks, where his group was engaged in clerical tasks rather than actual training. Fort Sill, Oklahoma, where he was supposed to be relearning his job, had no relevance with what he would be faced with in Iraq. Rather than receiving weapons training, he spent his two weeks watching movies about equal opportunity and sexual harassment. By the time he arrived in Iraq, he felt completely lost and didn't feel that he was ready to meet the challenges he would face. He soon found himself behind the wheel of a truck that he wasn't qualified to drive. Despite not being prepared, he suddenly found himself in a gun turret in a combat zone. This was deeply anxiety inducing, particularly because, after he returned, he remembered how some of his best friends who went to Iraq had been blown up.

When they arrived in Iraq, many US soldiers felt that they had been trained to fight a battle against a conventional, uniformed army. They believed that the US military had such great superiority that the war would not last long, and that peace would be quickly secured and end with Iraqi elections. Instead they discovered that they were saddled with a multiplicity of goals: holding elections, making friends with local sheiks so that they could work together, providing water supplies and electricity for farms, and more. Sergeants found themselves consoling their severely wounded soldiers, going to frequent memorial services, and trying to keep up the flagging morale of their troops. Ultimately, they learned that befriending Iraqis who cooperated with them could cause the Iraqis to be killed. One soldier remembers that the home of his battalion's translator was bombed and the man and his family fled to another part of Iraq.

During the first two years of the war, Iraqi men and women would try to run for office, campaigning for votes for the first election of the new national assembly. A number of political parties were created. But then patrols began to find the bodies of those hopeful candidates after they had been tortured and killed. Frequently, Iraqis who sought to become newspaper editors, judges, or politicians were gunned down by insurgents as they went about their daily lives. Soldiers found themselves caught in a confusing war. On the one hand, they had to deal with the insurgents and militias from Sadr City. On the other, they were trying to help the country and depose Saddam Hussein.

The US military began a program to train and equip Iraqi security forces, army divisions, and police forces. But soon they discovered that one of these groups went into Sunni neighborhoods killing and kidnapping civilians.[13] A short time later, al-Sadr began an uprising, and the Iraqi civil defense garrisons, police, and National Guard disappeared.

Besides the barrier of language, there were also two realities, one of which US soldiers were unable to fathom. There were always two conversations the Iraqis were having, one telling the Americans what they wanted to hear, to make them think that they were winning and to keep the money flowing, or even bring them a little peace. Then there were the conversations in Arabic they had among themselves right in front of the US forces.[14] The Iraqis lived a double life. They were concerned with their own survival and their need to look after their children. In their neighborhoods, they were endangered from all sides.

Another notable barrier was the dress and appearance of the insurgents: "It was everywhere and it was nowhere. The Americans would bring in the heavy artillery and the troops. They would roll into Iraqi towns ready for a fight, and would invariably discover that the enemy had disappeared. Often the people they were looking for were standing a few feet away."[15]

Shannon P. Meehan, a commander and a platoon leader, was in an impossible position, a situation with no clear winner, and the enemy was much more organized than the press revealed. He and his company were not confronting a formally trained army. They kept encountering new methods of inflicting damage with minimal manpower. They didn't know who the enemy was and they never felt safe, knowing that IEDs were all along the roads they traveled and that HBIEDs (house-borne IEDs) might detonate when the soldiers were inside. Once a soldier had to carry a wounded comrade down the stairs as his buddy's blood poured into his own mouth. That was an experience he could never forget and that marked him forever.[16]

The military established the Green Zone in central Baghdad, a heavily guarded diplomatic/government area of closed-off streets where the military commanders and Iraqi politicians live and work in relative security. It was surrounded by armed checkpoints; chain-link fences; and reinforced, blast-proof, concrete walls. There were constant lines waiting to go in. One soldier was ordered to shoot an unidentified man who was waiting in line in his car. The young soldier was devastated when he found out that the man he had killed was a physician.[17] But no one could tell who was a friend and who was an enemy. Soldiers and civilians in the Green Zone lived in a false and imagined sense of security while outside, the war moved from one province to another, one village to another. There was no front line, no demarcated area where they could do battle. According to an anonymous Iraqi source, sometimes, after leaving an area, the Iraqi military would blow up an entire village out of rage for what had occurred in one house.

The soldiers lived with the sound of bombs, mortars, and explosive devices like RPGs (rocket-propelled grenades) sometimes going off more than twenty times a day. Their bases were often mortared at night. When they were in their Humvees, soldiers would hold their arms behind their backs and keep one foot in front of the other so that their arms and legs wouldn't be blasted off if their tank was hit by IEDs, EFPs (explosively formed penetrators), or RPGs. After a while, everything began to sound like a bomb—a car backfiring, a door slamming. Sometimes the only sounds they heard were bombs and the call to prayer. When there was silence, the soldiers were worried about a deadly attack in the offing.

Servicemen and servicewomen were no longer able to distinguish between certainty and doubt. They lived and worked with constant ambiguity. Because they could not tell for sure who was an insurgent and who was not, they would often end up killing innocent people. And that was an experience that would haunt them forever. So when soldiers return home, they often have lost their pride and their sense of purpose. Because they have faced so many deaths and suicides in their units, companies, or platoons, they feel numb and they try to bury their turbulent and conflicting emotions. Many of them feel that they are losing their identity. Some of them have had so many close buddies die such horrible deaths, and have seen so many horrors, that they don't care whether they live or die. It will take years after they return before they are able to care about living and to acknowledge their feelings. One veteran told his professor that he felt every soldier who returns experiences Post-Traumatic Stress Disorder.[19]

AFGHANISTAN

The Soviet Union invaded Afghanistan in 1979 and withdrew in 1989, leaving behind 1.5 million dead Afghans and millions in refugee camps in Iran and Pakistan.[20] When they pulled out, the Soviet forces also left behind a country mined and economically ruined, without infrastructure, roads, schools, healthcare, or institutions that could provide legitimate governance. The destruction of the water supply for orchards and farms ultimately led to the production of poppies and a brisk trade in drugs.

After the Soviet withdrawal, there followed a long struggle between the mujahideen and President Najibullah until the latter was finally overthrown in 1992 and the mujahideen captured Kabul. Burhanuddin Rabbani served as president from 1992 to 1996, unable to abate the civil war between Uzbek forces, Tajik forces, and a number of warlord alliances whose fighters kept changing sides, including the mujahideen. The United States trained, funded, and armed the mujahideen.[21] This turbulence paved the way for the Taliban takeover.

In 1994, Pakistan intelligence officers began funneling arms, money, and supplies, along with military advisers, to guide the Taliban in battle. The Taliban was a cross-border movement led by Pashtuns trained in madrassas, Islamic theological schools for boys, where students are sometimes taught warfare in addition to the Koran. The Taliban was unique among Afghan political movements in the exclusively clerical origin of its leaders and in the refugee origins of its followers during the Soviet war.[22] The Taliban's goals included disarming the population, enforcing Sharia law, and defending the integrity and the Islamic character of Afghanistan. Sharia, which means "path" in Arabic, guides all aspects of Muslim life, such as daily routines, familial and religious obligations, and financial dealings. The sayings practices, and teaching of the Prophet Mohammed are the basis of the Koran and the Sunna.

There are distinct schools of Islamic thought. The Hanbali school, the orthodox form of Islam, is embraced in Saudi Arabia, where it is known as Wahabi, and it is also embraced by the Taliban.[23]

By 1996, the Taliban effectively controlled Afghanistan. They imposed strict enforcement of fundamentalist Islamic law and provided a haven for Osama bin Laden, a founder of al Qaeda. Osama bin Laden, an outspoken critic of the United States, fled his native Saudi Arabia in 1991 to Sudan, where he formed and financed al Qaeda as a militant Islamic revolution.

After 9/11, President George W. Bush declared that the United States was now at war with international terrorist organization and gave the Taliban an ultimatum to hand over Osama bin Laden. When it refused, the United States joined forces with the Northern Alliance, a collection of rebel groups that didn't accept Taliban rule and represented minority tribes. Shortly thereafter, the president demanded that President Pervez Musharraf of Pakistan support the US policy. The government of Pakistan switched sides from helping the Taliban to supporting the United States' invasion because it feared that its refusal might entail being bombed, having its nuclear facilities threatened, and having the United States create military bases in India, Pakistan's long-standing enemy.

On October 7, 2011, Operation Enduring Freedom began with heavy US bombing raids on Taliban bases and infrastructure across the country and against the Taliban troops outside Kabul defending a long front line against the Northern Alliance forces. Some of the first major combat of the war occurred in the mountains near Mazar-e-Sharif, where US forces were working with the Northern Alliance. The terrain and conditions were astonishing and extremely difficult for American servicemen and servicewomen. They trudged on mountain paths bordered by thousand-foot precipices. Since even four-wheel-drive vehicles couldn't maneuver on those winding mountain trails, they used horses to carry their equipment. Many of these troops had never ridden horses. Because of the sheer drop-off, they were told to keep one foot out of the stirrups so that if the horse stumbled, they could fall on the trail as the horse slid off the cliff.[24]

The first forays against the Taliban were in northern Afghanistan because Tajik and Uzbek opposition to the Pashtun regime was strongest there. The fall of Mazar-e-Sharif ended the Taliban's hold in northern and central Afghanistan. Only two months after the September 11 attacks, the strategically most important city, Kabul, was conquered. Within a month, the Taliban were routed, and soon after northern, western, and central Afghanistan fell to the Northern Alliance as the Taliban retreated to Kandahar in the south.

Afterward, Special Operations Forces advanced from the south toward Kandahar. Elements of the US 101st Airborne Division and 10th Mountain Division were involved. They faced insurgent fighters equipped with sniper rifles, machine guns, recoilless rifles, RPGs, and man-portable air defenses (MANPADS). The terrain lent itself for enemy fighters to hide in caves and along steep ridgelines. An al Qaeda manual captured by US troops during combat outlined the utility of rugged terrain for defeating large forces. The valley was eventually cleared of al Qaeda, but at a steep price in casualties as the insurgents shot down helicopters and killed American troops.[25]

Hamid Karzai, a relative of the exiled former king of Afghanistan took office as interim president in 2002. Following the 9/11 attacks, he was one of the few Pashtun commanders who took the risk of rallying the Pashtuns against the Taliban. Hamid Karzai was elected to a five-year term in 2004. He won with a high rate of approval. Although the Afghan people hoped that the new president would provide good governance and economic progress, they were soon disillusioned because aid never reached the many small villages that define the country.[26]

Months after winning the war in Afghanistan, US troops were training for the invasion of Iraq. Special Operations Forces were pulled out of key locations in Afghanistan where they were hunting members of al Qaeda. The US military focus on Iraq meant that Afghanistan had to use National Guard forces rather than active-duty soldiers to train Afghan National Army soldiers.[27] Ahmed Rashid, who has written widely about the Taliban, saw Afghanistan as the victim of the Bush strategy of diverting US resources, including funds and troops, to Iraq. In keeping with that decision, Americans made deals with the newly installed Northern Alliance, even though the majority of its members participated in the 1990s civil war and were hated by the Afghanis.[28]

After they were routed, the Taliban, al Qaeda, and the Haqqani slipped across the Pakistan border into Baluchistan, the Federally Administered Tribal Areas (FATA), and the Northwest Frontier Province, where they established new camps. The Haqqani is a group within the insurgency in Afghanistan that has maintained strong connections with Pakistan's ISI (the Inter-Service Intelligence) for decades.[29] Ynuis Khais Haqqani, the son of the founder of the organization, is fluent in Arabic and raises a great deal of money from Saudi Arabia and the Persian Gulf. He established a close relationship with Osama bin Laden in the 1980s. The Haqqanis run a network of madrassas and training bases, and they have invited foreign fighters from Pakistan, Uzbekistan, Chechnya, Turkey, and Middle Eastern countries into Afghanistan.[30]

Over the years, these insurgent groups recruited, rearmed, contacted supporters abroad, raised money, and planned their return to power. Yet until 2006, the United States failed to deploy sufficient troops to counter them or to maintain satellite surveillance of the south, where the Taliban was free to come and go unchallenged.

Although the United States was initially successful in removing the Taliban, it focused on killing Osama bin Laden rather than on stabilizing the countryside or rebuilding the economy and the shattered infrastructure. Also, it defined its strategy on the belief that stability could be achieved by helping create a strong central government, a policy that was difficult to achieve. Meanwhile, the Taliban began long-term efforts to conquer the real Afghanistan: tribes, subtribes, clans, and local institutions that were scattered in the mountains and valleys. For centuries, the country's terrain and population have prevented conquerors from dominating it.

Afghanistan is one of the most ethnically complex countries in the world. It includes overlapping cultures, languages, and tribal loyalties. Eighty percent of its people live in remote villages. The capital (Kabul), Kandahar, and the ancient city of Herat are the major cities where the rest of the population resides. Besides the Pashtun majority, ethnic groups include Tajik, Uzbek, Hazara (descendants of Mongols), Hindi, Kirghiz, and Turkomen. The major languages are Pashto and Dari, a dialect of Persian. There are seven languages, and many Afghans are multilingual. They do not consider their multiple ethnicities as impeding their national sovereignty.

By 2004, US intelligence officers concluded that Pakistan's ISI was running a training program for the Afghan Taliban, allowing them to raise funds like the Haqqanis in Pakistan and in the Persian Gulf and letting them import arms and ammunition from Dubai. Mullah Omar and senior Taliban leaders operated and held frequent meetings in the villages around Quetta, Pakistan. US troops reported to their superiors that the Pakistan army was protecting the Taliban on the Afghan Tajikistan border as they were either infiltrating Afghanistan or returning to Pakistan after a battle.[31] In 2003 and 2004, the Taliban were conducting low-level insurgency from bases in Pakistan. Insurgents also began attacking Afghans involved in election work, nongovernmental (NGO) workers, and Afghan citizens cooperating with Coalition forces of the Afghan government.

Zalmay Khalilzad, a former member of the National Security Council took over as US ambassador in late 2003. He was an Afghan who had lived in the United States for many years but was well qualified to develop a new political-military strategy to help rebuild Afghanistan. He worked closely with Lieutenant General David Barno, the commander of US forces there. Their goal was to disarm, demobilize, and reintegrate the militias in order to weaken the warlords.[32] This strategy shifted the US goal from counter-terrorism to nation building and counterinsurgency. Lieutenant General Barno assigned forces to territories where they were intended to secure the population and had achieved excellent early results.[33] Yet, in 2005, the State Department reassigned Zalmay Khalilzad to Iraq as the US ambassador, despite the fact that he had been one of the most effective ambassadors to Afghanistan because he spoke Pashto and Dari and had special relations with Afghanistan's political leaders. General David Barno was replaced by Lieutenant General Karl Eikenberry, ending the military-civilian coordination Khalilzad and Barno had carefully developed during their tenure.

Meanwhile, the military campaign by the Taliban demonstrated its expertise with new weapons and tactics. Trained by al Qaeda fighters from Iraq, it had improved its ambush tactics—its use of IEDs and suicide bombers to carry out attacks in urban areas and against troop convoys. Despite President Karzai's warning to President Bush that the Taliban was a growing threat and a greater regional challenge than al Qaeda, the United States directed all of its military efforts at trying to capture al Qaeda members. President Bush's close staff ignored the Taliban threat and the steady growth of insurgent violence throughout 2005, and it was not until 2006 that the United States began to engage the Taliban in combat.[34]

In 2008, the Taliban reentered the provinces surrounding Kabul from which they had been driven in 2001. The United States sent its forces to those provinces to safeguard the major roads that ran out of Kabul to the provinces. They were successful in opening the roads and increasing security in these areas.

Although Iraq claimed national attention during the US presidential election campaign of 2008, Barack Obama, as the Democratic candidate, promised to make Afghanistan his principal focus, and he criticized President Bush for overlooking the causes of international terrorism that lay in Pakistan and

Afghanistan. It was not until Barack Obama became president that the United States began sending the needed troops and funding and developing a new strategy. However, during that election campaign, the Taliban launched high-visibility suicide attacks in the cities, engaged in guerrilla assaults in the countryside, and increased its use of IEDs. For the first time, more Western troops were dying in Afghanistan than in Iraq.[35]

As soon as President Obama took office, he reviewed US policy toward Afghanistan and Pakistan, consulting with all branches of government, especially the military. His new policy promised major attention to Afghanistan and Pakistan. A new US Army doctrine established that stabilizing war-torn countries was just as important as defeating the enemy militarily.[36]

In 2009, the United States sent twenty-two thousand marines into southern Afghanistan, including military trainers, to intensify the build-up of the Afghan army and police. In 2010, President Obama launched a surge, sending thirty thousand additional troops to Afghanistan with the goal of forcing the Taliban out. This decision was backed by former secretary of defense Robert Gates and Secretary of State Hillary Clinton, but it was opposed by Vice President Joseph Biden, as well as by some of the president's political advisors. The latter advocated a more rapid exit strategy, keeping in place a force focused on counterterrorism and the training of Afghans.

As in Iraq, US soldiers sent to Afghanistan were unprepared for the language and cultural differences and for fighting in a terrain unlike any they had ever seen before. Many of those who are being redeployed don't want to return. Yet even soldiers who are suffering from psychological problems are being redeployed because there are too few available troops to afford giving them sufficient rest time in the United States. Some soldiers are aware that their comrades have come home with a myriad of problems, and they are worried that the same thing will happen to them. They worry that they too will feel numb, have difficulty making the transition home, and incur both physical and psychological damage. It is difficult for them to leave their families and not to see their children grow up.[37]

There are a few soldiers who want to be redeployed even though they were wounded by IEDs. Perhaps they wish to be redeployed because it is difficult for them to return to civilian life, to what has become an unfamiliar world in which their combat skills cannot be easily applied to other careers. One army wife described her husband's desire to be redeployed as "an addiction."[38]

As in Iraq, US units in Afghanistan don't have enough people who can serve as translators. One battalion had only two of them for forty soldiers.[39] American soldiers have difficulty maintaining a feeling of trust with the Afghan police with whom they work. Some of them are illiterate, and as soon as some are paid, they disappear. They are unreliable partners who sometimes skip planned missions or flee as soon as the shooting begins. The allegiances of the district police chiefs are also frequently unclear. In one instance, a police chief was using his men to help his brother, who was running for reelection in the parliament. And there were rumors connecting the chief's family to militias that smuggled drugs and weapons across the Tajikistan border.[40]

US troops were not prepared for the type of warfare they encountered, an insurgency that crossed borders and involved groups working hand in hand. Although they wore sixty pounds of gear that protected them, the vehicles they rode in, while useful in climbing winding and difficult roads, became death traps as explosive devices ripped through their light armor. Under former secretary of defense Robert Gates, some mine resistant vehicles have been developed. The Department of Defense is testing a revamped version of the Humvee equipped with a chimney to vent blasts from IEDs. The chimney, which rises through the passenger cabin, is intended to funnel some of the explosive gases that travel at supersonic speed and have flipped and mangled many of the conventional vehicles.[41] However, it will take years to make them available to servicemen and servicewomen. Thus, US and Coalition forces encounter hidden explosive devices too many times a day, use unsafe vehicles, and engage in combat along with the soldiers of a weak government in Afghanistan.

Hamid Karzai won reelection in 2009, but he exercises little control over the country and tends to remain secluded in Kabul. The hundreds of diplomatic cables obtained by WikiLeaks and released in December 2010 show that bribery, extortion, and embezzlement are the norm within the Karzai regime. They also include allegations of bribes and profit skimming in pilgrimages to Saudi Arabia, in purchases of wheat seed, and in economic aid. Many of the federally administered tribal areas, such as Waziristan, comprise isolated villages that, for years, never received any aid from the government and therefore do not support the Kabul regime. In those villages, when US soldiers seek out insurgents, they find the paths lined with IEDs. Sometimes they succeed in removing them, but it is not an easy task. They often get wounded or killed while the insurgents observe them from behind bushes in nearby fields. Even if they succeed in clearing an area, the Taliban or al Qaeda or another insurgent group soon returns.

There are Afghans who wonder why Americans occupy their country and who would like to see them to leave. Among them is Malalai Joya, who is widely known and celebrated for her important effort in providing education and healthcare for girls and women in concealed areas that are safe from the Taliban. Her mission is to liberate women and girls from Sharia practices that require them to remain at home, unseen and uneducated, and only able to appear in public when accompanied by a male relative. These are just a few of the Sharia rules governing the conduct of women: They must not wear adorning clothes. They must not wear narrow and tight clothes. They must not walk in the middle of streets. They must not talk to strange men, and if it is necessary to talk, they must do so in a low voice and without laughter. They must not look at strangers or mix with strangers. There are many more regulations that oppress women and girls. Malalai Joya's goal is also to bring down Gulbuddin Hikmetyar, who is one of the insurgents most hated by Afghan villagers and who is also a strategic ally of Pakistan and one of the leaders of the Taliban.[42]

At the 2007 World Economic Forum, Malalai Joya was named one of the 250 Young Global Leaders and nominated for the European Parliament's Sakharov Prize for Freedom of Thought. In 2005, she was the youngest person elected to Afghanistan's new parliament and, two years later, she was suspended for her persistent criticism of the warlords and drug barons. She voiced her anger about the fact that since the United States' invasion of Afghanistan, thousands of civilians have died from gunfire, mortars, bombings, and the ubiquitous IEDs.[43] The fact is the media do not cover the number of civilian casualties, most particularly those resulting from drone attacks.

The parliamentary elections that took place in November 2010 were rigged and thus exacerbated ethnic tensions.[44] The Taliban threatened Pashtun voters, ordering them to boycott the election. As a result, the Pashtuns lost 15 percent of their seats to the Hazaras and Tajiks. Thus these two minorities have achieved advantages that cause resentment among the Pashtuns. The Tajiks and Hazaras dominate the upper officer class in the army and police, even though the training and recruitment given by the United States involves a strict parity between ethnic groups. Traditionally the Afghan officers have been Pashtun. A Tajik general, Atta Muhammad Noor, and his fellow northern warlords are rearming their militias for a long war with the Taliban.[45]

However, as with the police, the attrition rate from the Afghan Army is 24 percent per year, most of them are illiterate, and drug use is a major problem. Although 80 percent of army units are fighting along with coalition forces, no single Afghan unit is ready to fight on its own without American help.[46] This leaves US soldiers with the responsibility to deal with many political tensions without much support from the population in trying to deal not only with the Taliban but also with many other different insurgents.

Besides tension between ethnic groups, there are also many other militias and gangs that go marauding through the country. They are referred to as *arbekais*, armed groups including semiofficial militias organized and paid by Afghanistan's intelligence service.[47] These gangs go through villages demanding food, shelter, and money from the local population. Some of these are headed by former mujahideen that once fought against the Soviet Union. Others are created by village elders. Others in Takhar Province provide protection for warlords who traffic narcotics along a drug transport corridor that runs to the Tajik border. These groups and growing disenfranchisement of Pashtuns make the Taliban more attractive to those already disillusioned with the government. Since the government hasn't protected people from either the Taliban or the militias, villagers feel caught between the two.[48]

In the spring of 2011, the United States launched a program considered by General David Petraeus, the former commander of US forces in Afghanistan, as a key part of his counterinsurgency strategy. Its goal is to convert insurgents into village self-defense forces, an Afghan Local Police that is distinct from the existing police force. It is organized and trained by the US Special Forces units in cooperation with the Afghan authorities and working at the village level. But they are paid half of what the national police officers earn. The local police who are intended to lure members of the Taliban into their cause are raising money the same way as the Taliban, by imposing an "Islamic tax" on people in their districts.[49] This has created a public outcry. During their meetings, elders and provincial government officials have expressed their concern. Many Afghans fear a return to the warlord days of the civil war of the 1980s even more than they fear the Taliban. A recent study by Oxfam and three other aid groups reported that the program had failed to provide effective community policing and, instead, produced forces feared by the communities they are supposed to protect.[50] For example, in Kunduz Province, armed thugs acting as local police even before they had completed their training were demanding their taxes just as farmers were harvesting their crops. The headmaster and assistant headmaster of a girls' school in Kunduz City, the provincial capital, refused. Two commanders along with thirty armed men stormed the school, beating both men unconscious with rifle butts in front of the students, and closed the school. A United Nations Report expressed concern regarding weak oversight, recruitment, vetting, and command-and-control mechanisms.[51]

As Iraq has an open border with Iran, Afghanistan has an open border with Pakistan, a country that harbors the Taliban and other insurgent groups.[52] Pakistan-based militants can cross unchallenged into Afghanistan while Pakistan's authorities refuse to shut down the sanctuaries used by militants to rest and resupply. The ISI is known to support the militants, including the Taliban, the Haqqani, and al Qaeda, and even Lashkar-e-Taiba (the Army of the Pure), the faction that the United Sates believes was responsible for the terrorist attacks in Mumbai in 2008 and in 2011.[53] Intelligence experts consider Lashkar to be even more of a threat in Afghanistan than al Qaeda because its operatives come from the region and are less readily identified or resented than al Qaeda's Arab ranks.[54] Even though the government of Pakistan claims that, under pressure from the Bush administration, it severed ties with Lashkar in the wake of the September 11, 2001, attack, the ISI still maintains its connection with it.[55] The Obama administration has estimated that Lashkar-e-Taiba has the capacity to quickly and inexpensively train young men from villages to be driven and proficient killers.

In Pakistan, domination by militants occurred in late 2006 after General Ali Muhammad Jan Aurakzai, the governor of the Northwest Frontier Province, brokered an agreement with Islamic districts. Since then, it has been ruled by Jalaluddin Haqqani, who created an alliance with the Taliban Movement of Pakistan.[56] General Ashfaq Parvez Kayani, who was formerly head of the ISI, views the Afghan Taliban as a means to ensure influence on the other side of the border and to keep India's presence there at bay. He also has close relations with Mullah Muhammad Omar, the spiritual leader of the Taliban.[57]

Even though America cultivates Pakistan's top military leaders and provides long-term development aid, the Taliban, al Qaeda, and Lashkar increasingly act as a syndicate, sharing skills and information. Besides, Pakistan is more concerned with its rivalry with India over Kashmir and with India's strong presence in Afghanistan than with the war in Afghanistan.[58] There have already been two major wars between these two countries over Kashmir. Further, in 2010, Pakistan closed its border to Afghanistan for weeks on end, keeping long lines of American fuel-supply trucks waiting at the border crossing and making them easy targets for terrorists to blow up.

Pakistan's economy is in deep trouble owing to bad management, widespread corruption, rising Islamic religious fervor, and worsening relations with the United States, its biggest financial supporter. Its turmoil is caused by a mixture of religious ideology and economic despair. It is also fueled by class differences, lack of support for the government, and resentment toward the landed and industrial classes. The government takes in little in taxes and provides few services to its people. During the catastrophic floods in July 2010, Islamic groups were bringing aid to the millions who were affected while the government provided virtually no relief.[59]

Since the May 2011 Navy Seal raid that killed Osama bin Laden in Abbotabad, his Pakistan hideaway, American officials have grown even more distrustful of that country.[60] The Pakistan military that, in effect, rules the country and has been deeply embarrassed by that raid, wants to alter its relations with the United States. While Americans at home cheered about the raid and wanted to increase pressure on Pakistan to break relations with militant networks, General Kayani was pursuing a strategy aimed at decreasing the United States' influence over his country while keeping the billions of dollars of American aid flowing in. In addition, the Pakistani government is already reaching out to China and Iran in search of new allies.[61]

There are many centers of power in Pakistan, which are often difficult to fathom or to criticize without creating diplomatic strains. For example, shortly after the killing of Osama bin Laden, al Qaeda commandos managed to overrun Pakistan's largest naval base and kill a dozen naval personnel.[62] There was also a suicide bombing in Islamabad, Pakistan's capital, the first one to take place in over a year and which was believed to be an act of revenge by the Taliban.[63]

General Kayani, who is the most powerful figure in Pakistan and has led the army since 2008, is now fighting to save his position and to respond to the outrage among the XI Corps commanders who are demanding that he get tougher with the United States.[64] The ISI, headed by Lieutenant General Ahmed Shuha Pasha, Kayani's partner, is also edging toward a break with the United States. It arrested more than thirty Pakistani informants who had helped the CIA in tracking bin Laden and ordered 120 US military trainers to leave the country as a way to express its anger over the US operation. Both leaders want to end CIA drone attacks against militants in tribal areas.[65]

The anger and disillusionment in the Pakistani army stem from the fact that the Obama administration decided against informing Pakistan in advance about the bin Laden raid. Thus Pakistan was unable to detect or stop it. That bin Laden was living in Pakistan caused little outrage in a country that is more sympathetic to al Qaeda than to the United States.[66] In fact, the US Navy officer who led the raid against bin Laden told senators that he had reasons to believe that Mullah Muhammad Omar, the Taliban's spiritual leader, was also hiding in Pakistan.[67]

There were other incidents by Pakistan's leaders that exposed their support of the militants and caused the United States to drastically cut its military aid.[68] A Pakistani journalist who wrote a scathing report about the infiltration of militants into the country's military was abducted from the capital three days after the publication of his article. The article revealed that al Qaeda was responsible for the commando attack on Pakistan's main naval base as a reprisal for the navy's arrest of naval personnel who had belonged to an al Qaeda cell. The journalist's mutilated body was found in a canal, and the ISI denied accusations published in the Pakistani news media that it had been responsible for the murder.[69]

Yet other events caused the United States to reevaluate its support of Pakistan. On four occasions, factories that produced bombs were evacuated shortly after American intelligence officials notified Pakistan's ISI of their existence. This caused suspicion that such intelligence was being shared with the insurgents. All of these factories produced IEDs that are the most frequent killers of US troops in Afghanistan. As a way to pressure the Pakistani government to end its support of the militants and to chasten the Pakistan military, the Obama administration is suspending or canceling hundreds of millions of dollars in aid, representing over one third of the more than $4 billion in US assistance. That move, it is hoped, will cause the Pakistani army to fight militants more effectively. It is indicative of the seriousness of the debate raging within the Obama administration over how to change the behavior of one of its key counterterrorism partners.

Because the United States is eager to withdraw from Afghanistan and is concerned about Pakistan's role as a nuclear power, it needs to avoid a rupture of relations like the one that occurred in the 1990s when it imposed sanctions on Pakistan over its development of nuclear weapons. Pakistan's military and the rest of the country are still bitter about the United States' cut-off of all military aid at that time. Although President Obama has shown that the days of unconditional support are over, he needs to keep working with Pakistan's leaders. In addition, Pakistan offers several strategic advantages, such as access to the Arabian Sea and the Persian Gulf and the opportunity to be engaged in pipeline projects transiting to the ocean through Afghanistan and Pakistan. It also serves as a counterweight to the neighboring powers of India, China, and Russia.

American policy needs and its ongoing differences with the Pakistan military have resulted in a very trying situation for US soldiers on the ground. American servicemen and servicewomen have been called upon to perform so many different duties at the same time, such as consoling wounded buddies, dealing with village elders, keeping in constant contact with helicopters to evacuate those who need immediate medical treatment, intercepting radio chatter, digging up and then detonating mines, interrogating prisoners, keeping surveillance of fighters' funerals, and recovering Taliban documents.

They are dealing with the Taliban, an organization that is widespread and unseen. Again, there are no clear perimeters or a front line for the fighting. As in Iraq, the battle is nowhere and everywhere. Like JAM in Iraq, the Taliban is an underground government of local fighters who have established a civilian administration to complement their fighting activity. They run schools, collect taxes, and adjudicate civil disputes in Islamic courts. Their combat is aided by intelligence and support networks that include villagers who inform them and provide shelter in tunnels where they can elude capture and receive medical care. The villagers signal movements of battalions' patrols with mirrors or smoke signals. The members of the Taliban are able to disappear by slipping away in canals or village alleys. And their supporters give false information to US troops. An American sweep of a village turned up a detailed terrain model of an FOB (forward operating base) where the battalion's headquarters are located. Suicide bombers infiltrate seemingly secure areas, exploding their mortar shells that can strike soldiers that are sleeping, standing in a shower, jogging around an airfield, or at meetings—all moments when soldiers are not wearing their sixty-pound protective gear. Local civilians who help Afghan and American troops are identified and assassinated by the Taliban, which operates a vast spy network.[70] Taliban fighters harass Afghan and American forces and lead a campaign of intimidation against residents who cooperate with or even acknowledge the Kabul government. Dressing as civilians, they engage in ambushes, set up IEDs, and conduct mortar attacks. Often wearing the uniforms of Afghan soldiers or police, they blow up buildings housing members of the Afghan government and Allied forces.

Besides dealing with well-organized insurgents, US soldiers are also involved in hearts-and-minds projects—helping to run schools, giving out cash to people in remote villages who can't find work. Mike Mullen, the former chairman of the Joint Chiefs of Staff, visited some of these schools, including those that Greg Mortenson has been building throughout the country, and voiced support for his work.[71] In 2004, the United States deployed one of eight military units known as Provincial Reconstruction Teams (PRTs) in Helmand. It sought to combine efforts to provide security, create small reconstruction projects, and help Afghan government officers build schools and health clinics and create jobs.[72] But two years later, several Taliban attacks shut down these American projects across the province, destroying America's most successful undertaking.

To make matters even more difficult, President Karzai has been pursuing conflicting policies from the United States, and this led to tensions between the two countries. On the one hand, he supports US efforts to train the Afghan army and police, while on the other, he has opened secret negotiations with the Taliban.[73]

There are two views of the war, the one in Washington, where policy is made; and the one on the ground in the crucial provinces of Helmand and Kandahar, where many US soldiers would prefer a quick withdrawal because they find that the Taliban continually retakes areas they have cleared. The Taliban routinely launches RPGs at a number of bases every night at ten o'clock. Thus, the war is one of conflicting stories one hears from the head of the US forces—General Petraeus—or a soldier crouching in a ditch outside a village. As usual, the governments of the Coalition forces only talk about policy, the big picture of the Afghan war, not the travails that soldiers face in combat and that make the war so difficult to pursue.[74]

DRAWDOWN IN IRAQ

Although President Barack Obama has officially declared that the US combat mission has ended and that American forces are now supposedly in an advisory role until their withdrawal from Iraq scheduled for the end of 2011, they were still in harm's way whether on their bases or moving around. Nearly a year after President Obama's declaration, American soldiers were still deeply engaged in fighting on two fronts: against Sunni insurgents in the Sunni-dominated areas north of Baghdad and against Shiite militias.

In June 2011, US forces suffered their biggest toll in three years. The casualties resulted from rocket or mortar attacks on US bases by Shiite militias and from increasing threats by IEDs on US convoys. Because of the security agreements between Iraq and the United States, American forces are restricted in their ability to act on their own to confront security threats. This creates a high level of anger and anxiety among the US troops who find themselves under attack but are unable to respond. They are also reluctant to target Shiite militias since they are linked to officials in the Shiite-dominated government.[75]

To make matters worse, the flow of arms from Iran to Iraq has increased along with Iranian influence. Weapons smuggled from Iran are being used against American troops by Shiite militias. The Maliki government's unwillingness to rein in the Shiite militias adds a new element to the discussions between the US and Iraqi governments. Those discussions are focused on the capabilities of the Iraqi security forces and on domestic political considerations in Washington and Baghdad, and not on the safety of US troops.[76]

Although the intention of the United States was to help create a democratic government in Iraq, power is rigidly contested on sectarian lines, a situation the de-Baathification policy helped to create. The unequal response by Iraqi security forces to threats from Sunni and Shiite insurgent groups is a legacy of the sectarianism that the US invasion unleashed. Deadlock occurs frequently with each community unwilling to compromise. Many Iraqis believe that the de-Baathification policy and disbanding the entire military in Iraq helped fuel the insurgency that pushed the country into sectarian conflict. Eight years after the United States–led invasion, there were still bombings and assassinations in Iraq almost every day. Yet almost everyone in Iraq regarded the United States as the arbiter even though Iraqi politicians ritually objected to its intervention, especially when it did not reflect their individual interests. The continuing US presence created a very complex and often-contradictory situation.[77] Special Operations Forces were sent there in 2011, but their mission is top secret. Also, depending upon political developments such as parliamentary elections, some sects have insisted that the US presence is needed while others increased their popularity by demanding that "the occupation ends."[78] This left not only US diplomats but also, even more, US soldiers in an extremely difficult position. Until they are finally withdrawn, they will still face an enemy, need to defend themselves, and continue to suffer casualties.

In August 2011, the powerful Shiite, anti-American cleric, Muqtada al-Sadr threatened to have his thousands of followers attack any United States troops that stayed past the December 31, 2011, withdrawal deadline. This threat followed the Iraqi government's decision to open talks with Washington about maintaining some troops in Iraq past the deadline. Worried about a potential backlash, Iraqi officials once tried to characterize American soldiers who would remain as trainers of the Iraqi military, not as combat troops. But

American servicemen and servicewomen not only are involved in training but they also assist in Iraqi counterterrorism operations. While security is improving, attacks against US service personnel are still common. June 2011 was one of the bloodiest months for the US military over the past two years.[79]

August 15, 2011, proved even worse, as forty-two coordinated attacks occurred across Iraq against civilians, security forces, and US soldiers. These widespread attacks compared with an average of fourteen attacks daily during this year and suggested that the Sunni insurgents, al Qaeda in Mesopotamia, were growing in power. The attacks occurred two weeks after the Iraqi government agreed to negotiate with the United States about the possibility of maintaining some troops in Iraq after the end of the year. A professor of political science at Baghdad University declared that the Iraqi security forces were more loyal to al Qaeda and to the Shiite militias than to the Iraqi government, and that the Iraqi army was not capable of protecting the country.[80]

The United States will be leaving behind a country that does not have a representative government and is caught in the throes of a civil war. In addition, Iraq has aligned itself with Iran and Syria despite the uprising in Syria that has turned many Arab countries against it. Again, the Sunni and Shiites have differing views on the demonstrations in Syria because of Syria's multireligious and ethnic fabric. Under these conditions, keeping a reduced number of American troops in Iraq does not bode well for Iraqi security.

On October 21, 2011, President Obama declared that all American troops would be "home for the holidays," and that only the usual number of troops stationed at American embassies around the world would remain. The decision was an unstated acknowledgement that the Iraqi government refused to agree to a key US condition for leaving American troops behind: immunity from Iraqi law. Some Iraqis in office feel that the consideration of Iran is now important, and many feel that freedom from Saddam Hussein was something to be celebrated, but that afterward they did not like being occupied.[81]

The United States is also scaling back diplomacy in Iraq because of fiscal concerns. For example, the State Department had a plan for 350 contract workers for a police training effort; now the figure is close to 100. There will now be ten Offices of Security Cooperation to manage the sale of weapons and training instead of the planned fifteen.[82] These results reflect the lack of interest in a Congress that is consumed with domestic issues. Even so, the war in Iraq will be a subject of contention in the United States for many years to come.

As of October 22, 2011, the Department of Defense identified 4,469

American service members who have died since the start of the Iraqi war and 32,213 that were left injured.[83]

DRAWDOWN IN AFGHANISTAN

In July 2011, President Obama announced that he would bring home thirty-three thousand troops from Afghanistan by September 2012 and withdraw the remaining sixty-eight thousand by the end of 2014. However, military leaders, including General Petraeus and retired admiral Mike Mullen, former chairman of the Joint Chiefs of Staff, publicly stated that they would prefer a slower withdrawal. General Petraeus was the leading champion of a counterinsurgency strategy requiring a large number of troops.

But much as in Iraq, the Afghan government appears unprepared to protect Afghanistan. During the week that was supposed to be the beginning of a transition to Afghan control, Kabul, which was supposed to be one of the safest cities and was scheduled to be the first to carry out the transfer, became the scene of mayhem. Nine suicide bombers penetrated the security rings of Kabul's premier hotel and killed twenty-one people. Many of the guests were provincial officials who had come to Kabul for a conference on transition. When the shooting started, instead of facing up the attackers, the police ran away from the gunmen and urged others to flee. The chairman of the Takhar provincial council in Northern Afghanistan who saw three of his friends killed commented, "The security forces cannot even protect a few people inside the hotel. How can they protect a whole country?"[84] The assault ended only after NATO helicopters joined in the battle. Another Afghan wryly commented, "If they gave the security responsibility to the current government at 10:00 am, the government would collapse around 12 noon."[85]

On the weekend of August 7, 2011, the Taliban shot down an American Chinook® helicopter in eastern Pakistan, killing thirty Americans aboard, including twenty-two members of an elite Navy SEAL team. It occurred in a valley crossing two provinces, Logar and Wardak, that are gateways to the capital, Kabul, and were liberated in the early years of the war. This represented the greatest loss of American lives in a single day of the war. Both provinces have become increasingly insecure as the Taliban has set up checkpoints on the main road to search people's pockets for ID cards and documents indicating whether they work either for the Afghan government or for Coalition forces. If the Taliban insurgents do find anything "incriminating," the people are beheaded on the spot as a way to instill fear and terror.[86] The Chinook attack demonstrated that the insurgents could entrench themselves anywhere they wished and that the Afghan government was weak, absent, and hated for its corruption. In these areas, the Taliban cooperate with the Haqqani and other criminal networks. US troops cannot assert themselves in every village or valley, and often when they do, their night raids and intrusions into people's homes cause resentment. In these provinces, there is little expectation of the American and Afghan forces gaining the upper hand in the near future.[87]

On September 13, 2011, two days after the tenth anniversary of 9/11, the Taliban and the Haqqani attacked the US embassy and NATO headquarters in the highly secured diplomatic district of Kabul. For twenty hours the insurgents rained RPGs and small-arms fire. Suicide bombers gained access to buildings and were aiming for Afghan and Coalition soldiers.

Political life in Afghanistan is conducted in ways that keep changing and are less than harmonious. For example, members of the Afghan parliament came to blows on July 7, 2011, as a majority began to discuss impeaching President Hamid Karzai, bringing the country to the brink of a constitutional crisis. The dispute was about the legality of a special court established by President Karzai to adjudicate allegations of fraud by candidates who lost their seats or were disqualified in the previous September's parliamentary elections. That court effectively stopped the normal workings of government for nine months. NATO insists publicly that Afghanistan is a viable democracy in formation; Western diplomats have remained silent.[88]

During the same period, President Karzai's half-brother, Ahmid Wali Karzai, was assassinated. He served as the center of the security and power structures in southern Afghanistan, and his death created a vacuum of authority in the important Pashtun region, the heartland of the Taliban insurgency. According to Ahmed Rashid, who knew him personally, the death of Ahmed Wali Karzai meant that three critical efforts were at risk, the war against the Taliban, the drawing down of US troops, and the US efforts to negotiate with the Taliban and forge a peace agreement. President Karzai's half-brother was involved in all three. He forged tribal alliances to defend the presidency and extend the government's rule outside Kabul. He helped US forces with strategic advice and his knowledge of the tribes, and he ran a clandestine Afghan special operations team for the CIA. He was also the first prominent Afghan leader to start talks with the Taliban to attempt ending the war.[89]

Soon after, the mayor of Kandahar, Ghulam Haider Hamidi, was also killed outside his office when a bomber blew himself up. Mayor Hamidi was a possible successor to Ahmed Wali Karzai, although residents in the area didn't trust him because of his closeness to Americans, his years of living in the United States, and his lack of tribal connections that are necessary to remain in power.[90] It was a great loss for Kandahar because Ghulam Haider Hamidi had dreams of improving his city, hoping to help create excellent schools equipped with computers, housing developments, and well-regulated shops and parks. Even though he lived through a bombing attack by the Taliban in 2009, he felt that they were only half of the problem. He intended to try to eliminate the vast corruption at the heart of the Afghan government, including the entrepreneurs who won city contracts for lighting, produced inferior goods, and lined their pockets with the profits. He had gone after the local power brokers who demanded their share of the opium trade, the military contracts, and the building projects. He had cleared away 460 illegal shops in order to build a school, had plans for 300 acres of sports fields and a special women's garden. He wanted to expand the road from the city to the airport and install solar lighting.[91]

The Afghan government itself is not secure. It has been trying to negotiate with the Taliban, but on September 19, 2011, Burhanuddin Rabbani, the leader of Afghan's High Peace Council, was assassinated, demonstrating how once again the government's enemies could reach into the most secure areas of the capital, a mile away from the American embassy. This assassination may be the most significant of the war. The seventy-member High Peace Council that had representatives of many different views was reaching out to senior Taliban commanders in Pakistan and attempting to persuade low-level Taliban leaders to join the government. Rabbani traveled all over the country, establishing reconciliation councils in every province and even in neighboring countries.[92] The United States has also made contact with the Taliban, hoping to gain momentum in the peace process. It has concluded that without strong Afghan involvement, peace will not be possible. This action will hamper the ability of the Afghan government to stay in power after the US withdrawal in 2014.

In late September 2011, the chairman of the Joint Chiefs of Staff of the armed forces, Mike Mullen, went public, addressing the Senate and criticizing Pakistan as a difficult ally. He stated what the US government has known for years, that the Pakistan army and the ISI had been shielding Osama bin Laden for at least five years and that they have long-standing ties with the Haqqani. He believes, as does retired General Jack Keene, that the Pakistani military leadership has never accepted that we could win the war in Afghanistan and is worried about India's influence in Afghanistan. Mike Mullen went public because he also thinks that we should change the terms of our relationship with Pakistan, which means reconsidering not only our yearly foreign aid of $4 billion. He is also concerned about Pakistan's relationship with Saudi Arabia. Thus US servicemen and servicewomen may be fighting in Afghanistan, but they are dealing with the involvement of other countries and with shifting political policies, as well as trying to gain the trust of village elders. The village *shura*, or council, is caught between the Taliban and its own wish for economic aid from Kabul.[93]

Meanwhile, US troops are discussing potential road projects, new dams and bridges, and other development projects that are important elements of their attempts to build goodwill among Afghans and restore the country's shattered infrastructure. They are running hospitals where Afghan children who were injured by IEDs are cared for, while they simultaneously fight the Taliban, the Haqqani, al Qaeda, and the Lashkar.

But talk among military officers has now turned from establishing a democratic Afghanistan to achieving a more practical and limited goal. Tactically, this means that US military units along the border with Pakistan, where the Haqqani cross unseen, are fighting these insurgents, and it is also placing more Afghan soldiers and police officers into contested areas. These units jointly are also trying to prevent the attacks that have reached Kabul and prominent targets.

A lieutenant colonel who commands a battalion used two companies to cordon off Charbaran Valley, one of the main routes used by the Haqqani to enter Afghanistan, and another to sweep the villages in order to prevent a spectacular attack in Kabul and gather intelligence as well. When they arrived, they found many signs of the insurgents' presence, from discovering armaments in villagers' houses, to turning up a bomb hidden in a woodpile, to hearing hidden fighters over two-way radios. But the valley, which fell silent after the insurgents managed only a small attack from outside the cordon, remained out of government hands as the company reached the other side.[94]

What complicates the work of our service personnel even more are the ongoing rocket, mortar, and artillery attacks on forward operating bases positioned on the border with Pakistan in Paktika Province that have occurred since May 2011, when a Navy SEAL team killed Osama bin Laden. The attacks occur from insurgent positions just inside Afghanistan, as close as two hundred yards from the border, where rocket crews fire and then rush to Pakistan. US officers and soldiers know that the Pakistani military positions are less than a mile from insurgent firing positions and are certain that the Pakistan military is involved.[95] They are frustrated and angry because they are limited in their ability to respond because of diplomatic relations between the United States and Pakistan. When receiving fire from Pakistan, they are permitted to return far fewer high-explosive rounds. Attack helicopters and aircraft are less likely to fire ordinance the closer their position is to the border, even if it is on the Afghan side.[96]

Here again, US government policies must be continually reevaluated given the differences between the Afghan political system, Pakistan, and the United States, and the heroic efforts of American soldiers on the ground. Over the course of ten years, the United States has lost 1,786 service members, and an additional 14,342 service members have been wounded.[97]

THE MEDIA

According to a study by the Project for Excellence in Journalism, an arm of the Pew Research Center, the war in Afghanistan accounts for just 4 percent of the nation's news coverage.[98]

American audiences are suffering from war fatigue, and deep cuts in budgets by the media affect the way the war is covered in this country. It is only in the past two or three years that the *New York Times* has begun publishing stories about returning veterans, although PBS has always ended its *NewsHour* program on a weekly basis with the names of the dead soldiers scrolling silently on the television screen.

A soldier returned to the United States with a member of his unit who had tuberculosis. When he was stationed at Abu Ghraib, tuberculosis broke out in the prison and infected a number of other soldiers. He stated, "There was actually a cover-up while there was this huge thing going on. The higher management of the camp wanted to sweep it all under the rug."[99] It never did get any news coverage.

The several insurgent groups besides al Qaeda that operate in Iraq are rarely mentioned in the press. Nor has the experience of soldiers who have seen their comrades blown to bits or who have piled dead and mangled bodies in their trucks. In his book *Beyond Duty*, Shannon Meehan wrote, "I just wanted to see some connection between our lives and the lives of our families back home. I just wanted to see some humanity in the news coverage."[100]

He and many others felt that their stories were invisible and that the news needed to have a central figure or major enemy to report, just as often as Muktar al-Sadr or President Karzai.

On May 19, 2009, the *New York Times* published a number of articles about soldiers in the war zone, including a five-page article, in a section titled "The Reach of War." It was like opening a window on the truth. Our soldiers were no longer just statistics, and we could learn what was really happening in combat. It included two full pages with the photos of soldiers who were killed in action in Afghanistan, with biographical information about these and other American casualties. The article included a color photo of an army helicopter arriving to evacuate soldiers wounded after their armored vehicle hit an IED in the Tangi Valley, Wardak Province.[101] It was both gruesome and heartbreaking.

There was also an article, "Life and Death Decisions for a Junior Officer," that revealed the many tasks the author performed in addition to combat, as well as his self-questioning, and a photo of soldiers placing a body into a military truck at the site of a suicide bombing. For the first time, a photo of six soldiers carrying a coffin of one of their buddies also appeared. It was poignant; losing a fellow soldier from a unit is like losing a member of one's family. There was also a video, accessible online, with interviews with the captain and other soldiers. It was a dramatic change in news reporting.

Under the Bush administration, the display of photos showing coffins returning from the war in Iraq was prohibited. Journalists and newspaper editors were told that showing such photos would undermine the war effort and put the nation at risk.[102] The media were thus used for political and social framing. And this is how a distance was created between our troops who were waging the war and the population at home.

In *The Good Soldiers*, David Finkel wrote that in the United States, "the news was all macro, not micro." It was about government policy, the different views of the political parties about the war and their quarrels. US soldiers felt that news reporters who were "embedded" (and therefore could only go where the commanders told them to go) and radio reporters knew nothing about Iraq.[103] The headlines were brief and far from the reality that soldiers witnessed and experienced driving in a Humvee, seeing their comrades with burns and multiple amputations.

Throughout the Bush administration, there was a concerted effort to have the government regulate the visual field, and the use of "embedded journalists" was widely practiced. They traveled in regulated transports that brought them only to carefully selected scenes, and they sent back images and narratives of particular action.[104]

It took this long for newspapers to write about how a war was really being waged and about its consequences. It took this long for parts of our country to recognize the travails of our soldiers. The economic costs for the psychological and health care of our returning veterans will require a budget that is larger than the war itself and will last for decades. But just as important is our attention and our time to inform ourselves, to honor the sacrifices that our soldiers have made, to care for them, and to help their families as well.

Chapter 2

HOMECOMING AND
PARALLEL LIVES

Fig. 2.1. Cameron Baker, veteran of the war in Iraq. *Photo by Jacques Bouvard.*

VA HOSPITAL CONFESSIONAL

Each night is different. Each night is the same.
Sometimes I pull the trigger. Sometimes I don't.

When I pull the trigger, he often just stands there,
gesturing, as if saying, *Aren't you ashamed?*

When I don't, he douses himself
in gasoline, drowns himself in fire.

A dog barks in the night's illuminated green landscape
and the platoon sergeant orders me to shoot it.

Some nights I twitch and jerk in my sleep.
My lover has learned to face away.

She closes her eyes when I fuck her. I imagine
she's far away and we don't use the word *love.*

When she sleeps, helicopters
come in low over the date palms.

Men are bound on their knees, shivering
in the animal stall, long before dawn.

I whisper into their ears, saying
Howlwin?Howlwin? Meaning, *Mortars? Mortars?*

Howl wind, motherfucker, Howl Wind?
The milk cow stares with its huge brown eyes.

The milk cow wants to know
how I can do this to another human being.

I check the haystack in the corner
for a weapons cache. I check the sewage sump.

I tell no one, but sometimes late at night
I uncover rifles and bullets within me.

Other nights I drive through Baghdad,
Firebaugh. Bakersfield. Kettleman City.

Some nights I'm up in the hatch shooting
a controlled pair into someone's radiator.

Some nights I hear a woman screaming.
Others I shoot at the crashing car.

When the boy brings us a platter of fruit,
I mistake the cantaloupe for a human skull.

Sometimes the gunman fires into the house.
Sometimes the gunman fires at me.

Every night it's different.
Every night the same.

Some nights I pull the trigger.
Some nights I burn him alive.[1]

—Brian Turner

Our soldiers don't come home. They can't come home. They are still in
Iraq or in Afghanistan and will be there for months, if not years. They
lead parallel lives, one that is similar to our daily lives, and another as depicted by
Brian Turner in his poem, a life where they hear mortars and gunshots, watch a
buddy die, see Iraqis or Afghans die, see wounds, blood, destruction. These memories will never go away. When soldiers drive down a highway or a road in Illinois,
Nevada, New York, Colorado, or any other place, they look at rooftops and overpasses to make certain there are no enemies waiting with rifles. When they park
their cars, they look around them. When they hear noises, they get startled and
think they are hearing gunshots. Some of them continue to carry weapons or sleep
with a knife under their pillow, check outside of their houses before going to bed.
They are unable to process their experiences and move beyond them.

They feel grief and guilt, but they have no answers. They ask themselves
how they could have killed a person. Like Brian Turner, they remember the

child throwing a grenade as their Humvee® passed on the way to Anbar: "We knew him. Or a woman walks by and blows herself up. There are no front lines or uniforms. Eventually, psychologically, everyone is a possible source of threat and injury."[2] The soldiers remember how many IEDs (improvised explosive devices) and even more lethal EFPs (explosively formed penetrators) they pass along the road, that are hitting their Humvee. These are weapons that blast molten copper into the surrounding area and pierce vehicle armor. The sophistication and cost of these weapons point to Iranian involvement in such attacks.[3]

Our veterans have nightmares and have trouble sleeping because of what they have experienced and because they were fighting 24-7 with very little rest. They want to be busy and work long hours. Most of them—including one veteran who was an infantry team leader in Iraq—continue working long hours after they return home. One veteran says, "When I came back, I had four jobs. I would get up at 2:00 in the morning and sell newspapers, just so my brain wouldn't be busy, until about 5:00 a.m., make breakfast. At 7:00 a.m., I worked voltage electricity work on construction sites until 3:00 or 4:00 in the afternoon, and Sunday through Thursday, I did online business communications until eight o'clock. On weekends, I took a basic guitar class. I wasn't sleeping much. Sleep in combat is not really sleep. It took me some time to get back to normal sleep with a schedule."[4]

In combat, soldiers work long hours and have to stay awake at night or sleep lightly to be alert so they can respond to possible attacks. One soldier, Amy Smee, works long hours in a grocery store besides attending college. She broke her hip in Afghanistan, and her wrists and shoulders hurt as well, and she suffers from intense headaches. She doesn't get much sleep and feels better when she is busy. She doesn't mind working "the graveyard shift."[5] Many veterans frequently work overtime or have two jobs because they are used to working around the clock in combat. That often means that they have little time for their families or the loved ones they left behind, and this may prevent them from having good relationships.

Amy keeps cleaning her room and rearranging her furniture. Perhaps it gives her a sense of control over a life that she feels is unraveling. She is "dealing with anger, with hatred against the Arab people, living in constant fear." She says, "When I came back from Iraq, I asked myself how could I hate these people. That was the hardest thing, all this hate that I felt in my heart."

Returning soldiers miss their buddies, the intensity of combat binding them as a close family. They lived and died together, and the ones who died often reappear in dreams and memories. They are overcome with grief and, for them, forgetting dead comrades is as dishonorable as forgetting dead parents.[6] In civilian life, no one speaks the language of wars, thus veterans feel that no one would want to hear their story—nobody likes bad news. Many of them feel terribly lonely.

The 3rd Platoon, 1st Battalion, 506th infantry, Charlie Company of forty-two soldiers referred to themselves as "the Band of Brothers." In one year, they encountered more than one thousand roadside bombs and captured 1,800 Iraqis. It took less than two months for the first death in their company to occur, and the memory stayed with some of them for years afterward.[7] Their combat medic was the first to arrive at the scene when a bomb plowed into their company. What he saw was smoke and dust, two kids just torn apart, and his sergeant covered in blood. He remembers what it is like to watch people die: "People don't die like they do in movies. When they die, you can look in their eyes, and you can tell that there is nothing behind their eyes."[8] That image haunted him. "I started behaving irrationally, realized that I was dangerous to my soldiers. I told the psychologist on my base that I didn't want to load my weapon."[9] But the psychologist told him that he was fit for duty.

Twenty percent of our soldiers return with PTSD (Post-Traumatic Stress Disorder), invisible wounds. Traumatic experiences can create a prison of isolation and the feeling that only a person who has been through the same experience can understand the intensity of this distress. Counselors from veterans' organizations interviewed on PBS's *Frontline* say that they are more concerned with the needs of returning soldiers than the military is.[10]

When soldiers return home, they struggle with what they did and with what they didn't do. They often have anxiety attacks. They blame themselves and feel like failures, as if they have let their country and their family down.[11] Some soldiers feel that they have lost hope and find that they can't read newspapers anymore or take an interest in the life around them.

The psychological cost of war is debilitating. Soldiers drink heavily to kill the pain inside them or take drugs to help them forget what they have experienced, to lessen the pain. Post-Traumatic Stress Disorder, as defined by the American Psychological Association,[12] includes recurrent, distressing recollections of traumatic events, such as causing death or serious injury to oneself and others. Its symptoms include depression, insomnia, feeling constantly threatened, and graphic nightmares. Many of those who come home feel reclusive and want to stay in their apartments or in their rooms.

Lt. Col. Dave Grossman, who has written extensively on combat stress, sees a deficit in military training. He feels that soldiers who are not emotionally trained to kill are unable to accept what they have done. "When you connect with your safety which is family, that's when you begin to realize where you were, acknowledge how scared you were. This is the most damaging kind of war psychiatrically. You have no protection anywhere, at any time. And therefore you are in a constant death threat and you are witnessing carnage and death at an incredibly close range."[13] One soldier remarked, "Coming back will tear you apart."[14] Another said, "The war took ninety pounds of flesh from me. Now that I've been through this, I have a profound look on a lot of things. I live in a whole different world."[15]

What makes it even more difficult to share these experiences is that they need to distance themselves from the death and destruction around them to keep fighting. As a result, soldiers don't talk about the tragedies that occurred.

Cameron, who attends Colombia University, is among two hundred returning veterans there and is in touch with fifty of them. He has a girlfriend who worries about him, and her family is involved in caring for veterans. It helps him deal with his PTSD.[16]

Many veterans lose contact with their friends in the military when they return. They miss their friends, and to many of them it seems like the more time goes by, the more they miss them. One soldier, Heather Demoines, says that her unit was like a close family as they went on missions together.[17] She regrets not seeing them anymore. It is difficult for veterans to make friends in the civilian world because their experiences are so different. They find that people complain about what seems to them like very trivial things, when as veterans they must adapt to and overcome even the most difficult situations. When soldiers are in a life-or-death situation, many things seem insignificant and meaningless, and they may feel that people who haven't had difficult life experiences are living on the surface.

Heather remembers how draining it was to adjust when she returned from Iraq. "It was very hard to be around people. They have such petty worries. They say, 'Oh, I've broken my nail,' and I think, *Oh my God, you don't know what it's like to live in a place where you think you are going to die every day, where you sleep in dirt, where you eat crap and wash your clothes in a bucket of dirty water.* They have no idea what soldiers go through."[18]

Sometimes when a soldier meets another veteran, it seems as if they had known each other for a long time and they are able to have a real conversation. One veteran told me, "In the civilian world it's hard to find friends."

Family members also have difficulties understanding their returning veterans. Amy recounts how her mother flew up to Washington, where she was stationed after being in Iraq.

I remember being at the airport waiting for her. When I saw her she ran towards me trembling and I just stood there. It was the most uncomfortable, awkward moment in my life. I knew I should be crying, but I couldn't. She was very emotional. My family assumed I was standoffish. They weren't sure who I was anymore.

My mom came to visit me for four or five days in the week that I returned. She was driving me to Walmart to go shopping. She was trying to get me out. I told her that there was a short way to get there if we go through the base. There's a long road behind the base, all wilderness and just one road. I saw this pothole on the side of the road. We were getting closer and closer to it and I thought, *Oh my God she's going to drive right next to this pothole and we're going to die.* I ended up grabbing the steering wheel and making her swerve. Even though I was home, it was a challenge to drive, even in daylight. I commented to my sister that there was a can on the road and she just ran over it. I knew that it bothered me because of Iraq. You still feel that your life is on the line and you have to be alert, so it's difficult to change.

It's lonely. People don't understand I have PTSD. There is one thing that soldiers know, even if they won't admit: that there is something wrong with them, that they have some anxiety. It's the civilians that have no idea what it's like to come back. People don't realize that we were in a place where it was hell on earth. When I came home from Afghanistan, I didn't fit in. People told me, "You're different. Now you're like a robot."[19]

Veterans return in combat mode, which gives them the ability to respond instantly with deadly force. They are in perpetual mobilization for danger, endurance, and hyperarousal. The capacity to adapt to harsh physical conditions that is required in combat may be irrelevant in civilian life. Veterans may feel pressure to suppress their feelings of grief, horror, and guilt.

Cameron says that

being over there is punctuated by intense hostile action. It was boredom. Maybe it's part of a desensitizing process. When you are getting shot at, mortared, rockets coming every day, everything else pales. When I was out in East Baghdad it got to a point when I just didn't care anymore. Mortars would start dropping. I would find myself getting infuriated. I was at my wit's

end. I didn't care anymore if someone killed me. We were on a forward operating base in Sadr City for two and a half years. The casualty rates were terrible. My job towards the end was to "just replace them." What made it more
difficult was when I knew the guy. Though we wanted to show respect for the
people, we didn't have time.

I felt as though the more challenging the environment, the more opportunity there was to excel. I was equipped and prepared for what happened.
Being able to deal with hostile fire is first and foremost. Usually we get hit
during the day when everyone is out working. My shipping container I lived
in got blown up and shot in two different camps. Mortars would come
through the roof and just destroy everything. It was very surreal to just walk
in that place afterwards. That was my bed. If I had been in that bed when that
happened, it would not be a good way to go. It got so bad with the IEDs, the
snipers, mortar fire, that we just shut all the convoys to and from unless it was
food or ammunition. Every single time a convoy came in or left, within two
minutes you'd hear the explosion, you'd hear the radio chatter, and they
would come screaming in on the base, offload the casualties. We actually had
a facility used for memorials. Instead of doing them individually, it got to the
point where Tuesdays and Fridays were memorial days."[20]

Many soldiers like Cameron have no time to mourn, and thus they bury
their grief. They become numb and stay numb when they return home. In
some bases, even in forward operating bases (FOBs), there were memorial
services and soldiers had the time to weep, but afterward they needed to
develop their own responses. Some walked around the base during the night,
some moved their furniture around to give them a sense of control. Cameron
had nothing but a bed in the small shipping container where he slept, and that
was destroyed. Suppressing the emotions that assail them is a way of continuing to be good soldiers.

Sadr City is where many Iranians came to join the battle in support of
Muktar el-Sadr, the radical and popular Shiite imam. It was one of the worst
places to do battle. Sadr City, Baghdad's most impoverished shantytown, was
home to more than two million Shiites. The Shiites were severely oppressed
during Saddam Husssein's regime when the Baathist army was Sunni. More
than 60 percent of the population in Iraq is Shiite. During the American occupation, and especially in the area of Cameron's forward operating base, young,
unemployed Iraqi men served as fighters who brazenly planted more than a
dozen hidden bombs, or IEDs. First, they set fire to tires. Next, they sank the

IEDs into the melted asphalt and let them cool. Within hours, there was no sign of the devices, which could be detonated with the remote control of a car alarm whenever American vehicles passed by.

US soldiers not only were in battle but also were involved in what is referred to as "hearts and minds projects," which often involved arranging for water supply or electricity and hiring unemployed people who put themselves at risk by working for the Americans. One group of soldiers was in the process of setting itself up in an abandoned warehouse and offered to let a homeless family live there, but then the warehouse was blown up with the family inside. Heather, who was stationed at Abu Ghraib, became friends with an Iraqi family that lived nearby and even sewed up a dress for their little girl. When she went by to visit them one day, she found the house had been destroyed by mortars and the whole family killed.

Cameron, like so many other veterans, felt that coming home was a shock to his system: "I had a lot of difficulty leaving all that behind and coming back." Even though he was no longer in uniform, he still felt as if he were getting shot at and caught in cross fires. One of his friends from his time in Sadr City came home when he did. They had difficulty communicating with anyone else. Cameron said, "We were so wound tight and our perspectives were so skewed, it was impossible to communicate." Too many of our returning troops become reclusive and feel more comfortable staying by themselves in a room or a trailer.

Cameron started seeing a psychiatrist because he felt that he was unraveling.[21] He was having difficulties doing the most ordinary things, such as getting up in the morning and preparing his meals. Like so many returning veterans, he was tired and worn out, and he stopped caring about life. When he went to Columbia University, he saw a psychologist there who offered him the opportunity to work through his issues. He knows that in the military there is a stigma attached to getting help because it is believed to represent weakness and failure. This is one of the many differences between the military and civilian cultures.

Many veterans of the wars in Iraq and Afghanistan suffer from brain injuries. They have constant headaches or may feel light-headed or dizzy and experience changes in mood or behavior. One can get injured just by the blast waves of an exploding IED. In fact, a study by RAND Corporation estimates that 19 percent of soldiers experience possible traumatic brain injury and that cognitive injuries may overlap with PTSD and depression. RAND found that of those reporting probable brain injuries, 57 percent had not been evaluated by a physician.[22] Traumatic brain injury affects executive and decision-making functions. The report suggested that educational programs could help soldiers recognize symptoms before these could become life threatening. But the stigma of psychological illness often prevents soldiers from coming forward and seeking help.[23]

Cameron recalls, "We'd get into a bunker and a mortar would come outside and it would just suck the air out of a van. You'd get the sound bouncing around and it would pop eardrums and my ears would be ringing for a couple of days." These injuries caused hearing loss. Cameron needs to sit in a front row in his class in order to hear his professor. People think of brain injury as only physical, and they do not understand that it also takes a toll on the emotions.

Cameron is doing very well at his university, but he recounts:

> The hyperaggression continues. If I felt threatened by my environment, I would have neutralized it. If I'm in a bar and if there is a threat coming from another guy, I would have immediately dropped him to the ground. Now when I do, I walk away from him. I don't like tight spaces with many people, but it's much easier when I am in a bar. I just feed off the vibes of everyone else. That's basically how I try to control my environment, to read other people's body language and attitudes. I feel much better now at identifying what's happening. There's nothing I can do that calms me down but just give it time and block it off. I'll go back to my room and isolate myself from everybody, turn my phone off, and just wait for it to get better.

He still experiences discomfort in crowds, especially in the subway, being surrounded by too many conversations, having someone walk behind him. In his political-science class, there was a video about Iraq where an IED went off, and that upset him terribly. He finds it hard to be calm and focus instead of reacting to things such as noises. He and his veteran friends like to go to the gym and burn off their aggression. Nighttime is difficult because of background noises. He tries to read twenty to thirty minutes before settling in for the night, to regain a sense of calmness. Heather's daughter is in the Girl Scouts, and when they have events, she feels very anxious and doesn't like being in a crowd.[24]

After returning home from a year in Kandahar, Afghanistan, a soldier wrote in the *New York Times*'s *At War* blogs that the battle he was involved in didn't stop when he came home, that he may have put aside his helmet and rifle, but that he still carried his armor.[25] He refers to armor as masculine armor, because for many soldiers admitting vulnerability is a "weakness." It is also considered an admission of selfishness, and every hour spent in a counseling session means time spent away from training his men for their next tour. The hardest part for the returning veterans who have life-altering PTSD is not only to accept their vulnerability but also especially to receive compassion, whether from a mother, a wife, or a friend. It seems that receiving a hug from a loved one or even a stranger takes a different kind of strength. After I interviewed a veteran one morning, we both reached out and held each other. He was relieved to be able to speak about his experiences, and I felt an outpouring of empathy for him.

Veterans who have the support of family and friends have an easier time dealing with their depression. The love and understanding of Brian Turner's fiancée helped him "come back to the world."[26] It helps many veterans to talk about their wartime memories. The wife of a veteran who is dealing with PTSD gives talks to church and community groups, sharing the important insight that "you need an environment where the warrior can be vulnerable."[27] Not many people know that Russian soldiers who had been in the war in Afghanistan met with American veterans of the Vietnam War. Vladislav Tamarov wrote a book, *Afghanistan: Soviet Vietnam*, in which he described their meetings. He observed that although none of the Americans spoke Russian and few Russians spoke English, "We knew we had found friends, blood brothers who understood us a lot better than our own people did."[28]

Some veterans prefer to deal with their problems in solitude. One likes to spend hours at a lake on his boat rather than talking with other veterans. Another works as a guide for hikes in the mountains.

Although the military acknowledges that 20 percent of soldiers come home with psychological problems, some commanders do not accept the validity of their problems and even expect them to return to war.[29] Since there are not enough volunteers, many soldiers are compelled to return to combat several times. "Stop loss" means that a soldier can be told to redeploy after his time is up and his contract is completed. In fact, 34 percent of our troops are deployed multiple times.[30]

Veterans like Cameron feel a sense of dislocation when they return. When he arrived at the airport, he didn't recognize his own mother, who was waiting there for him. Like Odysseus, he returned to a place he didn't recognize and where his peers had no experience of war. Returning veterans feel like strangers.

Their emotions come out rapidly and unchecked. They often behave in ways that they do not understand, and it may seem that the people around them understand even less. And like in the *Iliad* where Achilles was assured of fame only by dying, we are still uneasy about honoring our living soldiers.

The commemoration rites we observe each Memorial Day, parades, speeches, and graveside prayers are a way for the living to remember the dead. But there is no space for returning veterans to tell their stories of war and for it to be understood that they return to a psychological war at home. Movies like *The Hurt Locker* do not make up for the inability of a veteran to tell his story, to be personally heard and respected. It is difficult to come home after the traumatic experience of war. After the Vietnam War, soldiers came home to antiwar demonstrations. Now, veterans return from Iraq and Afghanistan to indifference and ignorance, responses that are painful, considering what they have accomplished in the war zone. Military families are helpful to their children, but some families fail to understand the emotional and psychological toll that the war has taken on their sons and daughters.

In fact, our society has changed. According to sociologist Jean Twenge, younger Americans are more self-absorbed and less empathetic than previous generations.[31] Although there are still older Americans who are concerned about others, the same phenomenon has appeared across the country. People seem to be focused on the issues of their own lives, with little interest in problems affecting other groups or the "at-risk sectors" of our society.

Most Americans have no idea about what our soldiers have experienced or the sacrifices they have made. Thus, they have little or no compassion for veterans and would like them to snap out of their new behavior, whether it's alcohol or drug abuse or the inability to interact with their loved ones or friends. Many people don't want to be burdened with the truth, or they are simply uninterested, remaining wrapped up in their own particular concerns. Civilians often fail to understand that when they ask a soldier, "Did you kill anybody?" he or she was doing it only for their country or to protect him- or herself during conflict or combat. Our country has largely removed itself from the fact that it has sent 1.6 million service members fighting into two wars, many of them in multiple deployments, and that the wars lasted far longer than World War II. A former SEAL commander broke his leg during an incident in Iraq. When he was shopping at a mall, someone asked him how he broke his leg. When he answered that he had been in Iraq, he was asked, "Was it a car crash or a cycle crash?" For a soldier returning with the memory of stepping over corpses with their entrails hanging out and of attending count-less memorial services, such naiveté is likely to make him quite angry.[32]

A lieutenant colonel would like to see more sensitivity toward home-coming soldiers:

> On the surface, it's polite. People say, "Thank you for your service." At the end of the day, what concerns me is that they really don't understand the level of sacrifice, the level of commitment that goes on. For a people to allow this government to remain at war for almost ten years is wrong. If the Amer-ican people were connected to the war and had to make some kind of sacri-fice, like being allowed only one cup of coffee a day or ten gallons of gas a week, we would have seen a conclusion in the war effort a long time ago. A lot of times, I've had people thank me, a little yellow ribbon, a tiny magnet on your car. If you really supported the troops, you'd be telling the govern-ment, "You need to support the troops and get them home." When a nation goes to war, the population should be engaged and understand that it is not natural to keep the government involved in the longest war. Many people don't understand that I've been through hell and I can't just sit down with them over a cup of coffee for an hour and tell them how it was.[33]

Our society is distanced from the experiences of our soldiers. A constant refrain I hear from veterans is that the people they meet do not understand or do not want to understand them. Further, our culture thinks of wounds as physical and has difficulty seeing the connection between emotions and physical pain or problems, the importance of memories, and how emotions such as hate and sorrow are confounded. Nor do we understand that wounds are also the memories, the hallucinations, and the nightmares our veterans experience.

Often we limit our conversation, marginalizing people who have suffered and are suffering. One percent of Americans are in the army, and it is a vol-unteer army.[34] They are carrying the weight of the war for our whole country, and they need people to listen to them—not just with their ears, but with their hearts—to be willing to become upset or sad, to empathize with someone who needs to share his or her feelings, which might include the depression so many veterans experience. They need recognition and respect for what they have accomplished. Returning soldiers often lose their pride, the perspective of their goals and lives; these are losses we don't understand. There needs to be a bridge of communication between these two worlds. When we think of human rights, we do not often realize that it means granting visibility to soldiers who have suffered, as well as honoring them by understanding their sacrifice and giving them our full attention.

One veteran who is a lieutenant colonel attended a party where there was a display of fireworks. One of his friends said, "This is kind of like Libya!" The colonel responded to that remark with anger and the feeling that people are disconnected from reality in this country. He believes that having a volunteer army is a step toward a private army, and that having a draft as we did in the past connected the American population directly to the war. He has noticed also that because it is so difficult for veterans to reintegrate in society and find a job when their adrenaline is still high, they end up reenlisting for multiple redeployments. He feels that we should have a national debate over mandatory service, whether in the Peace Corps or in the army.

Because of their isolation from our society, returning veterans feel more comfortable when they are talking among themselves. The psychiatrist Jonathan Shay, who works with veterans, has found that recovery from psychological injuries happens in a community, not just between two people.[35] That can include self-organized on-line support and blogs. A veterans organization started a new project called Not Alone, which is comprised of a community of soldiers and spouses. The new project was created to help them recover after the war. It lets the veterans anonymously talk about their problems through social networking so they can discuss what war was like and what they faced when they came home. It is intended to help them rebuild their lives after the devastation of war.

One veteran wrote about anger and isolation on the *Not Alone* blog, describing how when he was in Iraq he could focus his anger on his missions and the insurgents and his wounded soldiers. When he was home, he directed the anger against his family and the people he loved. He referred to the need to stop quarreling "as how to cease fire once the rounds started flying downrange."[36] He also shared what he learned about how to control his feelings. Another veteran wrote that he learned that the three hardest words for a warrior to utter are "I need help."[37] It takes as much courage for a soldier to accept his or her vulnerability as it does to engage in combat.

Many of the veterans who do have options to get help try to appear normal when they get evaluations. The mother of a recently returned veteran felt as if he flipped a switch, showing his anger at home and then appearing normal in an interview with a psychologist. One moment, he has his arms around his mother, and another time, he calls her names, which is something he never did before he went into combat. He returned with two lives, the one that people see on the surface and the war that still rages inside him.

Often veterans hear members of their family asking them to "please get over it," because they are frustrated with coping with so much family responsibility. But for too many soldiers, the war rages inside them for years, some for their whole lives. Even World War II and Vietnam veterans still feel lonely and misunderstood.

Not only do our returning soldiers feel dislocation, but also they need to gain social trust, to feel that they belong, that they are not outsiders. In our society, the kind of job we have defines us socially, and it is not easy for returning veterans who joined when they were only eighteen or nineteen years old to find fulfilling work. One veteran I interviewed became a janitor, another works in a supermarket, and a young female veteran runs a daycare center in her home. The unemployment rate among returning veterans is twice that of the general population.[38] Older veterans are more likely to find rewarding jobs because they have more experience. The lieutenant colonel remarked that if you are a midlevel manager, the transition to a civilian world is easier, and that one of his captains is now employed at Microsoft.

We all need to be able to have conversations about our common experiences, and if veterans are not in contact with each other, they feel isolated. Our college-educated veterans and those who attend college on the GI Bill will ultimately find better jobs, but unlike Cameron's situation, it is unusual for them to study with other veterans. They typically are older than the other students and they come with very different experiences.

Thousands of veterans remain homeless because they have difficulty reentering society. For them, reintegrating into civilian life and trying to find employment is overwhelming. The Department of Veterans Affairs has acknowledged that women are nearly four times as likely as men to end up homeless.[39] Lingering health problems and PTSD are contributing to the rise in homelessness among female veterans.

Women encounter problems in combat that most men don't. A shocking statistic is that one out of three women in the military is raped and sexually assaulted.[40] Given this kind of emotional and psychological harm, not to mention the physical harm, it is very difficult for them to go back into society. Many of them become addicted and homeless, sleeping in their cars or in alleys. About 5 percent of the 104,000 veterans who are homeless are women.[41] They can no longer fulfill their roles as wives and mothers. They return changed.

In February 2011, federal funding for women's counseling was due to be cut. US Veterans Initiative provided housing for fourteen of these homeless women and their children. Eleven percent of those living in federal housing are women.[42] There is also a transitional housing facility for female veterans at US Vets, a nonprofit organization at Long Beach, California. There are forty-three women in residence at that housing facility, and there is a waiting list.[43] The rest are left without the help they desperately need.

There are about nine hundred homeless veterans in the San Diego area who have periodic meetings called Stand Down. They sleep in tents called Alpha, Bravo, and Delta, and they parade, carrying American flags. But at their yearly gathering, there is room for only sixty-eight of the veterans who need rehabilitation and mental health. Stand Down is run by a clinical psychologist and a veterans organization.[44] Many of these veterans return from combat addicted to drugs, even though they are already taking sleeping pills and anti-depressants. It is extremely difficult to reenter society, given their multiple traumatic experiences.

Former secretary of defense Robert Gates saw a growing disconnect between the country as a whole and the relatively few who fight its wars. In a speech that he gave at Duke University in September 2010, he argued that the country is at risk of developing a cadre of military leaders who are cut off politically, culturally, and geographically from the population they are protecting.[45] Yet the wars were not an issue that was raised in that year's midterm elections when the political parties were bitterly divided over healthcare, government regulations, public debt, and the role of populist movements like the Tea Party. While the majority of Americans worry about their economic security, they rarely think about the fact that the country is in its eleventh year of fighting in Afghanistan and Iraq, which are the longest wars in our history. They also fail to correlate the cost of these wars in dollars or worry about the long-term cost to the health of returning soldiers.

WOMEN WARRIORS

About 15 percent of our soldiers are women who, like Heather and Amy, have been directly involved in combat situations.[46] Many of them were proud to serve. Most people think that women do not participate in combat but are only involved in safer roles. Women like Heather, who came home to a husband and children, couldn't cope like some men do, by going out drinking with their buddies. After performing critical work in the war, they must deal with friends who do not recognize them as real soldiers and with husbands, such as Heather's, who have little patience with their avoidance of intimacy and with the psychological harm that they are experiencing.[47] Women who return with PTSD are expected to act as nurturers, not as people who need nurturing themselves.

When Heather was with her unit at Abu Ghraib, she was subjected to mortar fire and encountered IEDs daily. When she returned home in 2004, she had two children to care for and she had a new baby in 2006.

> When I came back, I got the kids. That made it very hard for me to adjust. I had a lot of anger and anxiety when I got back. But I am worse now [2010]. For the first six months or a year, I went to counseling a couple of times a month. There were times when I called the help line. Nobody could understand that I couldn't control my fear. I felt a lot of fear and I had bad dreams. There were places where I felt very scared because I was on the road a lot, driving around town. When I saw scenes that were familiar, I had a flashback. When I saw a bush or a shrub, I would go back to Iraq. If things don't go the way they are supposed to go, I get really upset. My oldest son is fifteen and a wonderful person, but I stress around him because I am really on edge. I try to explain to him some of the things I've gone through. It's from being hyperalert. It just doesn't go away when you come back. I can't relax. When I go to bed at night, I have to make sure that everything is locked. I'm always scared. It's always in the back of my head, *am I going to get killed?* I am embarrassed to tell people that I have PTSD and to have them say you should just get over it.[48]

There is no membrane between life in combat and life at home. One young veteran struggles with her emotions and feels frustrated over where and how she sits. When she is in a restaurant, she wants to sit with her back against the wall so she has a view of what is taking place in every direction. She still feels at risk from the IEDs and mortars she encountered while she was on patrol. She gets agitated over what she describes as "small things." She told me that she wished that she could let go of those reactions and commented, "That was a long time ago, when I was normal."

Heather says that her unit was like a family, that they were very close and went on missions together. She regrets not seeing them anymore. It's hard for veterans to make friends in the civilian world because their experiences are so different. Veterans may feel alienated from people who know nothing about war. As veterans, they are used to adapting and overcoming problems, and they feel that people who haven't had difficult life experiences are only living on the surface.

These women veterans find it hard to have a real conversation. One veteran told me that in the civilian world, it is hard to find friends. Sometimes, when she meets another veteran, it seems as if they had known each other for a long time. When women return to a society unfamiliar with their wartime roles, they often choose isolation to avoid embarrassment. Many spend months or even years inside their apartments or homes, shuttered in a few rooms. A woman who lost her right eye in a mortar attack said that for more than two years after returning home, she rarely left a darkened garage.[49] Some psychiatrists feel that these women's need for help would not be considered valid in a military system that defines combat as an all-male activity.

A woman warrior felt embarrassed about having PTSD and was irritated because other people didn't believe her, as they thought that women didn't have the same experiences as men in war. She complained, "I may not have a purple heart and I may not have wounds you can see. I may not have been the one to kick down the door, but I was there. I drove on the IED-filled streets. I fell asleep every night wondering if this was the night I was going to be blown up. We got bombed every night. I worked the gates and roadblocks. I was shot at. I am still there."[50]

Women who suffer from PTSD are even more invisible than male veterans who struggle with the disorder. Our society doesn't realize how many women are serving in the military and that they may be wives and mothers. They are expected to resume their roles and to act as if nothing had happened when they were overseas.

FAMILY TRAUMA

Few people realize that family members can experience trauma just like the soldiers who return with PTSD. One mother found her loving and caring son transformed, as if he had become a different person. The once-kind son became sarcastic and often made nasty remarks to his mother. He was married with two children, but his wife left him because he began drinking heavily. His mother was beside herself with worry and didn't know how she could help him. She had suggested that he arrange for counseling, but he refused to go through with it. As a parent, she had a strong sense of guilt, and as two years passed with the complications piling up, and when her son went to prison, she became overcome with despair.[51]

One mother had been very close to her son. When he was out with his high-school friends, he used to call her frequently on his cell phone. When he returned from Iraq, he told her that he heard voices in his head and that he wanted to commit suicide. Once he sent her a text message telling her that she was a "shit liberal."[52] He was in the Marines and served as the tower supervisor that is in the middle of the Sunni Triangle. During his shift, bodies were flown out so often that he was deeply upset . He also witnessed a number of soldiers commit suicide. Then he began drinking heavily and getting into trouble. His mother was at her wit's end. She was worried about what he might do, that he might wind up in prison, but she felt powerless to help him. She too changed and found her life unbearable, yet there was no counseling for her. Her only solace was talking with the father of a young man who had returned with similar problems. Like her, he worried about what would happen next to his child, who didn't keep in touch with him. Would he commit suicide, would he wind up in prison? For parents of returned soldiers, having their children home was very much like having them at war, experiencing the same anxiety for their safety and for their lives.

A former soldier, now a minister at the United Church of Christ, had a son in Afghanistan. In a panel discussion about the consequences of war at the American Repertory Theatre, Cambridge, Massachusetts, on March 12, 2011, he spoke of the extreme pain and concern he was experiencing, referring to it as "double pain."

One father revealed that it was not just his son who came back from combat with PTSD, it was the entire family that suffered from combat stress. He had difficulty sleeping at night and lost his job. He used to train medics for the Special Forces. Worst of all are his nightmares, his recurring dream that he is working on a soldier who has been shot in the face. In that dream, he goes to his aid bag, but he is not attending that soldier anymore. Instead, he cares for his son and the soldier keeps asking him why he can't help him.[53]

Many parents of soldiers who have returned with PTSD and gotten involved in drugs, alcohol, or violence, leaving their family in deep despair and without help, have turned their anger and grief into political action.

One father, Tim Kahlor, has been very active in contacting members of Congress and the media on behalf of his son Ryan and Ryan's unit. He describes himself as suffering from secondary PTSD. He spends long days at work, caring for his ill wife at home, as well as supporting other parents whose children have serious PTSD as well as physical wounds. As a result, he too seeks counseling and is on antidepressants.[54] He has become his son's advocate, trying to get him proper healthcare, which has proved very difficult. He has contacted senators and members of Congress besides Barbara Boxer and Diane Feinstein of California, his home state. He continually contacts the media, even those in England. After articles about Ryan appeared, he received numerous telephone calls from other parents asking for his help.

Tim said, "Try to remove the image from my son's mind of cutting off a man's legs that were burned to the bottom of a vehicle [while] the soldier is still talking and they are trying to save him. Remove from his mind the smell of human blood and guts from a vehicle that was cleaned out and used again after men were blown up and their body parts were blown into the vehicle. Remove the image of a young man dying in my son's arms, and loading their bodies, and then a dead soldier's buddy chasing the vehicle with his buddy's legs in his hands. This is just a fraction of my son's memories."[55]

Tim Kahlor is very close to his son, and they exchanged letters and e-mails during Ryan's time in Iraq. Tim shared this page of Ryan's journal from his last year in Iraq,

On the ground, walls and roof tops were pieces of human flesh, bones and gear. I move to the first body that I saw and picking him up to put him on a stretcher. When I did I realized that everything that was in his head was pouring out of a hole in the back of his head. The blood and bone dropped as I set him on a stretcher. He was warm and still flexible like if he was still alive. I look closer and saw that there was a small hole in his forehead where whatever hit him had entered. We loaded him on the back of the medical vehicle and I ran to the next body. He was barely breathing and his body was limp. I grabbed his hand and said "You're going to be fine." His eyes rolled back into his head and I smacked him and told him "stay awake." By the time I had gotten him to the Bradley® he bled out. His left leg was gone and most of the backside of his body. His counterpart was running alongside us with his leg in hand. I took a breath and looked around again and just saw bodies and pieces of bodies. The true wounds are not just one of flesh and bone, but of the mind after experiencing such horror. Those are the ones you cannot treat only overcome it with a strong will.

Ryan's father said that this was just an excerpt from a small portion of that day and that Ryan was only twenty-two years old then, but his last sentence in that journal entry was that of a young man beyond his years.

Tim is extremely upset about the lack of proper care Ryan is receiving after returning from Iraq. He spent twenty-four months in combat and returned with PTSD as well as physical wounds. He had a detached retina, a ruptured disc, vertigo, headaches, memory lapses, and numbness in his arms. Fluid seeped from his ears. Ryan was a sergeant serving with the 1st Armored Division of the army. In Iraq, he survived seven IED attacks and falling off of a second-story building, yet he took narcotics and kept going back into combat. Ryan was also trapped and passed out in a vehicle that was burning. Luckily, a buddy was able to remove him. He had too many close calls.

During his first five months home, Ryan's speech was slurred, but slowly, the worst of the numbness along one side of his body receded. He was diagnosed with traumatic brain injury.[56] In those early months, he needed to write certain things down to remember them. Like so many soldiers returning with combat stress, Ryan kept having the same nightmare, a vision of walls painted in blood, men on top of houses throwing pieces of marines' bodies off rooftops. It was hard to forget what he saw in Iraq.[57] Because it was so difficult for him to sleep during the first years after his return, he began to associate a bed with the nightmares and found that he could sleep better on the floor.[58]

Ryan's first treatment was a counseling session on video from Fort Irwin, Washington. Tim spent time persuading a colonel to find a place for his son there and to accept him at that location. He also sought treatment at a variety of other places. According to that colonel, the best one was at the Balboa Naval Hospital transition unit. But when Ryan does see a counselor, he gets frustrated when he is told, "Everything is going to be okay." Once he became so upset that he grabbed a stapler and started stapling his arm.[59] Then he got involved in a motorcycle accident and burned his arm. His father constantly worries about Ryan's safety because he discovered that a very high number of veterans who have PTSD die in motorcycle accidents.

Tim became so angry at his son's experience that he confronted military recruiters. He intercepted young men outside recruiting offices, warning them about what was in store for them. He read them paragraphs from Ryan's journal. He even approached motorists in cars with yellow ribbons, demanding to know exactly how they were supporting the troops. He carried a poster of his son demanding the medical help Ryan needed. Tim wears a button to his job at the University of California in San Diego with an undated number of the war's dead and a question, "How many more?"[60]

Tim Kahlor made his first contact with the media in 2006 when Ryan's unit lacked sufficient body armor. He went on the Internet to find all the members of the Senate Armed Services Committee, and he telephoned and e-mailed thirty of them to inquire how they could help in providing his son with the required body armor. The typical response was that he should contact his own senator. Tim replied that he was contacting them on behalf of an entire unit that came from different areas of our country. He offered to purchase the armor himself and get reimbursed later. Senator Barbara Boxer did respond and gave him information on how to get reimbursed for that purchase, although she indicated that there would be a time lag for the reimbursement to get paid. In his case, it would take months. Thus, he had to buy what his son needed and send it to him on his own. That made him reflect about the soldiers who needed help but didn't have parents advocating for them.

That was just the beginning for Tim Kahlor. He realized that he needed to make certain that US politicians were paying more attention to the consequences of the war soldiers were facing. He actually met Michelle Obama when she was at a gathering with military families at a Democratic Convention, and he met Secretary of State Hillary Clinton at the State Democratic Convention in California.

His contacts with other policymakers were not as successful. Tim called a senator who had supported the invasion of Iraq to tell him what parents were experiencing. He expressed no interest. He had an argument with a congressman he met who told him, "Your son volunteered"—a reply he would hear over and over again. But he kept telling as many politicians as he could contact what soldiers like Ryan were experiencing in the wars the United States was waging, adding that his own son was only eighteen years old when he enlisted after being told about the educational benefits he would receive.

Tim refers to himself as "a media whore."[61] As a result of speaking out to politicians and the media, he has been deluged with calls for help from parents around the country. For example, a man from Florida called to tell him that his son became a security guard after he returned from the war but was sent to prison for shooting someone. He was able to get that sentence reduced because Tim instructed him how to use the media to publicize his son's problem.

Combat stress brings about recurring bouts of anger. Because soldiers have to distance themselves from emotions suffered during a horrific war, their feelings often flare up at unexpected times after returning to civilian life. The Kahlors have a hole in the wall where Ryan kept pounding to relieve his anger, which is not an unusual pattern of behavior for a returning soldier. Not many people realize how anger and grief are closely intertwined.

Ryan's wife left him, although she tried very hard to make their marriage a good one.[62] Since then, according to his father, he has had many short-term relationships. He gets easily agitated, as do so many returning soldiers. He finds that it is difficult for him to sit in a classroom and concentrate, although he wants so much to attend college.

In the early years of his return, Ryan went to Pathway Home, a privately run institution that offers trauma therapy, but Pathway ran out of funds. Ryan would drive there in the early hours of the morning to avoid traffic because it upset him. Once he saw a terrible car crash on the way, which triggered flashbacks and a difficult reaction. He not only reported the accident but also called his father, who spent an hour talking to him to help him recover enough to keep driving to his destination.

But Ryan has found an occupation that suits him, teaching surfing and kayaking to wounded veterans and their family members. It's very difficult for a returning veteran like Ryan, who has experienced so much, to integrate into civilian life and work in a job that has set hours. He is now twenty-eight years old, and his father still worries about him and wants people to understand what he experienced in the war and what parents suffer when their children return.[63]

TAKING SPACE

Because our soldiers are in a volunteer army, very few people are interested in their experiences or are aware of what is happening on the ground in Iraq and Afghanistan. Also, as the families of these soldiers have discovered, many people are focused on their own lives and are not really interested in learning about what is taking place in countries they know little or nothing about. The wars only became part of the national conversation when Sarah Palin and Joe Biden debated them during the 2008 presidential elections campaign. The 2012 campaign does include discussions about Afghanistan, but they focus mainly on the budget rather than our soldiers. As for news of the war, typically only sparse information will scroll for a few seconds along the bottom of the screen on CNN. The US public has never been so removed from the soldiers who work on its behalf. The suffering of our soldiers and their families has been so marginalized, and their voices often absent from the public discourse. A group of parents of soldiers founded Military Families Speak Out (MFSO) in 2002 to raise the voice of military families. The cofounders were Nancy Lessin and Charlie Richardson, who also worked with the labor movement and had a son in the Marines.[64] That nationwide organization spoke out on behalf of military families that were opposed to a war in Iraq. The membership includes more than four thousand military families and has racial and ethnic diversity. They developed a motto, "Support Our Troops, Bring Them Home Now, Take Care of Them When They Return." MFSO includes a chapter called Gold Star Families Speak Out (Gold Star Families are those who have lost a son or daughter in combat, while GSFSO is a member of MFSO).

Their purpose is also to untangle our attitudes toward war and our troops. Its members have many differing political views on the war, but the organization focuses on the needs of our soldiers. It also works with a number of veterans groups, such as Veterans for Common Sense (VCS), Veterans for Peace, Iraq Veterans Against the War, and many more. One of the many issues that anger the Gold Star families and other family members is a video game called Six Days in Fallujah, which is based upon the deadly battle that took place in Iraq.[65]

MFSO wanted to put a human face on the war and to let the country know what our troops were experiencing. They exposed how shockingly inadequate the planning for the war had been. They revealed how soldiers suffered from the lack of basic supplies, ranging from water to flak jackets. They shared what they had heard from their loved ones about the unconscionable decisions they had to make, such as riding in a Humvee® and seeing movement on a roof that could be an insurgent intent on killing them or just an innocent child getting out for some fresh air. MFSO members addressed religious associations and churches and spoke with print journalists, on television, on radio, and in many communities.

This organization was the first to start speaking about suicide and suicide attempts by returning soldiers. Members of MFSO were in the forefront of speaking about the psychological casualties of the wars. They organized the first conference on suicide, and they spoke out about the severe trauma that multiple deployments had on servicemen and servicewomen already suffering from PTSD.

In 2006, MFSO created Operation House Call and moved to Washington, DC, for the summer. It set up a display of the boots of service members that were killed in that year as well as those of soldiers who had committed suicide. The display was located right in front of the aisle members of Congress pass on their way to their meetings.

Military Families Speak Out meets nationally several times a year. As part of its goal to provide service to soldiers who return home, its members try to raise awareness about PTSD and the high rates of suicide among veterans. They accomplish this through their website, as well as by addressing these issues in interviews and editorials and by participating in demonstrations. Their members hold conferences, meet for a Healing Gathering with Native Americans on Memorial Day, and organize actions such as art exhibits and protest movements. They also travel in groups to meet with members of Congress and the Senate. They post military casualties online on their website. They have found ways to publicize what few people in our country are interested in hearing, and they have managed to avoid being sidelined by the media.

Given what our veterans have experienced during the wars and their continuing long-term needs, they require the support of family, friends, and their community, as well as that of agencies that are supposed to provide health and counseling services. The Department of Veterans Affairs health service is not monolithic. Some strides have been made, but much more needs to be done to help veterans reintegrate into civilian life, which is a goal we should all take part in. The losses and trauma that occurred on 9/11 at the World Trade Center, in Washington, DC, and in Pennsylvania were commemorated ten years after they occurred. There needs to be the same national recognition of our veterans from the wars in Iraq and Afghanistan that were a consequence of that event.

Chapter 3

MOTHERS OF SERVICEMEN AND SERVICEWOMEN

Fig. 3.1. Sara Rich and her daughter Suzanne. *Courtesy of Sara Rich.*

INSIGNIA

One in three females will experience
sexual assault while serving in the military

She hides under a deuce n'half this time—sleeping
on a roll of foam, draped in mosquito netting. Sand flies

hover throughout the night. She sleeps under vehicle exhaust
and heat, dreaming of mortars buried beside her, three stripes

painted on each cold tube, a rocker of yellow hung below.
It's you she's dreaming of, Sergeant—she'll dream of you

for years to come. If she makes it out of this country alive,
which she probably will. You will be the fire and the hovering

breath. Not the sniper. Not the bomber in the streets. You.
So I'm here to ask this one night's reprieve.

Let her sleep tonight. Let her sleep. Pause a moment
under the gibbous moon. Smoke. The gin your wife sent

from New Jersey, colored mint green with food dye
disguised in a bottle of mouthwash: take a long swig of it.

Take the edge out of your knuckles. Let it blur your vision
into a tremor of lights. The explosions in the distance

are not your own. In these long hours before dawn,
on the banks of the Tigris river, let her sleep.

In her dream your eyes are pools of rifle oil.
You unsheathe the bayonet from its scabbard

while she waits. On a mattress of sand and foam, there
in the motor pool, she waits to kiss bullets into your mouth.[1]

—Brian Turner

W hile we ignore the traumas our soldiers have experienced, we are also unaware of the sacrifices their families have endured. The mothers of our soldiers, who have shown great courage and given emotional support to their sons and daughters, have not received the attention and the respect they deserve in our society. They have spoken out in different ways about how our soldiers are treated and insisted that they should be honored and should receive the healthcare they need. Each one of them has a different political outlook, whether they are for or against the war, but what matters is that they are making unusual efforts to be heard and to protect not only their own sons or daughters but all soldiers.

Some mothers are in Gold Star Mothers, a national group of women who have lost their child or children in war; that organization was founded by a group of mothers in 1928 in Washington, DC. The organization was named after the gold star that families hung in their windows in honor of the deceased veteran. Gold Star Mothers Speak Out (GSMSO) is a political group and a member of Military Families Speak Out. Some members of GSMSO became politicized when their children or family members were deployed or when they were killed in the war. Every member has lost a loved one who was deployed in the wars in Iraq or Afghanistan or who died after returning home. These GSMSO members demand accountability from the government for the deaths of their children. They plan demonstrations, contact the media, and have their own websites and blogs. They have taken up the challenge of keeping the wars on the public agenda, a goal that is difficult to accomplish given the state of the economy and concerns about rising deficits and the government's budget. There are mothers who do not belong to such organizations and feel isolated because they live in towns that have few mothers whose children are at war.

Not many people think about the problems that the families of soldiers suffer. The mothers are afraid something will happen to their son or daughter, of someone ringing the doorbell and bringing bad news about their child. They live with worry while they continue to work and to care for other family members. They do everything they can to help their children, send packages, keep in contact by e-mail or letters, and sometimes telephone calls. Having a child at constant and serious risk of being harmed is a very difficult burden to bear.

The mothers' forbearance is also an excellent opportunity to ponder the meaning of strength and weakness. Their sons and daughters work in a military culture that emphasizes strength and believes that to display emotional distress is a sign of weakness. That perspective is held in different ways in a broader society that fears vulnerability. Yet what the mothers of our troops often reveal is that it is possible to show great emotional strength in supporting their children as well as to experience worry and grief.

The philosopher Sara Ruddick has given a widely read analysis of mothering in her book *Maternal Thinking*.[2] One of the important contributions of Ruddick's extraordinary work is how thought and feeling are connected. In our society, feeling, thought, and action are routinely sundered. Further, women are too often castigated for expressing anger, dismissed as bitches. However, anger that is not directed at harming anyone helps us to move beyond fear and to reframe political policy. What Ruddick refers to as *preservative* or *protective love* that extends beyond caring for our own child is reflected in the mothers of our soldiers. They reveal how grief can increase inner strength and endurance.

Patricia Hohl, whose son is a lance corporal in the Marines, is an arts/nonprofit administrator and an attorney. She creates arts and nonprofit organizations and raises funds for them. She is also a writer and a filmmaker.

She published a letter in the *New York Times* on August 31, 2010, describing how she traveled to Camp Lejeune to welcome her son home from Afghanistan. Waiting until 3:00 a.m. for the plane to arrive, she thought about all the families that weren't there because their sons hadn't returned or had already returned severely injured. In an interview she said, "More of us need to speak up, and more people need to realize that these troops we feed into the meat-grinder, these names and numbers we read in the newspaper, are our children and we want them home."[3]

In other words, Patricia Hohl was making an important statement that she supported the troops but not the war. According to philosopher Ruddick, Hohl's actions exemplify what many mothers do: their maternal political stand for peace.[4]

Patricia Hohl is angry because she believes that no one seems to care about the soldiers or the war in our country. She wonders, "How do you get people to pay attention in this culture where there are so many venues for expression? How do you find one that you can be heard in?"[5]

Patricia Hohl was distressed by her son Alexander's dream of joining the army since he was ten years old. He often watched history channels on television and movies that his mother regarded as glorifying war. She always hoped he would grow out of it. She gave him history books and took him to antiwar movies, but they made no impression.

In his last year of high school, Alexander was looking forward to seeing a military recruiter. Because he had gone to a nontraditional school in his town, the recruiter told him that his diploma and school weren't worth much and that he should get some college credits and earn a B average. That is exactly what he did, working very hard and earning quite a few credits. Like many young men and women, he was deeply affected by 9/11. It strengthened his resolve to become a marine.

His mother was upset when he was accepted into the military and sent to boot camp at Camp Lejeune, North Carolina, when he was only eighteen because she refers to herself as a "peacenik." But she realized that since he was grown up and had his own life, the best thing she could do for him was to love and support him.

Before he left, she gave him a journal so he could write down his thoughts about this period. They corresponded frequently. His letters reveal that he had entered a new culture, drill sergeants disciplining him by making him do one hundred pushups in sand whenever he didn't do something right, being woken up at 3:00 a.m., and other moments he found miserable. But he was also happy to be with his group. She went to his boot camp graduation and saw her beloved son in uniform among lines of well-groomed young men in his platoon.

Although she and her son are very close, they often disagree. Alexander had sent her one of his dog tags and asked her to keep it and remember that her son is a fighter. She does not believe that he is keeping his family safe or helping people improve their conditions overseas, and she tells him so during their long discussions. Yet he is very proud of what he is accomplishing, so she wears his dog tag under her clothes.

After President Obama announced the troop surge in November 2009, Alexander went to Afghanistan in early December and served there until the end of July 2010. He had become a lance corporal. He had access to satellite phones, and every few months his mother would receive a telephone call, and occasionally an e-mail or a text message. But he sent letters all the time because they are very close, and he shared as much of his experience as he was allowed to.

He did talk a bit to his mother about his time in Afghanistan when he returned. He came home with a lot of footage he had shot with his phone camera. But he wasn't able to tell his parents very much. There were times when he was with people and he'd say, "I'm not talking about war," because he just wanted to have fun and be with his friends.

By then Patricia was experiencing what Ruddick refers to as *preservative love*, thinking about soldiers who had died and mothers whose children would return severely wounded. She would pray and ask for help and then ask herself why her prayers should be listened to when there were so many mothers needing help and so many dying soldiers that might be praying.

As every military mother probably does, Alexander's mother feels that soldiers need help when they return, but she sees that there is very little counseling available. She views the army as a masculine culture with soldiers who are afraid of revealing that they have emotional pain lest they should be seen as wimps. In fact, some soldiers have actually been dismissed from the armed forces when they showed signs of PTSD (Post-Traumatic Stress Disorder).

When Alexander returned from Afghanistan, he gave his mother his journal, wrapped in an Afghan textile that was stained red from the sand. He even wrote in it, "I did this for my mom," and told her, "I did this for you." She felt it was a special gift because he was honest and open about his frustrations.

Her son was scheduled to go back to Afghanistan in August 2011. He had two more years in the marines. Then he needed to spend some years in the reserves. There was originally talk that he would go over on a ship, but she was very upset that he would be returning to Afghanistan at all. She regarded her hope for his safety as fragile.

Patricia feels that she is in a strange place because her nuclear family is not a typical military family. She is a liberal, and her political views are different—"left-leaning," as she calls them.[6] She feels that many people who support the war cannot distinguish between supporting the war and supporting the troops. Her brother was in the navy, and at the time she was very much against the war, causing his family to feel anger toward her. She knew that she needed to make the distinction she feels between supporting the troops and supporting the war, and she wants to be heard by the broader society.

She doesn't like the situation in Afghanistan, yet her sister-in-law told her that the war was very good for the United States since the company she worked for was prospering because of its connections. Referring to a term that President Eisenhower made in one of his last speeches, Patricia thought of Halliburton and Raytheon as part of the military-industrial complex. Like President Eisenhower, she thinks that more of our military budget should be used to provide for our citizens' needs.

In October 2010, Patricia was at a rally in Washington, DC, called One Nation Working Together. It took place on the mall in front of the Lincoln

Memorial. Peace Action joined with the NAACP, Service Employees International Union (SEIU), AFL-CIO, National Council of La Raza, Green for All, United States Students' Association (USSA), and hundreds of faith, community, immigrant-rights, and peace groups, to protest the wars and demand that the government create jobs for people. She believes that conflating the war and our economic problems would help the broader society pay attention to the wars instead of ignoring them.

Another political action that Patricia engages in occurs right on the outside wall of her house. In December 2007, she bought two cans of paint at a local hardware store, one red and one white. She made white rectangles, each with a painted red number and a hole drilled through the top, so they could slide on and off of the outside wall, with five nails as place holders. That is where she displays the number of soldiers killed in Iraq and Afghanistan. They read in December 2010, 4,430 (Iraq) and 1,440 (Afghanistan). She has placed them there to remind people of the costs of these wars. She is often asked what they mean, and those questions make her feel less powerless. She explains that "the more this war goes on, the more I want to talk to the mothers of soldiers. I listen to the radio. I hear a name. I read a name. They are not just names. It could be my child. It makes me cry every time. I don't know why we mothers are not screaming our heads off."[7]

Patricia has a friend who is making a film about returning veterans. He is a former marine who served for four years and is in his early sixties. He is disturbed by the thought that if a person doesn't support the war, he or she doesn't support the troops. What bothers Patricia the most is that she feels that nobody in this country seems to care about our soldiers. Her dual and conflicting goals are to support her son, whom she loves deeply, and to take a stand against the war in Afghanistan.[8]

• • •

Cheryl Softich is a quiet and reserved woman who works in a local bank in Sparta, Minnesota. Like Alexander, her son, Noah, started talking about joining the military when he was very young. Upon graduating from high school in June 2002, Noah decided to join the army. His mother knew this would happen and was uncomfortable with his decision. Since he had not yet turned eighteen, he needed her to sign his enlistment papers. She was in a very difficult position and repeatedly tried to talk him out of going to Iraq, without success. Despite her reluctance, she signed his papers. She concluded, "There was no way Noah was going to do anything without my support."[9] Caring mothers often find themselves challenged in many ways while nurturing their children who move away from them as they change. Mothers like Cheryl experience emotional and intellectual growth even though they feel conflicted.

Noah went to boot camp at Fort Stewart, Georgia, in October 2002. He served with the 3rd Infantry Division, first in Kuwait. He went to Iraq in March 2003 when the Iraq invasion began. He was a member of the 1st Platoon, Bravo Battery, First Battalion, 3rd Air Defense Artillery Regiment and was assigned to the front line. He drove a Bradley® fighting vehicle, was a gunner on a Humvee®, and entered Iraqi houses in search of the enemy. He turned nineteen and twenty-one in Iraq. Despite being honored for his bravery in combat, Noah faced many terrifying and upsetting situations in Iraq. He saw his close friend blown up, and he witnessed the deaths of many innocent people.

As a sensitive and caring person, Noah was distressed about the killings of innocent people he witnessed, and he was angered at the different views of the war in the United States. He kept his sister's photo near him as a source of comfort. Noah also wrote, e-mailed, and telephoned his mother frequently, telling her what he was involved in, even though this was not really permitted. He even sent her deeply moving poems he had written about his heartaches and despair.

Cheryl had foresight and tried to help Noah through his anguish. She experienced a new ability to support him and repeatedly told him, "Whatever you do in a war situation to keep your sanity and survive doesn't matter because you are not in the real world. If you did these things in my world, then you would be wrong and would have to account for them. But what you do in a war does not make you a murderer. You are following the orders of the United States government. That is not murder. A murderer is someone who kills a person on the street for no reason. Half of the time do you really know that it was your bullet, Noah? Sometimes you may know it was yours, but you don't know because you are not the only one who is shooting."[10]

Cheryl was not prepared for Noah's return. She was faced with a social response that sought to marginalize her and her son. Once when Noah was standing in line to renew his driver's license, some young adults called out, "Noah, did you kill anybody?" Veterans consider such a terrible remark as a slap in the face. Noah just picked up his papers and walked out without a word. He also quit his job at the mines and went to work as a machinist in his friend's company for the same reason.

Cheryl not only had to be a new presence for her son but also had to respond to social attempts to undermine him. She spoke out forcefully and wrote numerous letters of opinion that were published in the local newspaper, criticizing some of the reactions to Noah. She questioned those who had the temerity to ask any returning veteran whether he or she had killed anyone. She also demanded that they keep silent and be sensitive enough to realize that if a person wants to talk about his war experience, it is up to him to bring it up, not to ignorant bystanders.

Cheryl never tried to engage Noah in conversations about his problems because her friends who had served in Vietnam and in the navy for many years advised her against it. She felt that he had to be the one to decide when to talk about his time in Iraq. Meanwhile, she watched him drink to forget his experiences. She knew he wanted to return to Iraq for a third time so he could die, but she and his sister, Sarah, persuaded him not to return.

Like most family members of returning soldiers, Cheryl was unprepared for the changes in her son. Noah was coming home from another world with a psychological burden that was invisible. He was suddenly in a world he no longer felt part of because of his experiences with death and destruction. Her anger also caused her to publicize her outrage at the attempts to ignore his problems and at the inadequate medical treatment available to traumatized veterans. These experiences transformed her into a politically and socially active woman.

Noah didn't receive the help he required to deal with his symptoms, other than access to the veteran's hospital and clinic for checkups for a mere ninety days. He sought assistance for his nightmares, but all he received was a prescription for sleeping pills and appointments for return visits. He desperately needed medical care because he was losing his hearing and knew that he had brain damage from being so close to explosions. But he didn't keep his appointments. The clinic did not call him or try to reschedule. By then, the mandatory period of thirty to ninety days when Noah could receive medical help was over.

Meanwhile, Cheryl was educating herself about Noah's condition and she learned that the problems he experienced usually manifest themselves six to eight months after soldiers return home. She was irritated by the fact that whenever she failed to show up for an appointment with a physician, she would get a phone call, but Noah was never contacted by the clinic for missing his appointment. Cheryl began to acquire a great deal of knowledge about Noah's condition, including in a telephone conference with a psychiatrist in Massachusetts. She knew that like so many other troubled veterans, her son felt that if he had a visible wound, people would have acknowledged his suffering.

Cheryl has made an astonishing transition very much like some of the mothers from countries around the world unwillingly caught up in political situations. Like them, she has grown from caring for her own suffering child to working on behalf of other people's children and becoming a political activist.[11] She gives lectures at local colleges before mental-health workers and family members of veterans. She even gives interviews on television with a local congressman. In the fall of 2011, she became involved in a PTSD awareness project by telling Noah's story on the radio, on television, and to newspapers around the country.

Cheryl has gone even further by undertaking a tremendous effort to ensure mandatory counseling for soldiers during and after combat. She has written a letter about this to every member of Congress and the Senate, recounting Noah's experiences and explaining her mission to help create "Noah's Law."

Letter to members of US Congress and Senate:

December 2, 2008,

My name is Cheryl Softich, the mother of Army Specialist Noah C. Pierce. My son served two tours of duty in Iraq, and even though he physically returned home, mentally my son never came home. Noah had PTSD and was a prisoner of war in his own mind, and, left untreated, the PTSD progressively worsened.

When Noah was released from the Army after his four years were up, he did fulfill his mandatory 30,60,90-day appointments with the Veterans Administration. All he ever got for his efforts were sleeping pills which did not help, nor address the PTSD and that was just the beginning of many cracks my son fell through before finally taking his own life on July 26, 2007. Noah drove to a favorite childhood hangout and it was there that he put a pistol to his temple and wedged one of his dog tags between the temple and the gun before pulling the trigger producing a nice, clean and perfectly fatal shot. My son was dead in the blink of an eye and we are left to pick up the pieces. In my case, I have a mission, a goal. That goal is something I refer to as NOAH'S CLAUSE.

NOAH'S CLAUSE

As a member of the US Army, counseling is required for all service members (active and inactive) that have served in a combat zone. This counseling would start no later than six months after the service has been completed, and will continue up to and not less than twelve months. This MANDATORY counseling can be group, or one on one. If after the twelve months is up and a person wants to continue with counseling, they should be allowed to do so.

I believe that we owe it all to our servicemen and women along with their families to provide this service. It is a small price to pay considering all they have given to us. I have the right to speak my mind and try to make changes for the better. . . . I have this right because of all of our Veterans, past, present and future. We all do, and maybe it is time to remind those that have forgotten. If we added a Noah's Clause to the contracts that are signed, our soldiers would be protected from themselves. Getting help is not a weakness, and this would be an order. Soldiers follow orders. How can we not have a Noah's Clause?

I did have a chance this summer to speak to a group about PTSD and followed a lady bragging about the 30,60,90-day counseling rule and how wonderful that was. Well, when I came up to speak she told them that 30,60,90 days are great . . . if you don't want to hear or see the truth. Ironically, after the workshop was over that same woman approached me with her National Guard husband in tow and they told me that her husband is alive today because of a television interview I gave about PTSD and my son. Her husband was leaving the house when something about my voice compelled him to sit down and listen to more. When the interview was over the man was in tears. He reached into his pocket and handed his wife a pistol. That man was on his way out that night to die, but because of Noah's story and my speech he is alive and in counseling. Two kids still have their father; a wife still has her husband. Once again I ask you, how can we not have a Noah's Clause?
—Cheryl Softich

In November 2010, Cheryl was invited by the Pentagon to speak with General Casey about mandatory counseling for all returning soldiers. Her grief over her son's death is an important part of the movie *Wartorn*, which was aired on HBO.[12]

• • •

Sara Rich's outspoken help for her daughter's difficult situation in Iraq and the problems of her homecoming caused her to become politically active on a national scale. Her efforts help us all to revise our thoughts about mothers and political power. In Argentina during the Dirty War of 1976–1983, a group of women, the Mothers of the Plaza de Mayo, who were housewives, some of whom never finished high school, became activists against the government, a life-long career. They inspired women in the United States, such as the Mothers of East Los Angeles, to form an organization that would ensure their children's health and safety. The Mothers of the Plaza de Mayo even created an international organization of politically active mothers who supported each other even though they were on different sides politically, both within and between their countries.

Sara Rich is a social worker and family therapist who lives in Eugene, Oregon. Before her daughter went to Iraq, Sara was a human-rights commissioner for Eugene, a position that furthered her interest in human rights. Because her daughter suffered terribly from sexual harassment while she was in Iraq, Sara channeled her outrage into reaching out to other mothers whose daughters had the same type of experience and creating a widespread group of mutual support. This group helped her pay for her daughter's medical expenses and the lawyers Sara hired to represent her daughter. It also helped her contact members of Congress.

The way her daughter was treated by her sergeants and her NCOs (non-commissioned officers) in Iraq and after her return inspired Sara to become a national voice against rape occurring in the military. She gave talks at universities around the country, North Carolina, Salt Lake City, Los Angeles, and she also spoke in front of a Women's Law Organization in Seattle and at a Veterans for Peace organization national convention on September 11, 2006. She gave many interviews, and numerous articles were written about her and her daughter Suzanne, appearing in the *New York Times*, the *Washington Post*, and a number of other highly respected newspapers and journals.

Sara also set up a website about her daughter and created a large network of mothers whose children had similar experiences in the military. The e-mail list she created brought her and her daughter a great deal of support. She also came together with other military mothers whose children experienced difficulties when they were in combat. Sara was with five hundred military mothers when they had a demonstration in Washington, DC, in front of the White House in 2007.

When Suzanne was eighteen and had graduated from high school, she was working at a job she didn't particularly like. A military recruiter called their home and invited Suzanne to lunch. Sara comes from a military family and was pleased at her daughter's prospects, but Suzanne did tell her mother that if she signed up with the military police for five years, she would not be sent to Iraq. However, when she completed her basic training, she was immediately sent there. A sergeant kept calling Suzanne a few times a day to make certain that she was all right, and Sara was impressed by his concern for her.

Sara is very protective of her children. "My goal when she was deployed to Iraq was to focus on the positive. I didn't tell her once that I missed her or that I was worried about her. I wanted her to focus on staying alive and being strong. I'd say 'I'm so proud of you. You're so strong.' I did not want to show my worry to her."[13]

When Suzanne arrived in Kuwait in 2004, where she was supposed to be prepared for deployment in Iraq, she told her mother that her sergeant looked at her and asked her, "Why are you looking at me as if you want to have sex with me?"[14] She was so shocked that she walked away and told him that he had lost his mind. The following day, he made her get into a Humvee with him, just the two of them, and he told her, "You can keep a secret, nobody is going to find out." She looked at him again as if he was unhinged and immediately went to talk to the Equal Opportunity Officer, William Cox, to tell him what had transpired between her and her sergeant. But he did nothing for her. Sara believes that because Suzanne received no help, it was an indication that nobody would help her daughter. She believes that seasoned NCOs make bets about which of the women is going to be theirs. They separate these women, put them in different rooms, so they have easy access to them. There were four women and ninety men in the unit. Suzanne told her mother that she was coerced into having a sexual relationship that lasted three months. The sergeant in question would come to her room in the middle of the night, drunk.

Sara reports that Suzanne's sergeant frightened her. He kept punishing her, singling her out so she would appear as if she were a bad soldier by making her do push-ups for hours until she threw up in the mud and behind the barracks. Sara felt that he did this to prevent the rest of the unit from finding out how he was treating her daughter. Eventually he started asking her if she'd be his girlfriend when they returned and Suzanne replied, "You're kidding. You are the meanest person I've ever met." When Suzanne ended the arrangement with her squad leader, he retaliated by ordering her to do solitary forced marches from one side of the camp to another, at night and in full battle gear, and by humiliating her in front of her fellow soldiers.

Suzanne kept calling her mother and telling her about the sexual abuse she was experiencing rather than about the horrors of the war. She told her that they called all the women in her platoon "whores," "cunts," or "dykes" and that they didn't treat them like human beings. Because of this treatment, Suzanne became depressed and wouldn't leave her room until she had to. Then her sergeants started in on her again. Because they said that she was thirty seconds late, they made her carry a wall clock with her for an indefinite amount of time. Everywhere she went, she had to carry it—until one night she went to her sergeant's room and threw it at him.

As Suzanne told her mother, this treatment was happening while she was driving a Humvee in Karbala during combat patrol. Her camp there was hit by mortar attacks almost nightly for the first two months of her deployment. Suzanne worked sixteen-hour shifts, experiencing the death of a fellow company member in an incident of friendly fire and seeing a close friend injured in a car bombing. Suzanne's mother was so worried about Suzanne's safety that she couldn't bear to read the newspapers, listen to the radio, or watch television reports about the war. But Suzanne kept calling her mother and crying. Her mother really wanted to help her through this difficult time with her sergeants and kept asking what she could do. Suzanne told her that it was very dangerous for her to say or do anything about what was happening to her.

Sara sent her books and e-mails and had her support group send packages to her daughter every week so that she would know that people were aware of what was happening to her and that they cared. As a matter of fact, Sara knew the wives and children of the sergeants who were abusing her. Meanwhile, she kept in close touch with mothers of women soldiers who were experiencing the same problems, some of them even worse.

When Suzanne returned in February 2005, her mother made sure that she went to see a civilian therapist, where she was diagnosed with PTSD. She also saw a physician at the Veterans Affairs (VA) system in Eugene, where she received good treatment because she is partially disabled as a result of her soldiering in Iraq. Her mother asked her if she could do something to help her, but Suzanne replied that she had to deploy with the same group.

Again, she told her mother that when she asked him where he wanted her to report to him, he replied, "in my bed, naked." The other soldiers heard that and simply looked away. Suzanne reported this remark to her commander, and they were both interrogated about having a sexual relationship even though they weren't having one. Her sergeant was moved to a new unit, and she was treated like a traitor and called degrading names, she reports. Women soldiers like Suzanne suffer from PTSD not only because of their wartime experience but also as a result of rape and sexual assault.

Nine months later, Suzanne told her mother that she had been forced to sign a waiver ending her rights to eighteen-month leave. When she refused, she was told that her life would be hell if she didn't sign. Three days before her deployment with the 54th Military Police Company, she went home. She had sent her things off to Iraq and had packed her footlocker and put it in her car. On January 8, 2006, with her keys in hand, she looked at her mother and told her she just couldn't return. She went AWOL. For the first two days after she failed to report, she watched her cell phone light up with calls from her commanders. For the rest of that winter, she hid out in the seaside town of Brookings, staying in a friend's home, uncertain whether the army was looking for her.[15] In April she moved back into her family's house. Her mother hired an attorney and called the GI-rights hotline, and they began working on getting her emotionally and mentally stable so that she could turn herself in to Fort Lewis.

On the night of June 11, two local police officers arrived at Sara's house at 10:30 and took Suzanne away in handcuffs. They took her to a country jail where they strip-searched her and orifice-searched her and denied her medical care for an abscessed tooth. Her mother gave a press conference and had a vigil in front of the jail. She spoke to ten different radio shows (some nationally syndicated), three television stations, and three newspapers, and she received many calls.

Suzanne was in prison for three days until she was returned to Fort Lewis in the care of her unit and under the supervision of the original platoon sergeant that had harassed her. Sara and her attorney persuaded Senator Patty Murray to intervene and remove her from this sergeant's supervision with a no-contact order.

Once a week, Suzanne's mother came to pick her up at the base and take her out for a meal, and then they would check in to a nearby Holiday Inn, talking and watching television. At 6:30 the following morning, Suzanne would put on her uniform and her mother would drive her back to Fort Lewis in time for her to report for work.[16]

Her mother tried to get Suzanne honorably discharged. Her attorney told her that he talked to her captain and that she needed to prepare herself for a court martial. One investigation officer and a military psychologist focused on Suzanne's allegation for only one hour. The psychologist concluded that Suzanne had symptoms of PTSD, but not enough for him to give her that diagnosis. Meanwhile, two of the people who molested Suzanne had left the army and one of them was working for the private security company Blackwater (now called Academi).[17]

A 2003 report financed by the Department of Defense revealed that nearly one-third of female veterans seeking healthcare through the VA said they had experienced rape or attempted rape during their service.[18] Both rape and combat stress can create trauma. Like Suzanne, most female veterans from Iraq feel that reporting military-assault charges was not worth their effort. The Department of Defense statistics bear this out. Of the over three thousand investigations of military sexual assault, only one-tenth of them have resulted in a court martial for the perpetrator.[19] In addition, complaining about their treatment subjected women like Suzanne to constant ridicule and criticism. She was called all kinds of degrading names, and she told her mother that women are treated like traitors if they reveal the sexual harassment they have experienced.

Suzanne did have to face a court martial for being AWOL. Her mother sat through the proceedings with her and testified. Suzanne started to cry as she retold her story of being abused and humiliated by the sergeant who was supposed to be looking out for her rather than intimidating her. She did plead guilty of going AWOL, and she was sent to prison for thirty days as well as being stripped of her rank. Suzanne asked that her rank be maintained or suspended because she was proud to have been made a specialist and dreamed of being a sergeant. Sara arranged to have posters and T-shirts made with the words "Free Suzanne" and "Suzanne's My Hero" printed on them.

Suzanne was in prison during Christmas and New Year, but her mother couldn't visit her because she was helping her younger daughter give a home birth. Since she was unable to visit Suzanne during that time, Sara arranged for letters to be sent to her daughter and for friends to visit her.

After her release, the army transferred Suzanne to Fort Irwin, California. Sara was furious that they took away her support system, including her psychologist. Suzanne remained in the army on that base for two years doing what her mother calls, "weeds and seeds things. That means cleaning weeds at the volleyball court and answering the telephone." Her latest job was filing AWOL reports in another office.[20]

In 2008, in Maryland, Sara was on a panel with a woman who wrote a book about what was happening to women in the military. Eve Ensler, the author of *The Vagina Monologues*, wrote a monologue for Suzanne called "Going AWOL," and even Gary Trudeau fashioned a character after Suzanne, named Melissa, for his *Doonesbury* comic strip.

Suzanne is now out of the army and in college because of the GI Bill. Her mother sees or calls her every day. Sara is no longer involved in her political work, but she is still very much concerned about her daughter, who has made friends but is wary of men and still suffers from PTSD.[21]

• • •

Anna Berlinrut is a legal assistant in a law firm in New Jersey. Although she comes from a military family—her husband served in Vietnam, her father was a disabled World War II veteran, and her grandfather was a veteran from World War I—she was very upset that her son joined the Marines when he was only eighteen years old. He did so because he was patriotic and felt an obligation to serve his country even when he was a young child. When he was only ten years old, he started reading voraciously about World War II. Like so many mothers, she tried to persuade him not to enlist but was unsuccessful.

First her son went to Kosovo, but he was deployed to Iraq when he was married and had a six-month-old son. He's been deployed five times.

Anna feels that the troops are not adequately provided for in too many ways. When her son was in Fallujah, Iraq, his sergeant e-mailed the families to send in helmet kits because their helmets were not strong enough to prevent brain damage from IEDs. The parents sent $73.00 for each marine. Anna took up a collection for them. In addition, her son bought two GPSs for himself during his first two deployments there because they only have one per unit, and he was concerned about getting lost if he was separated from his unit.

She also sends him boxes of food. Marines are not located on bases and are given MREs (meals ready to eat) that do not suffice for the long term. Anna takes every opportunity she can to speak about the needs of our troops. For example, shopping for her son in the supermarket is a way of reaching out to people and telling them what is happening to our soldiers. When she was buying salmon for her son, deciding whether to take a can or a bag, she met a woman there and told her that she was sending this to her son in Afghanistan, and then they started talking. The woman was discussing the war, but Anna spoke about it from the troops' and the families' side, and they had a wonderful discussion. When a person learns something she or he never thought about, that person is usually eager to share that information, so that an individual can make a difference.

Her son is in Helmand Province, but he has not been able to call her since he has been there. They do have a satellite phone, but she told him that if he could only make one call a month, it should be to his wife. Anna and her son's wife are very close, and she e-mails her mother-in-law whenever she receives a phone call from her husband.

Like so many family members of active-duty servicemen and servicewomen, Anna has difficulty sleeping at night. The first thing she does every morning is to check a website, www.icasualties.org, which gives the count of how many soldiers were killed and in what location so she can find out where the action is and if it happened in her son's unit. In addition to updated numbers for Iraq and Afghanistan, there are short news synopses as well. She puts the number of deaths on a button she wears that has a coffin on it and the words "How Many More?" and she updates it regularly.

Anna has been interviewed on radio and on television. Recently (2011) she did a radio show *America Abroad* through the American University in Washington. They had four panelists, two Americans and two Afghans in Kabul. There were audio systems in both locations so that they could exchange questions. One person asked Anna a very difficult question—how she felt as a mother knowing that her child was killing innocent Afghans. She refused to answer the question, which she found inappropriate. She didn't mention that when her son was in Fallujah, there was a ten-year-old who threw a grenade at the soldiers. Nor did she say that one of the reasons why so many troops come home and attempt to commit suicide is because they were exposed to such horrific experiences in Iraq. Most of her radio interviews have been on CBS and NPR. The international press was more involved in the many demonstrations in which Anna participated. *Der Spiegel* sent a photographer to her home, and she had interviews with the British, Italian, and Japanese press.

She has also spoken with her congressman on several occasions and found him very responsive. However, she reports that her senators have shown little interest in her concerns. She describes military families as the "lost 1 percent because only one half of 1 percent of Americans have a loved one in harm's way. Therefore, the rest of the country doesn't even realize what is going on and our representatives generally don't care because military families do not represent enough votes for them."[22]

For three or four years, beginning in 2005, Anna had a vigil with some other military family members and veterans every week. She would stand on a street corner in an area of her town and hand out a two-page weekly newsletter she wrote. The back page had ten different stories about the wars and the front page was one long article. People would actually come up to her for the newsletter because this information was not covered by the media. Nobody ever dropped the newsletter on the ground as litter. One therapist came up to her during a vigil and said he would be happy to volunteer sessions with military families. She put him in touch with a woman who had PTSD and was sexually abused in Iraq. The vigils would begin at 5:00 p.m. on Wednesdays so it would attract people coming home from work. She found that some people were actually stopping by in their cars to pick up the newsletter. Her goal was to reach out to people who were not aware of what was happening in the war or who may have thought that the war was necessary. Anna found that after she talked to them, they would become more open to discussion about the war. She found quite a response from people who were not connected. Sometimes people would be very much opposed to the vigil, yet by the time they read the two pages, they seemed more open. Anna believes that being a military family member has a lot of influence on people because military family members are the ones who have so much at stake, and she considers herself to be very patriotic. She finds that discussions with different points of view are very useful.

After President Obama was elected, he didn't bring back the troops home any faster than President Bush would have done. This discouraged many people, and one by one they left the vigil. Anna found that she just couldn't get people to commit to join her. She believes that people have given up hope. She is also concerned about the military-industrial complex and finds that major corporations contribute so much money to elect politicians who will fund research on existing armaments and fund new ones. As a result, she believes that military families have the smallest voices in the United States because they cannot give millions to political candidates, and until there is campaign-finance reform, there is not going to be any change. She also knows that just taking care of our wounded veterans would take decades and cost trillions.

Anna has found that many soldiers who have enlisted in the Individual Ready Reserve (IRR) think that they are in only for the four years of active duty. Many of them, like Anna's son, forget that they can be called back any time for another four years. When they return from a war zone afterward, they find jobs, marry, and start families. Then, three or four years later, they are called back for another four years.[23] Even young mothers have been sent back as a result of their Individual Ready Reserve. Enlistees often forget that side of their commitment. If they are single moms, or if both parents are in the military, as is fairly typical now, the child or children are put into foster care. Anyone who has read about the problems of foster care, and they are legion, would be more than upset. Anna says that she doesn't know of any volunteer organization that a person is unable to withdraw from except for the military. Anna's son had five deployments and he still has six more years to serve. He knows a man who is on his thirteenth deployment. A marine stays in combat for only seven months.

Anna's brother is a retired air force officer, and he told her that, just before reaching the twenty-year limit to become eligible for retirement, many soldiers or sergeants were told they couldn't even reenlist and were withdrawn before retirement, thus they were denied their retirement rights. There is a bill before the Congress and Senate now that would lower the retirement benefits for veterans, although there are also some good proposals, such as helping veterans find jobs when they return.

● ● ●

Adele Kubein's daughter, M'kesha, joined the National Guard in 1999. Although her family's poverty was a motivation, her mother tried to dissuade her, but M'kesha replied, "There's never going to be another war."[24] She enjoyed her time in the guard because it gave her discipline and she was pleased to learn diesel mechanics and engage in public service. She told her mother, "The people of Oregon are sending me to college so I can pay them back."[25]

Neither Adele nor her daughter expected that she would be deployed to a war zone. In 2003, M'kesha went to Iraq. M'kesha's unit leader stated that she would not be in combat situations and that Pentagon regulations prohibit women from being assigned to ground combat.[26] But once in Iraq, she was ordered to operate a 50-caliber machine gun without body armor and with minimal ammunition to protect convoys of an engineering and construction company. She remained in Iraq for ten months.

Before she left, she gave her mother a cell phone and told her, "I'm going to need to be calling you." Adele kept that telephone with her every second. They talked at least twice a month. As Adele recalls, M'kesha once called her when she was in the middle of the desert and told her, "Mom, I'm never going to be able to come home again and live a normal life. I killed a fifteen-year-old boy today. He was just defending his family and I attacked him because I thought he was going to kill us." Adele replied, "You did what you had to do. You're not a bad person." It was 3:00 a.m. in Oregon because, like most family members of soldiers, they are used to being available at all hours, and sleep is not an issue. Adele realized that the emotional impact of this horrible event would last forever in her daughter's life.[27]

M'kesha was in a helicopter that was shot down near Mosul. Her leg was badly broken, but her commanding officer didn't believe her, so she stayed in combat for another two months because he thought she was malingering. She kept on working until a general saw her and asked why she was limping. As a result, they evacuated her and sent her to a hospital. When the physician did a pre-op screening, he told her that she was pregnant. The officers never told her that birth control failed because of antimalarial drugs. They discovered that she was three and a half months pregnant and told her that she needed an abortion because she had been exposed to toxic waste and depleted uranium. She refused to have an abortion because, as she told them, she had killed enough people. Adele noted that a lot of female soldiers come back pregnant and some marriages break up. Apparently M'kesha, like too many other female soldiers, experienced serious sexual harassment.

They were unable to repair her leg at the hospital because it had remained mangled for so long that it became twisted and is missing muscles and tendons. It's incredibly painful for her because the bones rub on each other. Now she can only walk the distance of a block with her cane.[28]

As a result, she was sent home to a base in Colorado. She returned from the war zone with PTSD and suicidal thoughts. At that time, injured soldiers were required to sign a waiver and remain on active duty to be treated. M'kesha refused.[29] To protect her daughter, Adele contacted her congressman, and he was more than helpful, issuing an Act of Congress. Her daughter came home, was treated by doctors, and received disability.

But M'kesha wants her leg amputated so she can receive a prosthesis and walk again. She went to consult with a prosthetic rehabilitative clinic and the physician assured her that her life would improve considerably, but the VA refused to amputate her leg. Adele believes that it's simply because the VA didn't want to pay for it. However, M'kesha does receive free counseling from the Soldiers Project.

M'kesha has made a remarkable return despite all of her psychological and physical problems. She has a home in the countryside with a partner and is devoted to her son, who is disabled. He's seven years old and is unable to talk or write. Adele believes that raising this child has saved her daughter's life. Although raising her son is a full-time job, M'kesha is running a Doberman rescue service, saving dozens of dogs every year, then retraining and finding homes for them. She finds that it brings meaning to her life. Adele sees many veterans that are re-creating their lives even though they are unable to hold full-time jobs.

Adele sees her role as to listen to her daughter and to be available whenever her daughter calls her, since she doesn't have people who understand what she has experienced in combat. They talk four hours a day because Adele wants to help her daughter carry the burden of her time in Iraq, since she understands what happens psychologically to soldiers.

She is also in touch with mothers whose children are at war. She is a member of Military Families Speak Out, which not only engages in lobbying and demonstrations but also is available to families that need a place where somebody can understand what they are experiencing and share their worries. Adele said, "Nobody can deal with other mothers who haven't been there because there are so few serving. You can be crying, your child can be killed at any moment, you may be unable to function."[30] She knows when to talk to a mother, when not to, when she needs a hug, and that every mother has a different way of dealing with this stress. She is also very annoyed at constantly hearing from other people, "Your child volunteered, it was her choice."

Once she took to the governor's office a woman who badly needed help. The woman's husband was one of the few recruiters that had been deployed to Iraq. He became increasingly destabilized, and his wife kept telling his commanding officer that he desperately needed attention, but the commanding officer ignored her.[31] Then her husband cut his throat in front of his family, but she managed to get him to the hospital in time to save his life. Before doing this, he had removed her from their bank accounts and his commanding officer was going to remove her from their house.[32] Adele took her to the governor's office and he helped her out.

Adele is a member of a support group in Portland, Oregon, that meets once or twice a month and makes packages to send to soldiers in Iraq and Afghanistan. Although she has also been demonstrating and writing articles for the media, Adele now sees that her greatest opportunity is the one she has as a professor. She can teach her students to think about things that are important and create a change in their consciousness.

• • •

Few people realize that grandmothers are caring for their grandchildren while their son or daughter and their spouse are serving in Afghanistan. One grandmother's daughter is in Afghanistan while her husband is in Iraq with the Special Forces. She is concerned that the newspapers publish articles about the number of soldiers who are withdrawing from Iraq but never mention the fact that new forces are coming in.

This grandmother is not only working but also caring for her five-year-old child. Her daughter misses her son very much and he longs for his mother and father. Sometimes he goes through periods when he chews his T-shirts or has anxiety, but he is too young to articulate his feelings. Even though she loves her little grandson very much and finds much joy in his presence, caring for him is not easy.

This grandmother is concerned about all the children whose parents are active in the war. Not all of them have loving grandparents. She knew about the case of a nine-month-old baby whose parents were deployed and who has no one to care for him. The daycare workers each took him for a week.

Her daughter wanted to join the military to create a new life and receive the education she so wanted because there was not enough money available for college. She was active in Germany, but when she became pregnant she decided to leave the army. Twelve days before her papers were filed, she received notice of a new requirement that everyone who wished to leave would have to spend six years in the reserves.

The mother communicates with her daughter in Afghanistan by e-mail when the Internet service works. Sometimes they are able to speak to each other. Recently her daughter called to tell her that things had changed for the worse and there were many traumatic injuries coming into the hospital and it would probably be days before she could be in contact. As of this writing, she was due to return in January of the following year, but she has already received a letter that she might be taken from her present unit and sent back to her previous one, since they don't have anyone to fill her position. This means she will have to spend another year in Afghanistan.[33]

Her mother writes letters to the president and members of Congress. She has written to President Obama, telling him that he should begin the policy of drafting people for the wars, that the price we pay for recycling people has severe mental and emotional consequences. She added that the federal budget did not include the constantly rising costs for the care of our veterans. She had bumper stickers made that declare "There's a War Going On," and "Mothers of Soldiers."[34] She distributes them at public events.

• • •

Patricia Alviso is a very politically active mother. Although she has been a high-school teacher in Cerritos, Los Angeles County, California, for thirty-eight years, she spends a great deal of her time organizing and participating in peaceful protests against the war. She wants to create a space the popular media doesn't provide for servicemen and servicewomen to express the traumas they experience. She especially wants to have access to our political leaders so that she can discuss their decision making about the wars.

Like many young men, her son dreamed of joining the armed forces. Also, like Patricia Hohl's son, he left high school against his parents' wishes and went to a continuation school so that he could graduate at eighteen and join the Marines. He married his high-school sweetheart and started a family. Before he left for Iraq after 9/11, Patricia was actively speaking out against the war.

When he left, she was devastated, so she traveled to New Mexico, to the Indian Market Festival, where she saw a woman wearing a peace T-shirt. She walked over to her and began a conversation, and they both ended up crying and hugging each other. That new friend told her about the demonstration at Crawford, Texas, outside of President Bush's ranch, and she immediately packed her bags to join in. She thought that she would see only Cindy Sheehan, whom she believed was there alone, protesting her son's death. There was a large tent with a huge crowd of people, a table for World War II veterans, one for veterans from Vietnam, and one for Military Families Speak Out. Although Patricia's husband accompanied her, he was not pleased that she was critical of the military. He had a twenty-year career in the Air Force and still works for it as a consultant for satellites. However, Patricia has a different opinion and is deeply concerned about the well-being of our troops.

When Patricia returned home, she started a county chapter of Military Families Speak Out, in Los Angeles as well as in several other counties in her state and in other states. The following December, she joined a march with thousands of people in front of the White House. She was arrested with a very large group of people simply for demonstrating. This was her first of many arrests. She reports that she and the other mothers were cordoned off from all facilities for hours while they waited to be arrested in front of the White House and taken off to jail in buses. It was the largest arrest by park police in front of the White House.[35] There were so many people taken that they had to be divided into three groups. They were in jail all night and released at dawn, but their court date was in the winter. Patricia represented MFSO in federal court, assisted pro bono by an attorney. She pleaded not guilty and looked right at the judge and told him what she felt about the war. She and the group she was arrested with were subsequently released. The protest was held in hopes that President Bush could come out and speak with Cindy Sheehan, who was with MFSO.

While there was a campaign for a congressional seat in her district, Patricia went to meet with each candidate and ask them to sign a pledge to vote against funding for war. There were twelve people running for that seat, and Patricia got four of them to sign the pledge. She then discovered that one of the candidate's aides belonged to her group.

Patricia's chapter of MFSO also held a sit-in at the congressional office of Loretta Sanchez in Garden Grove. Congresswoman Sanchez had an open house, and Patricia's group presented her with a document, asking her to sign a pledge to vote against funding the war. She refused but told them she wouldn't fund the next war and that she thought the war was wrong. She left in a huff. She asked her deputy in charge to stay with them, but she still refused to sign. So Patricia and her group remained and were locked in the congresswoman's office. They spent the night there until they were finally arrested and released on their own recognizance after posting bail.

Patricia was also a part of a mothers' march that took place in Los Angeles and Washington, DC, on the eighth anniversary of the invasion of Iraq. Her group headed toward Mann's Chinese Theater, where Hollywood's actors' and actresses' handprints and footprints are on the sidewalk. The mothers arrived with photos of the soldiers who died and were wounded. The theme of the march, which took place on March 19, 2011, was "War Is Not a Hollywood Movie." The group sat down and got arrested again. Eleven military families were arrested. They posted bail and are waiting for their court date.

Patricia says that she is always involved in civil disobedience. The norm has been to charge her group with civil trespassing or disorderly conduct, even though they are quiet and peaceful while demonstrating. She has made certain that everyone is trained for the consequences and knows how to handle them. If the demonstrators are asked to leave, they just refuse. Then they are handcuffed and brought to jail to wait while the paperwork is completed, and then the mothers are released without bail. Sometimes they have to post bail, and sometimes the police are understanding when her group tells them who they are and what they are doing. MFSO aims to never disrupt traffic, stop motorcades, or interfere with the city in any way.

Her group also had what Patricia referred to as a somber service, a mock funeral with cars in a funeral procession, with stickers on the windshield and headlights turned on. They had a procession through a local cemetery and stopped at a recruiting station, carrying life-size caskets for American and Iraqi war dead. They then had a memorial service on Memorial Day in front of Representative Laura Richardson's office with a Catholic priest and a Methodist minister. "Taps" was played and lilies were placed on the caskets. Then, the city commissioner told them that their march was illegal because it wasn't in a "free-speech zone," and Patricia replied, "What is a free-speech zone? Remember Freedom of Assembly and that this is public property."

Nothing stops Patricia. Along with members of her group, she has challenged the speeches of Senator McCain, Representative Nancy Pelosi, and former governor of California Arnold Schwarzenegger. She found him to be the most tolerant and willing to listen. Her worst experience was when her group entered a large arena where Sarah Palin was speaking and the MFSO group actually was attacked by members of the crowd.

Patricia has found that being arrested has been very hard on her and her family, although she believes that these difficult times are minor compared to what soldiers experience in the war.

Patricia also started several peace clubs in California and, along with another person, she helped to start the Recruiter Awareness Project in Long Beach. She tells the young people who attend that they may need a job, but that the recruiters are lying to them about what it means to join the military during wartime. Every day she comes to her school with the number of deaths in the wars written on her blouse or jacket.

Her school, like all the high schools in San Diego, was given free television sets that were programmed with "Channel One." Students had access to the news during class time, but the Channel One program included commercials for military recruitment. Patricia turns off that program, believing that when she does that, her students have a few minutes to think about the war.

She is also invited to speak before different high schools. She once brought with her a member of the Iraq Veterans Against the War and a mother who spoke about her son's problems with PTSD. Sometimes she brings a Gold Star Mother.

She describes herself as an angry mother whose son has had two deployments to Iraq as a combat engineer who helps to set up bases, and two deployments to Afghanistan. She discovered that he lost quite a few of his buddies and didn't want other people to pick up their body parts. Part of his job was just to retrieve the ammunition from the bodies, but he insisted on removing the body parts himself. When he returned from his deployment in Afghanistan, he told his mother that he kept forgetting things. His vehicle was hit six times, and Patricia believes that he incurred a traumatic brain injury. But he didn't want to get diagnosed officially because, as he told his mother, he is afraid it would go on his record, affect his status, and prevent him from getting a promotion. Nor does he want to get counseling because, he tells his mother, he doesn't need it. This refusal is partially because he is only three years away from retirement. Despite his injury and his need for counseling, he was deployed for the fifth time in November 2011.[36]

Like so many mothers' groups around the world, from the Mothers of the Plaza de Mayo in Argentina to the Mothers of East Los Angeles,[37] Patricia has shown that there are different kinds of anger. Her anger is intended not to hurt anyone but to make the public aware of what our soldiers are experiencing and to help them recover. She speaks out, organizes and participates in demonstrations, and sends packages to the soldiers and supports them when they return.

When angered, mothers cannot be silenced or proved helpless. They will find ways to celebrate the value of human life. The mothers of soldiers have proved that their power to become outspoken and active originates from their maternal work. As with so many other mothers' groups around the world, this activism ensures that we will not forget their lost children. As such, mothers' groups lend a moral compass to our society.

Chapter 4

SPOUSES AND CHILDREN OF SERVICEMEN AND SERVICEWOMEN

Fig. 4.1. Peter, Sophie, and Angela Buckley. *Courtesy of Angela Buckley.*

SITUATIONAL AWARENESS

These past few weeks I'm more than just aware
of where he is—I'm hypersensitive,
stretched thin as a length of wire, a hair—
trigger mechanism. Nothing can live
near me. I twitch each time the telephone
rings through the dark, so like a warning bell
I want to run from it, escape the Green Zone
of this house. Who said that war is hell?
Well, waiting can be worse. Show me a guy
shipped overseas, and I'll show you a wife
who sees disaster dropping from the sky.
The ambush always comes, her husband's life
a road of booby traps, and blind spots made
to hide the rock, the shell, the thrown grenade.[1]

—Jehanne Dubrow

Army spouses are socially invisible. Yet they too are living with courage, fear, and anxiety. Burdens on military families are intense, from the logistics of moving from base to base to the challenges of parenting alone when a spouse is deployed. Moving from base to base often means that a spouse has to give up a job that means a great deal to her or him or live far away from extended family. Some of them wonder if they should stay in one place and keep a job that is important to them, having relinquished work after moving so many times. Multiple deployments make those transitions even more complex. Wives may be surrounded by friends, but not many people understand what it is like to endure both separation from a spouse and much more responsibility because of that distance. Holding a job and caring for children and a home by oneself is more than demanding when added to one's concern for the well-being of a deployed loved one. A website for military spouses sponsored by Military Families Speak Out has published an interesting demand, "give a medal to a wife and child as well as to the soldier," making clear that the efforts of family members left back home need national recognition and that the public should have a greater understanding of the sacrifices they have made.

Preparing for deployments is highly stressful for both soldiers and their families. Soldiers face the distress of uncertainty and the anguish of separation from their families while serving in a distant and dangerous place. Spouses may feel a combination of pride, anger, and fear. Also, multiple deployments are occurring at a faster rate than they did in previous wars. Instead of the eighteen months to two years between deployments, some soldiers and their families are facing redeployment within nine to twelve months after a return from combat. As a result, soldiers and their families suffer from increasing anxiety. As Angela Buckley points out in this chapter, much of what her husband experiences in combat is classified, which makes it difficult for both partners. Although they do communicate by e-mail and sometimes by phone, such communication is a matter of minutes, and this makes it harder for them to reestablish their prior relations when he returns from combat.

Although many mothers have been politically and socially active on behalf of their children in the military, a wife or a husband usually doesn't have the time and energy for such pursuits. Mothers, brothers, and other family members are the ones who are active in contacting members of Congress to provide appropriate healthcare for the soldiers and their families and to demand that they be able to return from the war, which is the longest one this country has been engaged in.

Some recent studies have found that the risk of mental illness for the wife who remains at home rises significantly during her husband's deployment. The stress and fear provoked by those absences can be debilitating and have a profound impact on women's health. A medical study of deployment and the use of mental-health services among army wives has revealed the challenges they face as a result of repeated, and uncertain duration of, separation from their spouses.[2] They may experience marital strain and dissatisfaction, divorce, and declining emotional health. The Armed Forces Health Surveillance Center found that out of a sample of over six million visits of more than two hundred thousand wives, 36 percent had at least one mental-health diagnosis when their spouses were in combat.[3] These wives suffer from depression, anxiety, and sleep disorders.

One spouse, Keli, experienced considerable anguish when her husband was severely injured and, like Angela Buckley and many other wives, she traveled with him to hospitals. Over just three years, her husband was sent to Afghanistan twice and then to Iraq. Like Angela's husband, Peter, he was wounded and endures traumatic brain injury and PTSD. Keli sought help from her army physician one day because she was having panic attacks.

Instead of receiving counseling, she was handed three prescriptions, one for sleep, one for anxiety, and one for depression. It took years to get the help she needed: free counseling from a local therapist. She also received support from local army wives.[4]

A veteran's PTSD has an impact on family relationships. Combat trauma includes emotional numbing and anger, which can cause wives to withdraw from their returned spouse. Because their husbands have had to suppress very painful emotions, it is difficult for them to trust their feelings or reach out to their partners when they return. And even though family problems are created by a veteran's trauma, his psychological turmoil is increased if there is any disruption in his family relationships. People don't understand that a soldier who returns from deployment with PTSD will create what can be considered almost a secondary PTSD in his loved ones. A person who used to make the decisions, such as suggesting that his family goes out to dinner, is no longer able to do so. Typically, he prefers to remain at home and sometimes no longer pays attention to his children, with whom he once may have had warm relationships. Keeping a marriage intact is often overwhelming for spouses. Some of them see psychiatrists and spend years persuading their husbands to also seek help.

Some wives are deeply upset by the lack of intimacy when a husband returns. One female veteran insisted on sleeping in a separate bedroom to avoid being with her husband. A wife or husband yearns for a hug, a kiss, and the words "I love you," which they used to hear before the spouse was deployed. In addition, the wife will be the one spending months or years persuading her veteran husband to get the help he needs and speaking before groups about the problems of PTSD.

As in any war, the prolonged absence of a spouse can create tension when a soldier returns; the husband or wife who was left behind has become more independent and, while welcoming his or her return, may feel put upon or distanced. Military wives' blogs reveal the issues, from small to large, that assail them upon their husband's return. There are not only "milspouse" blogs but also SpouseBuzz.com, which keeps them in touch constantly and has created an online community where they can share their anxieties and their worries. The practice of "milblogging" developed in 2003, and by 2007 there were thousands of military blogs, written not just by troops in Iraq and Afghanistan but also by parents, spouses, and veterans. Spouses even have their own aggregator, Milblogging.com. Although military families have long used blogs to share experiences, blogs by military spouses are the main growth area in the military-blog world. This digital world has proved to be a comforting place for spouses, where they often enjoy instant responses and where they can share their loneliness in dealing with raising children by themselves as well as facing household problems, such as an overflowing toilet, construction jobs, or shoveling a driveway after a snowstorm. In short, they all experience multitasking that is exhausting, and they are lonely. They tend to continue communicating after the return of their husbands, sharing their problems, large and small, about stress in their relationships, the changes they experienced, and the changes in the loved one they must deal with. One of these issues is that their husbands may feel more comfortable talking with their buddies or watching a military channel while the spouse may need to develop an understanding of the importance of their units. Further, because the United States eliminated the draft, and the Bush administration put some restraints on media war photographs, the civilian world is not interested in the war. Thus bloggers remain engaged in the tribulations of their families. Perhaps they are the only ones to realize that we are still at war.

Given the national economic decline, military wives are exhausted by struggling to make ends meet while their husbands are in Iraq or Afghanistan. Although National Guard members are guaranteed their jobs when they return, many of their employers are going out of business. The unemployment age for combat veterans ages eighteen to twenty-five is 14.1 percent, compared with 11.6 percent for civilians that age, according to the Bureau of Labor Statistics.[5] One woman's husband is due home in a few weeks, with no job to return to. They have four children and a mortgage and are deeply concerned about their economic situation. The wife's real-estate business has slowed down considerably because she cannot work the extra hours to make up for the lost income. Sundays are her big day for work, but she has two children aged four and seven years and can't always find a sitter. She wants to be with them and finds it hard to focus.

Before being deployed, a mechanic worked a second job as a superintendent at a building that provided his family with a basement apartment rent-free. After he left, his wife took over that job. She had to teach herself how to snake out toilets and sinks, something she does once a month. She also learned how to drain a boiler and change valves when the apartment lost heat. The couple has two children, one six years old and one eighteen months.[6]

Often members of the National Guard chose redeployment for economic reasons, creating additional anxiety and strain for their family members. During the wars in Iraq and Afghanistan, too many soldiers have returned physically and psychologically wounded and unable to work. Their wives' salaries and their own small disability payments may not suffice to pay the bills that would support their modest lifestyle.

One military spouse, Jehanne Dubrow, commented that there are a number of books on how to be a good military wife. The dominant messages are that as a wife you are also making a sacrifice. Her problem with that view is that while it's true that the wives do make sacrifices, the husband is paid for his and the wife isn't, in a country where money and financial security are especially important in a period of economic decline. She found these books strange, upbeat, and anachronistic. That inspired her to write poetry about the difficulties a wife faces during deployment.

As in any war, soldiers sometimes return to find that their wives have been having affairs with other men, and too many of these marriages end in divorce. One soldier returned from the longest of three consecutive deployments, only to be told by his wife that she no longer wished to live with him, that she and the children wouldn't accompany him to his next assignment, even though it was only an hour and a half away to another post in Germany.[7] Another returned to find that his wife had been living with another man. One of the problems veterans' families face when there is not adequate support is painful separation or divorce. A veteran who has served in Iraq and comes from a military family has noted that the rate of divorce is very high. Jennifer Baldino, whose husband served two tours in Afghanistan, remarked that out of thirty-five returning military personnel, seven of them went through a divorce.

Although there have been studies of the families of returning soldiers, every spouse's life is unique. One army wife feared that her husband would change, and she was terrified at the possibility that he would die. At her job and sometimes among her friends, she felt surrounded by people who didn't understand or who thought that she shouldn't worry. She wanted to be recognized as an army wife who missed her husband terribly. There were also times when she was resentful that he was gone. They were separated for two years, and each of them had grown in different ways. This particular wife felt that her husband was protective of her when he returned, and she felt that she wasn't very helpful to him. Typically, there is a very difficult adjustment in a relationship after a return. Loving a husband or a wife is not an easy experience under such circumstances.

Just as our soldiers do, spouses feel a combination of anger at the way the war is being conducted, and they experience loneliness and fear for their loved one's safety. Like the mothers whose sons and daughters are in Iraq and Afghanistan, spouses left at home often display courage and understanding that are not visible to those who are not in similar situations.

Brooke Kinna's husband was deployed in Iraq twice. When her husband went the first time, his job was to go into new areas and create a post to prepare for the army's entry, a role that terrified her. She was glued to the news day and night. She was more than irritated about the way the media portrayed the war and felt that it didn't provide an honest portrayal of what was taking place in combat, that the news was negative.

When Brooke's husband returned from his first deployment, he had become so thin that she burst into tears when she caught sight of him. Fighting forces spend months living on MREs (meals ready to eat, which have chemical mixers to warm up the food). She sent him large packages of baby wipes because that's all his unit could use to wash. She also sent cookies and brownies for everyone who was with him because she felt that they weren't treated properly.

It was very difficult for her to stay in touch with him the first time he was in Iraq because he didn't have access to cell phones or computers. They had occasional phone calls and letters, but letters were difficult because his address was always changing, since he was in constant movement between posts.

When her husband left for Iraq the second time, she was left caring for a three-month-old baby and felt very much alone. Accompanying him to the plane that would take him from her for a long period of time was very upsetting. "It's almost like you go on autopilot. I felt empty. It's awful, horrible. You live in fear every day, afraid that someone is going to be knocking at your door."[8] What made it more difficult for her was seeing the resemblance between her child and her husband over time. She felt that it made her miss him even more.

During her husband's second deployment they were able to communicate with e-mails, cell phones, and computers. Brooke discovered that after working fifteen hours or more, soldiers had to stand in a long line for hours to be able to talk to their loved ones for just a few minutes. Her husband would walk a mile up a hill and stand in a line of fifty people just for five minutes on the phone. Sometimes he would try in the early hours of the morning, one or two o'clock, and have easier access.

She also noticed changes in her husband's outlook. As was the motivation for so many soldiers, he joined the army because of what happened on 9/11. During his second deployment, he conveyed to Brooke that he felt that the war was about oil and not about providing freedom and security for the United States and for Iraq. Brooke discovered that soldiers don't necessarily support the war. They enlist with the thought that they are going to protect their family and ensure their country's freedom. As is the case with many soldiers, Brooke's husband returned with a different view of the war.

Brooke tried her best to make him feel welcomed and loved when he returned, but she knew that he was thinking about his buddies back in Iraq and felt guilty that he was back home while they were still in combat. Her husband is a sergeant and is twenty-eight years old, and that is not young for a soldier. She considers that when most soldiers are first deployed they are "just babies," eighteen or nineteen years old. She was able to get her husband to talk about the time he spent in Iraq, but he spoke mostly about his buddies in his units. She knew that he was thinking that his "brothers" who were over there needed him, that he should be there to help them, and that he was safe while they were not. She understood that this closeness is all they have in Iraq and when they are in combat. "You don't leave a brother behind," she commented.

Brooke rightly felt that there was insufficient preparation for the war, even though she may not have known the underlying reasons for the war. For example, L. Paul Bremer unwittingly helped foment a Sunni insurgency and empowered the ardently religious Shiites, thus creating an insurmountable situation.[9] The first wave of soldiers who went to Iraq was stretched so thin that ammunition dumps were left untended. There were conflicting views of Paul Bremer, and he did receive an award from President Bush. Even though Brooke and all the military families are well informed about what is going on in Iraq and Afghanistan, what matters most to them is what concerns their children and spouses. They are both proud of their family members' mission and yet upset about what some of them see as policies that overlook their families' needs and safety.

Brooke is also upset by antiwar rallies and feels that they are actually against soldiers. She would be happy to see a demonstration to bring the soldiers home. In addition, she wants people to talk to soldiers who are against the war. She wants them to be heard in a country that knows very little about what is happening in Iraq and Afghanistan and shows even less interest in what our soldiers have experienced.

She also found that the healthcare for soldiers is often inadequate, which is deeply upsetting to her. She discovered that in Georgia, where she resides, veterans have a lot of problems getting adequate medical help. Ultimately her husband was fortunate enough to find a civilian physician who confirmed that he had PTSD, and he was given the care he needed instead of being sent back to Afghanistan. Brooke knew that the army would redeploy soldiers with PTSD.

As time passed, she became pregnant and looked forward to her growing family, although she knew that there are events in the war that her husband still thought about and didn't share with her.

Jehanne Dubrow, whose poem opened this chapter, is a professor and a poet; her husband is in the navy. He has been on frequent deployments near Afghanistan and Iraq but also near Africa and in Bahrain. He began his first substantial deployment in January 2010, for nine months. It's hard for them to stay in contact because he has to turn off his cell phone on a ship and is not allowed to use Skype®. She receives brief and unsatisfactory e-mails from him that are short on details. She would send him as many as she wanted to, but sometimes they didn't get through and her husband asked her why she didn't contact him.

She knows that even if his ship is docked, he is potentially in danger because of the large number of casualties or fatalities on a destroyer that are the result of explosions or fires, which are quite common. Her husband's ship has been in dangerous areas, but naval officers in his situation are not allowed to tell their spouses when such events occur.

Her husband is an electrical engineer and had a number of positions on the ship. He was a weapons officer, oversaw what is called the *aegis weapons system* of a cruiser, and is working to become a commander of a ship. She finds that he is frequently on call or having to extend his stay and that as a result they have very little time together. He will get ten days off between deployments. Her career and his support of her work as a professor helps her deal with his absences.

Jehanne's husband has been in the navy for ten years and was recently promoted to the rank of lieutenant commander. However, she comes from a family that worked in the Foreign Service, a very different culture. Politically she is a liberal, and she is also Jewish; she feels alienated from the military culture. She believes that the fact that she is Jewish could adversely impact her husband's career, something she felt keenly during the Bush administration. Her husband is very careful not to overtly identify his political beliefs because he knows what the dominant view is in the military. As Jehanne mentioned, once, he was on a ship when there was a fundamentalist Christian chaplain who was trying to proselytize over loudspeakers. Her husband was one of the few people who stood up and said that that was not appropriate behavior.

There was a time when her husband was going to be sent on an Individual Augmentation, which is a program whose positions in the army and marines are usually filled by the navy in places like Afghanistan and Iraq. She started panicking because a naval warship is a profoundly dangerous place. It's a situation that frightens her because officers are given only a brief amount of training before being sent into areas that are extremely different environments from being on a ship. While she is pleased that her husband is not in a nuclear submarine but in surface warfare, a safer position, it's still upsetting for her.

One of the activities that helped her feel close to her husband while he was away was teaching a class about the poetry of war. Having that experience helped her deal with her feelings about the war and her husband's career. On the first day of class, she told her students, "I'm teaching this class for a very important reason: my husband is deployed right now."[10]

She is also teaching a creative-writing workshop for returning veterans. The Writers' Center in Washington, DC, sponsors community workshops financed by grants from the National Endowment for the Arts. She has found that it is not only a way to deal with her husband's deployment but also an opportunity to do something for the military community.

She has also written a book of poems, *Stateside*, because she felt that the experience of being a military wife surviving her husband's deployment is a meaningful and emotionally complex subject matter. She finds that it is an important way to give authority to a perspective that is usually ignored, and that it places military wives in a larger historical and literary context. "It means that people who don't care about the military, who are touched by poetry, will suddenly care."[11]

Jennifer Baldino's husband has been in the reserves for eighteen and a half years. Reserve soldiers don't have different combat experiences from active-duty soldiers. However, they and their families experience very difficult adjustments, swinging back and forth between military and civilian life. That means that they often have to deal with important changes in their lives that none of them is prepared for. Jennifer had to learn how to live as a single person, not as part of a couple, and found it hard to maintain friendships and her former activities while her husband was away.

After 9/11, her husband enlisted in the Massachusetts National Guard. The reserves are on a five-year rotation, so he was only deployed every five years. He was in Iraq for fifteen months and then again in 2010 for a year. He was deployed under the troop-withdrawal process.

As with most military families, Jennifer and her husband had difficulty communicating when he was abroad. They communicated primarily by e-mail. Once her husband was installed in a permanent barrack, they could send instant messages and she could talk to him once or twice a week. But there were times when she didn't hear from him at all and periods when she could only talk to him for five consecutive days. As in most cases, the soldiers have to provide their own communication equipment. There are WI-FI spots on his base, but they are public and of limited use. To have a private conversation or talk for any length of time, soldiers need to sign up for a private service Internet that they have to pay for themselves. Jennifer's husband has a wireless satellite card that he uses on his computer, five minutes at a time. It costs $60.00 a month, a sum that is quite expensive for a soldier's pay.

Their daughter, Rachel, was twelve years old when he left in 2005 and fourteen when he returned. It was very hard for her to have him away because she was very close to him. When a child is twelve years old, it's very hard to process changes in family life. She celebrated her thirteenth birthday at Fort Dix. There were twelve men in the room singing "Happy Birthday." All of them had children. Jennifer's daughter was afraid that her father was going to die, and she burst out crying. She and her mother drove home crying.

Jennifer's daughter was going through puberty and expressed her feelings of missing her father through both anger and sadness. She and her mother went through a period when they were so much at odds with each other that her father actually called home to speak to her about her behavior. She later looked back on it and told her mother, "I knew I was in trouble when Dad called me all the way from Iraq." Her mother feels terrible that her daughter had difficult years dealing with her father's absence, especially beginning her teenage years without him.[12]

Jennifer had to deal with several trying issues at the same time. Her father was living with her because he was suffering from cancer. In May 2010, her father died. Then she had a career change when a school principal, who was a close friend of hers, persuaded her to teach there but left his job soon after. In July, her husband went to Iraq, so the three men in her life left at the same time.

While her husband was in Iraq, Jennifer coped by keeping very busy. Her father had gone to a rehabilitation hospital, and she and her husband had decided to build an apartment for him in their house. She was responsible for that project while her husband was away. Two of the most important people for her at that time were the contractors who worked at her house. They were with her from September to March. They shoveled the driveway for her and ran her snow blower. One of them went to school and picked up her daughter when she couldn't get her car started. They even took care of her dogs.

During the summer, she worked with a construction crew. She did roofing and used a jackhammer and power tools, loving every minute of it. She also drove the van for her daughter's softball team and did maintenance at the school where she taught. Her adrenaline was high, just like that of soldiers, and she was suffering from a different kind of trauma. She was unable to deal with her father's death for a year and a half after he died, and keeping busy had some connection with the 24-7 schedule soldiers keep at war.

She and her husband had a very hard time adjusting when he returned from his first deployment. She had been on her own for fifteen months. She thought he would take over and pick up where he left off, assuming some of the many responsibilities she was burdened with. But part of the training before soldiers return home advises them to not try to make changes to routines that were established while they were not home or to take over tasks their spouse had assumed when they were gone. She wanted her husband to pitch in, but he was following the advice he received not to make any changes. They both had very different expectations, and that created a lot of tension in their lives. Jennifer felt that she did fine when he was gone, that she was able to cope. But she felt unprepared for the challenges she faced when he came back from his first deployment. Her husband returned depressed and suffering from PTSD.[13]

Jennifer's friends thought it was wonderful that her husband was home. Thus the support of family and friends stopped because they thought his homecoming meant her difficulties were over and she didn't need that extra help anymore. It was the beginning of a very difficult time. She found that part of the problem with reintegration was that she too had to change, and she found that she had difficulty not functioning at a very high level, such as doing everything around the house and at work. That meant altering her survival mode. Her husband felt that when he left, everything stopped and his home remained what it was when he was away. He didn't understand why so much had changed in their household. Because of these different perceptions, they experienced a lot of conflict.

Her husband didn't know how to relate to Rachel because she had changed into a young woman. Once when he and Jennifer were quarreling, their daughter lost her temper. She told them, "Well, listen, the two of you are acting like children. Someone in this house has to act like an adult." While Rachel was upset, she learned that married couples go through difficult times, work through them, and remain committed. It was difficult for their daughter, as well as for Jennifer, while her father was deployed or in army preparation. Rachael had to cope with her grandfather's death as well as her father's absence at important events. Thus, he wasn't there for her prom, for her high-school graduation, or the day she went to college, missing all the milestones in her senior year.

Jennifer feels that one of the hardest things for her was to drive her daughter to college by herself, say good-bye to her, and come home to an empty house. In fact, she put a sign on the back of her car, "Daughter in first year of college, husband on second deployment to Iraq. Please excuse my driving."[14] On Facebook®, she wrote, "My daughter is in her first year of college, my husband is on his second deployment, I have three dogs, one is a puppy. I am having construction and I teach Junior High. Do you really want to mess with me?"[15]

When he came home from his first deployment, her husband was depressed and began to gain weight. The last thing he wanted to admit was that he was depressed, because if he would be given medication, he would become grounded. Because he was in an aviation unit, he was based in Kuwait and flew missions in and out of Iraq daily. He was under fire and transported dead bodies, but he returned feeling that he didn't sacrifice as much as the ground units and thus felt a sense of guilt.

Jennifer found that soldiers like her husband are very resistant to even talk about what they are experiencing and at times don't even know what is going on themselves. At one point, she asked her husband whatever was wrong with him, and he answered that she was going leave him because she didn't need him anymore and he didn't have any purpose in her life. She answered no to the first comment and insisted that she did need him. She had been told at the briefings not to change anything, such as rearranging the furniture, or make any significant purchases, yet life goes on and her daughter became a teenager. She was emotionally exhausted and wanted her husband to pick himself up and become who he once was, something he was unable to do. That was the major source of conflict between them. At that point, Jennifer felt that she just couldn't do everything anymore. She had been through so much, with her father dying, her daughter going through puberty, the construction project, being in charge of more than she felt able to handle. She found herself struggling with depression and feelings of worthlessness as a result of her marriage problems, which drove her to find a marriage counselor.

Part of the problem for the families of our veterans is that soldiers have to reach out for help. Jennifer found that during that time the support for the family is not as good as it is now. It took Jennifer many months before she finally got her husband to agree to get medical help. She threatened to leave him and told him that she couldn't stay in the house and watch him suffering and spiraling down, not trying to get help for himself when it was available. She told him that she was not going to divorce him, but that she was not going to stay with him, so he had to make a choice, either get help or she and her daughter were leaving.

That threat worked, and they did go for marriage counseling for a year. Just sitting down to talk was very helpful. The person they saw made them think about the issues they were facing. Oddly enough, more than anything, he helped them unite against a common enemy because neither of them could stand that experience. They went to counseling first and then went out to dinner afterward to complain about their sessions.

They also had help from the National Guard in Massachusetts, which had recently developed a program called Strong Bonds. That program is a free weekend that is available to anyone who has been on a recent deployment. That proved to be a turning point for them and helped them reunite.

But it took almost three years for them to get back to their former relationship, and then he was sent to his next deployment in 2010. Jennifer discovered that a marriage subject to their circumstances would never be the same. She went through a period of time when she had to mourn because she felt that it was a death of something and that their relationship would never be the same because they had such different experiences. By the time they both got ready for his next deployment, they were very close, but she felt that something was missing. They were both concerned that they might have the same problems as they did after his first tour in Iraq. Jennifer thinks that they are both a little wiser now and are in a better place.

Jennifer learned that suffering makes a person stronger and able to see beyond his or her own needs. As a result, she assumed new responsibilities for the families of returning veterans. Now, the reserves in Massachusetts have outreach programs available for families before and after deployment. During her husband's first and second deployment, she became chair of the Family Readiness Group, a volunteer group that provides social networking for military families. It puts families in touch with programs that can help them with such problems as dealing with landlords, a broken furnace, or a need for counseling. She found that wives who actively participate in family-readiness groups managed to deal with the return of their spouses much better than those who tried to deal with the issues of reuniting alone. There are a number of agencies that can provide support. There are also Yellow Ribbon events prior to and after deployment where there are speakers and tables set up with resource information.

When Jennifer's husband returned from his last deployment in 2011, she was once again faced with the challenge of having to adjust to his presence. She feels that it was harder on her husband than on her this time. However, her daughter and husband have become very close after this return, and he is amazed at how much she has grown up. The fact that she was leaving for college in August was upsetting for him because he didn't have to face that departure when he was in Iraq. When soldiers are at war, they not only miss their children but also are not part of their important transformations as they grow up and develop new activities and experiences. Luckily, Jennifer and her husband are looking forward to the time they will be together just as a couple, even though their daughter is away at college.[16]

Leah Curran is one of many wives who find themselves in a financial bind. She has to deal with her husband's physical and mental problems as well as caring for their children while struggling to keep their dwindling finances afloat. Her husband had a good job before leaving for combat as part of the National Guard, but because he came back with physical and mental-health problems, he was unable to return to his prior job. Leah's job as a preschool teacher is insufficient to maintain their modest lifestyle and to pay the mortgage on their house.

When he was first deployed to Iraq in 2003, he returned with PTSD and physical problems, Leah reports. She says it was like living in hell and that it took at least seven months to get him adjusted to his household. He frequently lost his temper, which made it difficult for her to keep family relations calm.

He was receiving disability payments, and yet they reactivated him in 2010. As a result, she called the VA and told them that they couldn't reactivate him while he was on disability. In fact she called them several times, yet the disability payments kept coming in while he was away. This shows poor oversight on the part of the VA. Leah misunderstood their lack of response and was using the money to pay the mortgage on their house. Months later, she received a telephone call from the VA telling her that she had to pay back the disability. By May 2010, she had fallen behind on her mortgage and was obliged to pay off a large sum within the next six months to retain her mortgage. What's more, she was required to reimburse the disability payments her husband had collected, as well as pay back her husband's drill pay for weekends spent with the National Guard, even though he was doing his drill and weekend service despite being on disability.

A civil service act prevents Leah's house from being foreclosed, yet when she is unable to meet her monthly payments, the bank adds an additional charge on her mortgage. She is terribly worried about losing their home, about being able to pay the bills for her car payments, electricity, and food, which are adding up. She is also concerned about health payments for her children. Her son has asthma and needs medical care. He also needs braces, but Tricare, the military health insurance, will only pay $1,500 of the $5,000 bill. As a result, she is working long hours, mornings and evenings, so she can earn more and still spend afternoons with her children.

She is deeply upset because during his second deployment in Iraq, her husband was injured a number of times, was hospitalized, and yet continued going out on missions. His truck went over an IED that blew the whole back of the truck off. He lost consciousness and incurred a traumatic brain injury. As a result, he lost part of his hearing and his eyesight began to fail. Leah is furious because her husband wasn't sent home after being seriously injured.

He is stationed at Fort Drum in New York for medical care and therapy. He is able to come home on weekends and commutes with his buddy. Leah is distressed because her husband is unable to participate in the running of the household. One of their four children is ten years old and has a hyperactive disorder and thus needs a great deal of attention. She feels a lot of grief because her husband used to be a very involved father and was concerned about his children. He is now unable to help her with their care, especially for their son. So she is running the household all by herself while taking care of her husband during the weekends. She drives him places to get him out of the house, and sometimes she takes the children out of the house so that he can have time for himself. Like too many military wives, she is doing the job of six people and is exhausted and frustrated.

Not only was her husband physically wounded, but he also suffers from

PTSD. He is unable to communicate with her, which is frustrating. They have lost their intimacy because, like so many soldiers, he feels reclusive and is numb. Leah yearns for a hug or a kiss from him. He used to be close to their son and is now unable to reach out to him or to his wife.[17]

Since her husband is unable to walk, she knows that he will not be able to work again and will receive disability. Disability payments are low, and that means that they will lose their house because they won't be able to afford mortgage payments. She is burdened with so many problems and so many worries about the future that she often feels despair. Because she wants to protect her children from these feelings and concerns, she uses the death of her sister from lupus as an excuse for her sorrow.

She also takes care of a disabled mother, which means driving back and forth to her mother's home as well as going to work and running errands. In addition, she is undergoing two surgeries, one for melanoma on her face and one for glaucoma.

Like so many military wives, she is concerned about the cocktail of medications her husband has been prescribed. Leah doesn't trust the psychiatrist he is seeing and finds that her husband gets dizzy and light-headed and sometimes faints. He has also been given pain medications that he is supposed to take during the day, and they both decided that he shouldn't take them. When her husband was home for a week, she insisted that he stop taking all of his medications. She has a good friend who is a physician, and she consulted with him as well as doing a lot of research on the computer herself. Leah feels that she can be his doctor because she's lived with him for twenty-five years.

A fifth of the soldiers who return with PTSD receive prescriptions for an antipsychotic medication that has serious side effects. The use of such drugs have increased sharply as thousands of returning soldiers have found that their PTSD does not respond to antidepressants.[18] This was a finding by Dr. John H. Krystal, director of the clinical neurosciences division of the Department of Veterans Affairs' National Center for PTSD. These findings come at a time when the Department of Defense and Veterans Affairs are trying to provide treatment to returning service members who not only are concerned about the stigma of mental illness but also are skeptical of the value of the treatment. Studies have found that talk therapy alone or in combination with antidepressants could relieve nightmares and reclusive behavior.[19] Yet returning soldiers who intend to stay in the military are also concerned that treatment would be a blot on their record and would prevent them from being promoted.

It would be helpful if the concerns of the families of our service members over the "cocktail" of drugs given to the returning soldiers were taken into consideration because the majority of them worry about the short-term and long-term effects of these drugs. Many of them, like Leah, either deny their loved one access to those medications or persuade him or her not to take so many.

Leah has a deep faith, and though she is upset and sad, she knows how to be positive and that she can manage such a difficult life, day by day. She says that even if she loses her house, her family will still be together. She is a remarkable woman who knows that inner strength and the vulnerability she feels go hand in hand.[20]

Angela's husband is a member of the National Guard who served two tours in Bosnia. He decided to continue his service because he had already been with the National Guard for ten years and thus would be eligible for its retirement benefits. He told his wife that it would only entail weekend drills and training once a year, and he transferred to the National Guard in Massachusetts after 9/11. Twenty-four hours later, he was sent on an airport mission for security because he is a military police officer. He was sent to Baghdad for a short period, where he was a driver and a gunner and was responsible for sending six mine-resistant armored vehicles to various units but remained on his airport mission. He came back after eight months, and two weeks later he left for Afghanistan for a year.

Angela's personal history is a testament to her inner strength and her ability to demand proper care for her husband when he returned. Her Polish father, who was in the Resistance during World War II, was sent to a concentration camp, and he taught her that it was important to speak out on behalf of people who are in trying circumstances. She had continually expressed herself to the people in charge when her husband was at the Walter Reed Army Medical Center. Equally important was her ability to engage her husband in conversation about his experiences in Afghanistan. She understood that much of what occurred there was classified but told her husband that she didn't care if it was classified, and that if he couldn't tell her everything, they could at least talk about some of the events during his combat. She engaged him in conversation because she told him that she had to live with his experiences as well.

When he was in Afghanistan, her husband, Peter, patrolled the mountains, working with Special Forces units. He was shocked at the poverty he saw, at all the children waiting by the gates, always trailing behind the soldiers and wanting help. Peter sent the children shoes and jackets. It was a horrible deployment, dealing with cold and hungry orphans and being among so many corpses.

There was no counseling available for Peter when he returned because of the stigma of asking for help with PTSD. Angela is angry that our veterans are expected to fit back into the civilian world as soon as they come home.

When he was deployed, his daughter Sophie would ask her mother, Angela, every day, "Do you think my daddy will be safe?" and she replied, "Of course he is, don't you think he's a good soldier?" Then Sophie would say, "I miss my daddy but I know he's going to be okay." Angela had tried to prepare her for her father's return and told her, "When he comes back, he's going to be a little different and tired so don't overwhelm him. Please give him some space and some time."[21]

It was difficult for Sophie to be the only child at school who has a father in either Iraq or Afghanistan. Angela had to insist that Sophie switch classes because a child was bullying her and told her that because her father was at war, he was going to die. Sophie was so upset that she came home crying. Her mother told her, "Honey, your daddy is a good soldier and he is going to be fine." The two of them had to deal with his absence day by day, and often Sophie would get tense.

Because of his PTSD when he returned, Peter had very little patience and was easily upset. Sophie was surprised at his behavior and asked her mother why he had outbursts because he was never like that before. But Sophie became mature for her age, given what she has experienced with her father and the time that she spent with him at the Walter Reed Army Medical Center. Despite all her father's problems, they have remained very close.

Angela's husband went directly to the hospital when he returned from Afghanistan. She tried to prepare her daughter on their drive to the hospital. He returned with a brain injury as well as PTSD, and even more physical wounds that needed attention. She was shocked when she saw her husband and felt that he looked like a broken man. He had nerve damage, and thus one side of his body was paralyzed, his head was leaning, almost resting, on his shoulder. His hair had turned white. Because of the brain injury, Peter had lost his memory. He repeats something every forty-five minutes. Although Peter came back from Afghanistan in 2004, Angela understands that his wounds are also emotional and that the signs of the pain of this war will be with him a long time, not just in his nightmares when he can sleep, but in his inability to sleep at other times.

A few weeks after, Sophie had a meltdown in school because she was afraid her parents were going to die and she kept telling her mother, "I don't want you and Daddy to die. I won't have anybody. What's going to happen to me? I'm going to miss you."[22]

After her husband's long stay at the Walter Reed Army Medical Center, Angela began driving her husband to medical appointments every day of the week. She drives one thousand miles a month and is exhausted and overwhelmed. She addressed her concerns to the person at the highest level of the chain of command. She told him that she takes her husband wherever he needs to go, but that she has a school-age child and no support network. For her, not only is time an issue, but also financially these trips are a huge burden. She pays $400.00 dollars a month for gas. According to army regulations, an appointment has to be fifty miles away or more for a spouse or parent to be reimbursed. Angela's husband's appointments are forty-eight miles away and thus they are not eligible for financial help. She told the commander that he was putting a big financial burden on her family, that her husband lost half of his income compared to his civilian pay, so he is already taking a pay cut by having been on active duty. She is furious because they are reaching into their savings and she feels that she is paying for her husband having gone to war.

Too many wives of returning servicemen find themselves spending all of their time caring for their husbands. Some of them have to give up their jobs and many of them develop health problems such as hypertension or suffer from depression. They experience considerable emotional strain. In the past few years, advocacy organizations like the Wounded Warrior Project lobbied Congress to enact a law providing financial compensation and other benefits to family caregivers of service members. In 2010, the VA approved 1,222 applications for monthly stipends of $1,600 to $1,800.[23] Caregivers can also receive health insurance and counseling.[24] The VA estimates that three thousand families will benefit from the new program, but while that is an important step forward, it represents a fraction of the families that need financial help when spouses return from Iraq and Afghanistan. The monthly stipends are a recognition of the family's sacrifice, but they are hardly sufficient if a spouse has to give up her job to care for her husband.

Angela is working 24-7 to care for her husband and is not only fatigued but upset about the way veterans are treated. Fortunately, her daughter and her husband have become very close, and Angela has always been a supportive and loving wife and mother.

Children suffer from anxiety even though they may not speak clearly or even understand what is happening within a family, but they don't miss anything. They are very sensitive to any changes in parental relationships or events that affect the family. Whether their mother says anything or remains silent, a child knows his or her parent is under pressure. Younger children have difficulty processing their parents' experiences and have no framework for understanding the return of a parent who has been at war. They may act out in a number of ways, such as having tantrums, arguing with their mother, or continuing to ask her questions about what will happen. They fear for their parents and for themselves and wonder if they will be left alone because if one parent dies at war, maybe the other parent will die too. Younger children may have meltdowns while the older ones go through life changes, such as puberty, that may distance them from their father or mother when they return. A child's life is filled with special events, such as birthday parties, high-school graduations, musical performances, or sports activities, where they miss their parent's presence.

For most of their lives, their father might have been in either the army or the National Guard, with multiple deployments that may entail multiple moves and missed school events. Sophie Buckley missed eight months of her school because she and her mother accompanied her father while he was at the Walter Reed Army Medical Center. Another child discusses her father's recent absence, "Like, in your heart you have your mom and dad, and then you have the rest of the people. So that was like a third of my heart gone for a while."[25]

When children grow up living near military families or near a base, they feel part of society. Often, they may be the only one at school who has a parent in the military. Not only does this make them feel lonely, but they may receive neither sympathy nor support. For Sophie, one of the most wonderful moments was when she told a child at school that her daddy lost his memory every forty-five minutes and a friend responded that hers had only a five-minute short-term memory. It made Sophie feel wonderful and less alone.[26]

Sophie was also fortunate because while she was with her parents at Walter Reed Army Medical Center, she received some counseling that was very helpful. As a result, she keeps a diary where she can record her deepest feelings in privacy and over time see what she has learned and the progress she has made.

Sophie's mother helped prepare her for her father's return. Children as well as spouses need to have good communication with a parent when he is deployed. Of course they miss waiting for their father to come home at the end of the day or having dinner with him. Being in touch by telephone or e-mail is very important. While parents are away, a family develops its own routines and practices. When parents return from combat changed, it takes months and sometimes years for parents and children to reintegrate.

There are sixty-three free camps nationwide for children from military families that are sponsored by the National Military Family Association. The mission of these camps, called *Operation Purple*, is to help children to meet others who have experienced parental deployment and to cope with the stress of war. The RAND Corporation did a study of some of these children and in 2008 published its research and proposals for helping military youth.[27] However, speaking to military families and reading their blogs reveals these issues. What is also needed is for our country to realize the burden that deployments place on wives, children, and parents of servicemen and servicewomen. The entire family is dealing with the stress and pain of war, not just the soldier.

Chapter 5

THE HIGH RATE OF SUICIDES

Fig. 5.1. Noah Charles Pierce. *Photo courtesy of Cheryl Softich.*

SPECIALIST NOAH CHARLES PIERCE

When he returned from the war
they called him a killer.
He was not a murderer.
He befriended a child, gathered

the limbs of his fellow soldier
who was blown up beside him,
lost some of his hearing from the blast,
obeyed his colonel's orders to gun down

a man driving into the Green Zone
who turned out to be a physician.
When he came home, the weight
of his guilt, displacement and pain

was invisible. He didn't come home.
He was still in Iraq. The people
in his town couldn't hear the nightmares
that haunted him or his heart

pounding at sudden noises.
They couldn't understand how he left his house
to protect his parents and his sister
from his anger, closed the door of his apartment

to release his sorrow. Then one night
he drove to the mine dumps
near his favorite fishing spot,
wrote "Freedom isn't Free"

on the dashboard of his truck
beside the nine medals of honor
closing yet another door
to liberate his own life.[1]

—Marguerite Guzmán Bouvard

THE FACTS

How many veterans came stateside and didn't care whether they would live or die? The number is shocking: More active duty soldiers and veterans have died from suicide than from combat wounds.[2] Each one of them deserves to be remembered and honored. In November, CBS News reviewed data from all fifty states in 2005 and found that there were at least 6,256 cases of suicide among those who had served in the armed forces.[3] According to military records, the wars in Iraq and Afghanistan have the highest rate of suicides.[4] Veterans in the range of twenty to twenty-four years old are the most frequent victims.[5] The Department of Defense has revealed that an average of eighteen veterans a day from all wars are committing suicide, including one veteran of Iraq and Afghanistan every thirty-six hours.[6] Multiple deployments and redeployments of personnel who are suffering from PTSD are among many factors causing this high rate.[7]

The Department of Defense has released some data about suicides yearly since 2005. But there is insufficient accounting of how many of our soldiers take their own lives because so many of them do so months or even years after they return home. Captain Shannon Meehan, a former leader of a tank platoon for the 1st Cavalry Division of the US Army and author of *Beyond Duty*, has clearly expressed what too many people fail to understand, how combat can lead to suicide. "War erodes one's regard for human life. Soldiers cause or witness so many deaths . . . that it becomes routine. It becomes an accepted part of existence. After a while, you can begin to lose regard for your own life as well. So many around you have already died, why should it matter if you go next? That is why so many soldiers self-destruct. The deaths that I caused also killed any regard I had for my own life. . . . I fell into a downward spiral, doubting if I even deserved to be alive. The value, or regard, I once had for my own life dissipated."[8]

According to Dr. Nassir Ghaemi, someone considering suicide feels despair, the loss of hope for the future. In fact, the future gives way to a horrible present and a painful past. Family, friends, and military comrades can no longer serve as protection if the despair is deep enough.[9]

When our soldiers return home in need of mental-health support, they find a country that is obsessed with budget cutting. Legislation to repair damages for members of the Army's Individual Ready Reserve, a category that does not enjoy the unit-based care of other reservists, was on the congressional agenda. That bill was approved by both houses of Congress in late 2009, but it got stuck in final conference for supposed budgetary reasons. According to Representative Rush Holt, Democrat from New Jersey and a sponsor of the bill, one of his constituents, Sergeant Coleman Bean, was a unit-free reservist who did two tours of duty in Iraq and committed suicide while on a waiting list for PTSD treatment.[10]

The US Department of Veterans Affairs (VA) recently hired 3,500 mental-health professionals and said its policy is to assess new veterans within twenty-four hours if they are in crisis.[11] It also has created a hotline for veterans who feel at risk. Despite these recent improvements, the mental-health system has been known to be failing the United States' veterans for years.

At a time when the Pentagon is attempting to remove the stigma surrounding mental healthcare in the hope of stemming the rapidly rising number of suicides among service members, the question of whether their survivors deserve recognition has taken on new significance. Under an unwritten policy in force across several administrations, President Barack Obama continued the practice of not sending letters of condolence to families of soldiers who had died by suicide. According to *Politico*, a Washington, DC, news source, eleven senators—along with the American Psychiatric Association—have been advocating for this policy change since last year.[12] On July 5, 2011, President Obama reversed himself and announced that he would be signing such letters in the future, "to de-stigmatize the mental health cost of war" and help prevent more tragic deaths.[13] Unfortunately for the families whose sons or daughters committed suicide in war zones or after returning home, this decision is not retroactive. Suicides among veterans should be regarded as the direct result of untreated PTSD. Families that mourn these losses deserve that recognition for their son's or daughter's services, along with the compassion and comfort that such a letter would bring. Cheryl Softich, whose son committed suicide after he came home from Iraq, spoke about it on ABC Eyewitness News on July 9, 2011. She said that the letters should be retroactive and apply to all soldiers who die by suicide, including those who die after returning home.

There has been little public accounting or recognition of the war's toll on these men and women. Bob Herbert wrote in the *New York Times*, "Because we have chosen not to share the sacrifices of the war in Iraq and Afghanistan, the terrible burden of these conflicts is being shouldered by an obscenely small portion of the population."[14] Yet there has been some public protest about not honoring these soldiers, with families such as Cheryl Softich's in the forefront.

The distressing reality of suicide makes people very uncomfortable about discussing it or even admitting that it occurred in their family. Imagine a soldier speaking about his or her desire to end his or her life to a platoon leader or a general. Navy admiral Jonathan W. Greenert spoke before the Senate Armed Services Committee, "Suicide destroys families, devastates communities and unravels the cohesive social fabric and morale inside our commands."

Air Force general Carrol H. Chandler remarked that "the number of airmen taking their lives has been rising despite our commitment to prevention." General James F. Amos, commandant of the Marine Corps, observed that "with every suicide case, there is a unique life to understand." And the army's vice chief of staff, Gen. Peter W. Chiarelli added, "Many more suffer from behavioral health issues such as depression, anxiety, traumatic brain injury and post-traumatic stress—often referred to as the invisible wounds of war."[15]

Private organizations are actively expressing their concern and contacting members of Congress. Military Families Speak Out (MFSO) held a conference on military suicide awareness and prevention in March 2011. The speakers included Congresswoman Barbara Lee (CA) and Congressman Walter Jones (NC), a veteran, a representative of MFSO and clinical social worker, and presidential hopeful Dr. Ron Paul. The organization Veterans for Common Sense met with members of the administration to express concerns about the need to reduce the stigma against suicide.

The data on suicide is deeply troubling. Twenty percent of Americans who commit suicide are veterans, an extraordinary number, since veterans compose less than 1 percent of the population. It is the fourth-leading cause of death in the United States for adults eighteen to sixty-five years old and the third-leading cause of death in teens and young adults from ages fifteen to twenty-four years. A high percentage of soldiers in the US Army, Marines, and Air Force fall into that age group. The number of suicide attempts by army personnel has increased six-fold since the wars in Afghanistan and Iraq began.[16] Suicides happen in war zones, at their bases, at home, and in their communities.

Young women veterans are nearly three times as likely as civilians to commit suicide, according to new research published at Portland State University and Oregon Health and Science University. It found that female veterans aged eighteen to thirty-four are at the highest risk.[17]

When veterans return from war, they come home as different people.

Their scars are buried deep inside them. Some of them feel guilty that they survived while their buddies in the same unit were blown to bits. Some of them remember picking up the pieces of friends' bodies and putting them into bags. The constant sounds of IEDs, RPGs, and EFPs still haunt them, and any sudden loud noise can be deeply upsetting. Many of them return with traumatic brain injuries, and many have trouble hearing. They come from a culture that focuses on bravery, heroism, strength, and endurance, but their war experiences have filled them with shame, have silenced them, have caused them to become reclusive, and are constantly troubling them. That is the reason why so many returning soldiers turn to alcohol or drug abuse as a way to help them forget their sorrow.

The military created thirty-two Warrior Transition Battalions, special units that provide closely managed care for soldiers with severe psychological trauma. There are 7,200 soldiers in such units across the country, including 465 at Fort Carson outside Colorado Springs.[18] A specialist returning from Iraq after suffering two concussions and watching several of his buddies burn to death was admitted at one of these units. He was prescribed a list of medications for his anxiety and nightmares, but instead of helping him, they made him feel disoriented. The unit was run in military fashion. Noncommissioned officers (NCOs) would harangue or discipline him when he arrived late to formation or violated the rules. That specialist attempted suicide with a combination of alcohol and an overdose of painkillers. Like many other soldiers, he felt that being in those units was worse than being in Iraq. Four soldiers in the Fort Carson unit have committed suicide since 2007, the highest rate of any transition unit.[19] Because of the medications they are given, some soldiers have become addicted to prescription medications or have turned to heroin. There are so many psychotropic drugs available that some soldiers openly deal, buy, or swap prescription pills.[20]

Soldiers and healthcare workers in transition units such as in Fort Carson complain that soldiers there were given complex cocktails of medications, which raises concern about accidental overdoses, addiction, and side effects from interactions. The wife of one of these soldiers who was in a trauma care unit complained that the medications disoriented him and that he would often wander in the house late at night before falling asleep on the floor. He died after taking morphine and the sleeping pill Ambien®, although the coroner ruled that his death was from natural causes.[21]

This is not the kind of care that soldiers or their families had hoped for.

In Veterans Affairs centers, many of the clinicians have never been in a war and have no understanding for what the troops experience. For veterans, dealing with the VA can be difficult and often humiliating. By 2010, there was a backlog of 951,000 medical claims, many of which have been pending for years. It can take up to fifteen years for a claim to be decided, and waiting for mental-health services is one of many causes of the troubling high rate of suicide.[22]

On May 19, 2011, the United States Court of Appeals for the Ninth Circuit ordered an overhaul of mental healthcare out of concern over the high rates of suicide among veterans and what the court called the "unchecked incompetence" and unconscionable delays in caring for veterans with mental-health problems by the Department of Veterans Affairs.[23] The court's decision found that the VA bureaucracy was so extremely slow and unresponsive that veterans were being denied their rights to mental healthcare and to timely adjudication of disability claims. It cited as evidence the high veteran suicide rate. The judges pointed out that the agency had no suicide prevention officers at any of its outpatient clinics and that 70 percent of its health facilities had no systems to trace potentially suicidal patients. The court agreed with the plaintiffs that "system-wide" changes were needed at the VA, given the rising flood of veterans returning from Iraq and Afghanistan, and ordered the case back to the district court so that a plan could be devised. Judge Stephen Roy Reinhardt, in writing for the majority, stated that from October 27, 2007, to April 2008, "at least 1,467 veterans died while their appeals for mental health treatments were pending."[24]

The delays are getting worse as more troops are returning from Afghanistan and Iraq. The judges noted that the system for screening suicidal patients was ineffective and cited a 2007 inspector general's conclusion that suicide-prevention measures were not available. The ruling occurred two years after the appeal was filed, when lawyers for the government and Veterans for Common Sense and Veterans United for Truth were trying to negotiate a plan for improving the system. Since they didn't succeed, the judges have remanded the case to the district court to order that a new plan be enacted. Unfortunately, the VA appears to be determined to overturn that ruling and is seeking a rehearing from the full appellate court.[25]

Benefit claims are supposed to be acknowledged within days or weeks after they are filed, but it takes an average of more than four years to fully adjudicate a mental-health claim. When a veteran appeals a disability rating, the process takes even longer. The problem, as previously mentioned, is one of inadequate resources and planning.

THE SUICIDE OF SPOUSES

A soldier's spouse, who had been multitasking during her husband's too many deployments, working and raising children, confided that she thought of committing suicide. She thought she couldn't share with her husband how she felt because he had returned from war a different person, with mental and physical problems of his own.

The shocking revelation of military-spouse suicides has only become public since 2010, when Deborah Mullen, the wife of the former chairman of the Joint Chiefs of Staff, Admiral Mike Mullen, spoke out about it. She stated that there is no information about how many military spouses have killed themselves. She added that they were reluctant to seek mental healthcare because of the stigma it still carries and because they were concerned that seeking help might have a negative impact on their husband's military career.[26] A recent study published in the *New England Journal of Medicine* established a clear link between the incidents of army wives attempting suicide and the number of deployments by their spouses.[27]

The army is keeping track of the rise in mental-health problems of its soldiers, and it is collaborating with the National Institute of Mental Health. But it does not take account of, nor does it have programs to help, the military spouses who are at risk. Coincidentally, the results of the study on servicemen and servicewomen were announced at the same time that the wives of two husbands who had multiple deployments were reported dead as a result of suspected suicides. One of the women was a pregnant forty-year-old army wife from North Carolina who called 911, threatening to harm herself. When the police arrived, she was dead of a self-inflicted gunshot wound. A few weeks earlier, army officials had begun investigating the suspected suicide of an army spouse in Schweinfurt, Germany.[28] In 2009, another Fort Bragg wife committed suicide by carbon monoxide poisoning, locking herself and her children in her car, parked in the garage, with the engine running.[29] Carissa Picard, founder of Military Spouses for Change, wrote "Here at Fort Hood, Texas . . . they cannot give me figures on spouses' suicides but they . . . see so many attempted suicides in the Emergency Room that the medical staff have become quite adept at handling them."[30]

The reality of the situation of these highly stressed spouses is revealed in the many blogs they have created, including *Unlikely Wife*, *Left Face*, and *Milspouse Mutterings*, among others. In these blogs, wives complain that they cannot be employed, despite their college degrees, because they are required to remain where their husbands are stationed in the United States. One wife encouraged her husband to get help because of his erratic behavior and his alcohol abuse. But all he received from his physician was a prescription for antidepressants and sleeping pills without the counseling that might have helped him. As their marriage deteriorated, she realized that he was involved with another woman. She checked herself into a hospital because of her suicidal thoughts.[31] Another wife wrote, "In the Army, we are only as good as our husbands."[32] Too many intelligent and highly skilled women are regarded as appendages to their husbands and find that the military has no concern for their mental health or employment. It is only in their community of blogs that they find sympathy and a way of sharing their problems and heartaches.

PEOPLE, NOT STATISTICS

Philip was a sergeant who recruited several young men into the army, including one who had a terrible childhood in a dysfunctional family. He befriended him, and they became as close as brothers. Philip was one of the soldiers who helped capture Saddam Hussein, and he was touted in articles in his hometown newspaper for his accomplishments. His family was so proud of him. But then this young recruit killed himself, and he was the subject of yet another article, although a very painful one.[33]

Mark drank heavily to forget the pain he felt and then drove his car at top speed, only to die in a crash. A thirty-five-year-old specialist argued with his girlfriend over the phone and then sent a despondent e-mail message home: "I can't explain how ashamed I am. I said some things out of anger. I can't cope without each and every one of you there by me the whole way. I feel alone and unappreciated. For some odd reason this deployment is ending up to be like the last one. I thought about killing myself. . . . I realize I need help and I need to have family put first. Please forgive me and accept my apology."[34] Then he killed himself.

Specialist Armando Aguilar Jr. committed suicide by overdosing on pills after returning from a rough tour in Iraq a year earlier. His job was to drive an armored vehicle in search of roadside bombs. The army's physicians put him on medications for depression, insomnia, and panic attacks. What he needed was prolonged psychological counseling. Even though the army has increased its number of therapists and psychologists, it is still experiencing a significant shortage. As a result, army physicians must rely more on medication than on therapy. Also, the services screen too few soldiers for mental problems after deployments.[35] This places the burden to seek help on the soldier rather than on the officers. Few soldiers are willing to seek help unless they are ordered to do so.

Armando Aguilar was stationed at Fort Hood in Texas, where fourteen soldiers killed themselves in one year. Fort Hood is the largest base in the United States. Its surrounding communities have suffered high rates of crime, domestic violence, and suicide, as wave after wave of soldiers return home, often after multiple tours of duty.[36]

On January 16, 2009, Staff Sergeant Thad Montgomery returned to his unit from a harrowing patrol in Afghanistan. A few hours later, his company suffered its first casualty when one of its members was killed in an ambush. After the patrol, Thad withdrew from his friends and said that he could no longer fight. Because he insisted he wasn't suicidal, he wasn't immediately evacuated from the base. Four days later, as his condition grew worse, his company commander arranged for him to be flown out on a resupply helicopter. But Thad killed himself that morning. His mother feels a deep anger against the army for having failed not just her son but all the soldiers who were there with him.[37] She faults the army for not doing more to educate its officers about PTSD.

The daughter of Angela Buckley's neighbor returned from combat in Iraq in a wheelchair, paralyzed from the waist down. She was a captain and was also eligible for a purple heart. She was about to enter a program that would have provided her with a dog to help her navigate, and Angela believed that it would also have given her comfort as well. But the young woman killed herself in her bathroom on Christmas Eve after her mother stepped out of the house.

Staff Sergeant David Senft died alone and despondent in Afghanistan from a self-inflicted gunshot to his head, leaving an unsent text message typed on his cell phone, "I don't know what to say. I'm sorry." The army had deployed David to Afghanistan despite several suicide attempts and a stay in a mental institution. He remained in Afghanistan even after receiving mandated counseling and after his weapon had been removed from him. "If he was suicidal and they had to take away his gun, why was he allowed to stay in Afghanistan?" his father asked.[38]

Lieutenant Elizabeth Whiteside tried to kill herself on a number of occa-

sions. Her father said that she took two weeks' worth of four different medications at once in an attempt to end her life. He claimed that her suicide
attempt was brought about by stress as she waited to find out whether she
would be court-martialed for an earlier suicide attempt and for discharging
her weapon into the ceiling. After she was interviewed by a *Washington Post*
reporter, all charges against her were dropped.[39]

Yet another soldier had a dispute with his wife one evening. It was like
lighting a match near a flammable place. His colonel thought he was highly
intelligent, stable, and efficient, yet the soldier was troubled because many of
his buddies were in harm's way. After that quarrel with his wife, he put his
army uniform on and shot himself. His wife thinks that somehow she was
responsible for his death, not realizing the extent of the burden he was carrying since his return from Iraq.

Chance Keesling joined the army in 2003 at the age of eighteen because
he wanted to serve his country after 9/11. He was trained as a combat engineer for the rebuilding of Iraq and then was retrained as a tactical gunner sitting on top of a Humvee®. During his first deployment, Chance suffered
mental-health issues so severe that he was placed on suicide watch. After he
returned home, his father realized the huge toll that the years of war had taken
on him. Chance sought mental-health treatment from Veterans Affairs. Then
his marriage failed, and he knew that he needed help. He turned down the
offer of a $27,000 redeployment bonus because he felt that he could not
handle it; nevertheless, he was sent back. Because he enlisted, he had to spend
four years in the army, with an additional four-year commitment to the
reserves. His father suggested that he talk with his commander and tell him
about his mental-health issues, but Chance told his father that it would be a
waste of time because his commander would think that he was trying to fake
his mental condition to avoid being redeployed. Two months after returning
to Iraq, Chance took a gun into the latrine and shot himself. The Pentagon
reported his suicide as a "noncombat-related incident." As if that wasn't
enough of an insult, five months after his death, the VA sent Chance a letter
asking him to complete a post-deployment adjustment report.[40]

In his poetry book *Here, Bullet*, Brian Turner wrote a eulogy to his friend
Private First Class Bruce Miller, "And it happens like this, on a blue day of sun
/ when Private Miller pulls the trigger / to take brass and fire into his mouth:
/ The sound lifts the birds up off the water / ... and nothing can stop it now,
no matter what / blur of motion surrounds him, no matter what voices /

crackle over the radio in static confusion / because if only for this moment the earth is stilled / and Private Miller has found what low hush there is / down in the eucalyptus shade, there by the river."[41] Brian Turner wrote this poem to commemorate his friend Private Miller because the colonel spoke about each soldier who had died in his platoon but didn't even mention Bruce Miller.

When Jason, an infantry soldier, returned from the war, he experienced depression and suffered from hopelessness and despair. He complained about having suicidal thoughts. He eventually was sent to a psychiatrist, whom he told that he meant to commit suicide. Yet the psychiatrist who examined him wrote down in his report, "This person does not meet any of the criteria for mental disorder." He told Jason, "Just be a man." When Jason called his father, he told him that the psychiatrist who had seen him had spent only ten minutes with him and had told him that he was just faking everything. His father was outraged and replied that there was no way anyone could spend ten minutes with him and make such a diagnosis. He wanted him to return and see that psychiatrist again, but Jason told him that it wouldn't do any good and that they had the paperwork and were after him like sharks because they needed more troops. His superiors told him to go back to his barracks and clean his weapons. They also told his buddies to stay away from him. Shortly thereafter, Jason killed himself.[42]

Oftentimes soldiers who committed suicide while in combat were the bravest and the best. This war is not the kind of war our soldiers were prepared for. Too often they must endure a 24-7 schedule in the midst of heartbreaking and enraging situations.

NOAH CHARLES PIERCE

Noah Charles Pierce, a soldier honored for his bravery in combat, faced many terrifying and upsetting situations in Iraq. He saw a close friend being blown up and witnessed the death of many innocent people. Like so many other members of the army who were on the front lines, Noah suffered brain injury from the proximity of deafening explosions. He was afraid to be tested for it, so he did not show up for his doctor appointments. When he returned home after his second tour of duty in Iraq, he began to experience nightmares and bouts of anger as well as a profound sense of grief and loss of self-worth.

Cheryl, his mother, said that Noah was slowly dying inside, "PTSD kills you from the inside. He couldn't escape the horrors of his two tours in Iraq.

He thought of himself as a murderer. The Army trained him to kill to protect others. They forgot to untrain him."[43]

Soldiers in combat feel as if their unit is a family and that they need to protect each other. When a member of a unit is killed and a buddy like Noah has to pick up his friend's remains, he cannot avoid rage and despair.

Cheryl was looking forward to Noah's return from Iraq but, like most family members of returning soldiers, she was unprepared to deal with the changes in her son. Noah was coming home from another world with a psychological burden that was invisible. He took the plane back from Iraq to Sparta, Minnesota. Despite all he had been through, there was no preparation for his homecoming. Because of his experiences, he no longer felt a part of the world he was suddenly thrown into. Traumatic experiences can create a sense of isolation and the feeling that only a person who has been through the same experience can understand the intensity of one's distress.

Cheryl found the son she loved transformed. Although he was home in body, the person she knew wasn't there. She said, "The guilt just ate at him. He was too kindhearted."[44] She knew about the terrible things that had happened to him, his best friend struck by a bomb by his side, the Iraqi child he had befriended and worried about when he lost track of him, the memory of the physician his sergeant had ordered him to kill as a suspected enemy. This sensitive young man was haunted by the memory of an unarmed man he shot during a house-to-house raid and the memory of that other child who he hoped might run away but was crushed beneath a Bradley® vehicle.

When soldiers return home, they struggle with what they did do and what they didn't do while on duty. They often have anxiety attacks. Many of them, like Noah, hope they will die and that it will all end soon. Soldiers often blame themselves, feeling like failures, as if they had let down their country and their family.[45]

Noah lived in the small mining town of Eveleth, Minnesota, where he and his stepfather, Tom, used to go fishing and hunting together and where he had a circle of close friends who shared his love of fishing. When he returned, his stepfather, who loved him as if he were his own son, continued to take him fishing to their favorite spot and tried to get his mind off of his troubles.

But now that he was home, Noah didn't know why he couldn't drive down a road without his heart racing, why he was having repeated nightmares, bouts of anger he couldn't control, feelings of guilt that tormented him. He was still worried about roadside bombs. He was still in Iraq. The psychological cost of war is debilitating. The RAND Corporation has put out a booklet on post-deployment stress that lists common experiences associated with PTSD, such as reliving bad memories of being attacked or ambushed, having to handle the remains of a friend, having thoughts of suicide, and experiencing situations that trigger flashbacks of traumatic experiences. Noah had all these symptoms. He drank heavily to kill the pain inside him, to help him forget what he had experienced, to lessen the anguish that was invisible. He was experiencing PTSD. He kept reliving his worst experiences, had difficulty falling asleep, and reacted with exaggerated startle to any sudden noise. He had feelings of detachment or estrangement from others. And this gentle person also had outbursts of anger that surprised his mother and his sister.[46]

Once, Noah turned on his sister Sarah with inexplicable rage. Because of his unpredictable anger, he decided to leave home and move in with Tyler, the best friend he had spent a lot of time with as a child. Tyler also gave Noah a job as a machinist in his company after Noah quit his job at the mines, where he was being harassed about his PTSD.

Cheryl's way of responding to the different Noah was to be there for him, to express her love, and to reassure him that he was a wonderful person. She was deeply troubled by the lack of support she was receiving in helping him with his suffering. She found herself on her own, just as her son was. She knew that in his own mind, he felt like a prisoner of war. She felt very protective of him but at the same time felt angered at the lack of understanding manifested by some people in her town who began to belittle him and treat him badly when they found that he had PTSD.

The only help that Noah received to deal with his symptoms was access to the VA hospital and clinic for checkups for a period of up to ninety days. Counselors from veterans organizations interviewed on PBS's *Frontline* say that they are more concerned with returning soldiers than the military is.[47] But Noah didn't receive any counseling.

He sought assistance for his nightmares, but all he received was a prescription for sleeping pills and appointments for return visits. He desperately needed medical care because he was losing his hearing and he knew that he had suffered brain damage from being so close to explosions of IEDs that occurred around him daily. But he didn't keep the appointments. The clinic did not call him or try to reschedule. By then, the period of thirty to ninety days when Noah could receive medical help was over.

Noah told his mother that if there had been a clause in his enlistment papers requiring him to seek counseling on his return from combat, he would have followed those orders. A number of returning veterans told Cheryl that they would have done the same, but they didn't want to go on their own because they were afraid it would make them look weak, like wimps. In the military, there is indeed a stigma against receiving mental-health services. When the army did its own survey in Iraq, nearly half of the soldiers who needed psychological support reported that they felt that if they asked for such help, their leaders would have blamed them for their problems, and that their unit would have had less confidence in them. Soldiers are immersed in a culture of disciplined stoicism that leads them to see weakness in sharing their emotional distress.

Although Noah had moved in with his friend Tyler, his mother stopped by every day to see him when he was home from work or sent him text messages or engaged in short telephone calls if he wasn't there. Noah tended to be abrupt with her, but despite his difficult behavior, she kept telling him, "When you need me, I'm still here, Noah. I am not going anywhere, no matter how badly you treat me."[48] How can a family understand that the traumas of war create walls around returning soldiers that prevent them from expressing their love?

On July 24, 2007, Cheryl, her husband, and her daughter, took a day off, a break that they had planned for a month. Cheryl thought about calling Noah and asking him to join them but decided not to. She blames herself for not contacting him and wonders whether, if she had, she could have affected his decision.

The following day, she didn't drive by his house or his place of work as she usually would do. When she returned to deliver the bank's mail, as she did every day, she didn't see his truck at home, so she thought he was at work, but his truck wasn't there either. She was upset and wondered if he might be at the recruiting office. At a quarter of five, she called his cell phone and said on a voice message, "It's me. I want to know if you would like to have dinner, see me, talk to me, but I guess not."

On her way home from work, Cheryl's cell phone beeped, and she found a text message from Noah. It said, "I love you very much and I'm so sorry." She knew instantly that her son was going to commit suicide, and she immediately typed back, "You are my heart, Noah." Her daughter called right after, asking if she had received a text message from Noah. When Cheryl replied that she had, Sarah started to scream, and then his mother knew what was happening.

Noah shot himself on Wednesday, July 25, 2007, in the mine dumps near his favorite fishing spot. The words, "Freedom isn't free," were carved on the dashboard of his truck. In his final note to his mother, he had written, "Mom I am so sorry. I'm freeing myself from the desert once and for all. Time's up. I'm not a good person. I have done bad things. I have taken lives. Now it's time to take mine."[49]

After Noah died, Tyler found his friend's moving poem written on a wrinkled page of a newspaper: "Got home almost a year and a half ago / We were so happy / that beer never tasted so good / Iraq was the farthest thing from my mind / That was the best week of my life / It crept up slowly / First just while sleeping / More real and scary than when it happened / After it's on the mine awake / Never ten minutes goes by without being reminded / Been home a year and a half physically / Mentally I will never be home."[50]

On August 1, 2007, Cheryl kissed her son for the last time. Her grieving family stood by his grave as members of the military fired a salute and "Taps" sounded. There was a preacher there beside the largest group of military that had ever attended a funeral in the area, with standing room only. Cheryl felt that so many people are unable to understand the necessity of affirmation. She believes that being for or against a war is not what matters. What a veteran needs to hear is that he did the right thing, fought to bring peace to the world, and that everyone is proud of him.

As Cheryl sorted through her son's belongings, she discovered nine awards for bravery that she never knew anything about. However, what mattered the most to her and was the most dear to her heart is the fact that after his return, he gave blood as often as possible. "This son of mine who thought he was a murderer. Until the day he died, he did it quietly, and he did it faithfully." She reflected on how much he had given to the world during his short life. She discovered how "Noah left footprints in everyone's heart he met. Anybody that knew him walked away a better person."[51]

Cheryl has created a memorial to her son in their home that covers an entire wall. It includes photos of Noah as a child and two photos of him in Iraq in the same frame, his nine medals of valor, and the insignias from his uniform. Above is a triangular frame with stars. On one side of the frame is the image of an eagle with the American flag and a crucifix.

Cheryl, her daughter Sarah, and many of Noah's friends memorialized him by getting tattoos. On her leg, Cheryl tattooed the last words she spoke to him, "You are my heart Noah." Out of the broken heart, an eagle is flying that represents the peace, freedom, and the patriotism Noah felt. Sarah and Noah's friend

Tyler had Noah's name tattooed, as did about twenty other people who knew and loved Noah. Tyler's younger brother, Jake, was close to Noah, and Jake's fiancée, Casey, who was also a friend, wears a pendant around her neck with Noah's photo. Cheryl and her daughter Sarah go to Noah's grave as often as they can to be with him in spirit. His stepfather, Tom, returns to their special place in the woods for hours and comes back red-eyed. Noah left behind a loving family and friends who grieve over his death. There are many memories of Noah in the town of Eveleth, and they cause much anguish for those who loved him.

There are also painful memories beyond Eveleth experienced by Noah's friends who were with him in Iraq. His friend Keith, who suffers from PTSD, was still in Iraq when Noah died.[52] Brooke, Keith's wife, considered Noah her best friend and spent time with him and his other friends when he was at boot camp in Georgia. She flew up to Minnesota to be at his funeral.

But Cheryl was heartened by the growing public recognition of the trials of returning veterans. Members of a national veterans organization flew up to Eveleth to take footage for the HBO documentary *Wartorn*. The AMVETS Club in Virginia, Minnesota, asked Cheryl if it could name its post after Noah. It is now called AMVETS Noah C. Pierce Post 33. Cheryl was happy to know that Noah's name would live on long after she was gone.

Yet in 2011, four years after Noah died, Cheryl experienced a new emotion, a deep anger that led her to contact other parents of soldiers who had committed suicide. Looking back, she discovered that her son should not have been sent back for a second tour in Iraq. He had tried to harm another soldier in his unit. Despite this, he was given a promotion from private first class to specialist. She said, "They could have sent him to prison for doing that. Then, he would still be alive."[53] She came to feel that the army had been using him and all the soldiers, not giving them the care they needed, and she thought of suing the army as the parents of other returning soldiers did after their sons committed suicide.

Somehow, Cheryl still feels guilty about Noah's suicide, even though she was such a loving and supportive mother. She feels that because she and her family took the day off for a motorcycle ride on the day Noah died, it was her fault that he killed himself, even though she had called him every day and kept in constant touch with him. She has since put her motorcycle away and decided never to use it again.

JEFF LUCEY

Jeff lived in a small Massachusetts town, was a popular young man who excelled at sports, and wanted to join the Marines after finishing high school to help pay for his college tuition. He felt that it would be an honor for him to serve his country. He and his best friend met with Marine recruiters. His parents were alarmed when he told them that the recruiters had invited him to meet in a hotel because they knew that meant he was given the "red carpet treatment." They begged him not to sign up. But the next morning, he returned and told them that he had.

This was in 2000 and Jeff was nineteen years old. His mother, Joyce, wanted to scream and take him to a safe place, but she felt helpless. His father, Kevin, was also upset. In addition to Jeff, they had two daughters, and their family was very close. They all worried about Jeff's time in Iraq, especially after he wrote to his parents, telling them about the pain and heartache he felt about leaving them. His letters home hinted at despair and included the comment, "I did things I didn't want to do."[54]

The last entry in the journal Jeff kept mentioned news of a scud missile landing nearby, "The noise was just short of blowing out your eardrums. Everyone's heart truly skipped a beat and the reality of where we were and what's truly happening hit home. We just had a gas alert and it is past midnight. We will not sleep. Our nerves are on edge."[55]

As for so many families of young veterans, Jeff's was not prepared for his homecoming when he returned in July 2003. The week before, his mother had a stroke. She thinks it was caused by all the pressure and stress she felt while Jeff was in Iraq. She had been constantly watching television to understand what was happening in Iraq. Even though she was exhausted, the whole family and Jeff's girlfriend, Julie, whom he planned to marry, went to greet him on his arrival. Joyce thought he appeared wonderful but thinner. He was looking forward to college and had been accepted as a transfer student for a course in business at Holyoke Community College. She felt blessed that the nightmare was finally over.

But neither of Jeff's parents could foresee the year of anguish and bewilderment that would follow, nor their son's inability to get the medical care he needed so badly. And neither Jeff's family nor his girlfriend, Julie, were prepared for the changes in his behavior after his return. His parents saw puzzling, isolated instances that were difficult to cope with. One of the differences that surprised everyone was his refusal to walk on the beach with Julie, even though it had been a favorite pastime of his. He felt that he had seen enough sand to last him a lifetime. Like many veterans of the wars in Iraq, Jeff started to show signs of PTSD. He became afraid of open spaces and uncomfortable in crowds, and he wanted to remain in his room. There were times he was able to attend college and times when he just stayed home. Since Julie's courses were scheduled at periods different from Jeff's, she didn't notice his absence. He began having panic attacks and nightmares and became depressed. Neither his mother nor his girlfriend could recognize the person he had become. It took them months to persuade Jeff to get the help he needed.

The events of Jeff's downward spiral are engraved in his parents' hearts. Jeff began drinking, as many veterans do, to kill the pain he felt, and he became an alcoholic. Sometimes by 10:00 a.m., he had already downed a six-pack of EKU 28®—a German beer, one of the strongest in the world, with more than twice the alcohol content of a Budweiser®.[56] He was drinking at the wedding of his older sister, Kelly. During the reception, he went to talk to his grandmother and told her, "Grandma, you can be in a room full of people and still be alone."[57]

Then his mother discovered that he had physical problems as well. Julie's family lives very close to Jeff's, and he stayed at her house very often. Joyce found out that Jeff was vomiting every day and that he wasn't eating his breakfast. He was also having bloody stools. She sent him to a primary-care physician who referred him to a specialist, but Jeff refused to see him.

On Christmas Eve, the Luceys went with their youngest daughter, Debbie, to Joyce's parents' house for their traditional celebration, but Jeff refused to accompany them. His sister stayed with him a little while. He was drinking and told his sister that he was nothing but a murderer. She tried to calm him down, telling him he wasn't a murderer but her brother. After she called her parents to tell them that Jeff was having trouble, they came home immediately. The following day, he seemed just like himself again, and Joyce thought it was the alcohol that had caused his reaction.

In March 2004, Jeff had a troubled week. He argued with Julie and stayed home even though it was his birthday. He seemed very sad and depressed. He was also showing a typical reaction of veterans, becoming startled and upset at noises like a door slamming. Jeff's parents told him that he should be seen at the VA, but he felt that if the Marines learned about his situation, it would affect his career. He was also concerned that it would hamper his chances to find a job in the civilian world, since he had already taken an exam to become a state trooper before he had left for Iraq. Being steeped in the military culture, he was afraid that if his problems were known, they would make him seem weak.

Jeff's parents sent him to a private psychiatrist and to an internist. He was given a prescription in order to help him cope with his depression and allow him to resume his college classes. Joyce saw on Jeff's card, "Call me if you don't feel safe," and thought the note referred to feeling safe in his surroundings, not to feeling that he might harm himself.

In mid-May, Jeff took his mother for a walk through a field. He had her listen to a song, Shinedown's "45," which had lyrics alluding to suicide. He told his mother that the song was about him, and that he was looking down a dark tunnel. They went down to a brook and sat there, talking, and then walked through the woods. It was a time Joyce cherishes and holds in her memory.

By the end of May, Kevin and Julie convinced Jeff to go for treatment at the psychiatric ward of the VA hospital in North Hampton. He was put on a suicide watch, a locked ward, meaning that only a medical attendant could be with him. His attendant, Ken, was a Vietnam veteran. Yet Jeff's parents and Julie came to the hospital every day to find out how he was doing. Even though he showed suicidal signs and the doctors saw clear evidence of PTSD, he was kept for only four days and then discharged. Jeff's records noted that his suicidal thoughts included suffocation, hanging, or a medication overdose. His records also stated that he had bought a garden hose that he might use to kill himself.[58] None of this was ever shared with his parents. The nurse who handled his case told Joyce that he would not be accepted into any program until he had his alcohol problem under control. Jeff left with a cocktail of antipsychotic drugs. Each one came with a warning label stating that it should not be used with alcohol.[59]

The VA never contacted the private psychiatrist Jeff had been seeing.[60] Years later, Joyce and Kevin learned from the National Center for Post-Traumatic Stress Disorder website (www.ncptsd.org) that PTSD and alcohol abuse needed to be treated simultaneously. When they told Jeff's story at a meeting of the American Medical Association in Pennsylvania, one woman stood up and said that she worked at the VA and that she was sorry to say that they do tell patients they can't do dual diagnostics.

When Jeff was released, Joyce spoke with a nurse who suggested that she could call the police and get him arrested so that he could get involuntarily committed. She did get in touch with the police. In case he might get into trouble, she wanted them to know that Jeff was suffering from psychiatric problems.

Soon after that, Jeff began to drink again. His girlfriend, Julie, told him that he had to make a choice between her and his drinking. But Jeff was unable to make that decision because he was helpless to control his emotions and his struggles.

That week, Jeff asked his father to take him for a ride, and Joyce knew that he wanted Kevin to get him some beer. Joyce called the VA and spoke with the Vietnam veteran who had been Jeff's attendant. He told her that he was afraid this was what would happen, and he mentioned that it had taken him over ten years to recover from PTSD. This made Joyce begin to think that she and her husband might have to be working with Jeff for years. They did not realize how close he was to killing himself.

The first week in June, while Joyce and Kevin were attending Jeff's sister Debbie's graduation, a policewoman arrived escorting Jeff. She had stopped him for drunken driving. She mentioned that she herself had two sons who had been in the military and that she just wanted to help Jeff. Joyce's son-in-law and Kevin took Jeff for a walk so that they could keep him away from the crowd. He hadn't shaved and looked unkempt, unlike the person he used to be. But he insisted on seeing his sister and went right up to the front of the room before they called her name to receive her diploma. He hugged her and wouldn't let her go until someone separated them, telling him she had to get on the stage because they were about to call her name. That was the last hug she would ever get from her brother.

Joyce and Kevin asked their son-in-law to take Jeff home. When they came back home, they found Jeff laying down on his bed while their son-in-law sat next to him. In his own way, Jeff was crying out for help as he kept listening to Shinedown's song "45" over and over again.

The Luceys didn't know how to deal with the troubles of the son they loved so much. Kevin called the VA and went over the list of problems Jeff was experiencing. He wasn't eating enough. He was drinking too much. He kept isolating himself in his room. He could no longer hold a job at the university career center where he studied, as he once did. His relationship with his girlfriend was troubled. He couldn't sleep, he had nightmares, and he heard voices. The VA physicians concurred that Jeff's condition sounded worse than during the week he had been committed, so they suggested that the Luceys bring him in.

Jeff got into the car with his sisters and his grandfather while his brother-in-law drove. Meanwhile Joyce was pacing frantically. The hospital never called in a psychiatrist—just Ken (the Vietnam veteran) and an intern who happened to be on call. A few weeks before, Jeff had told Debbie that he had gotten a rope, so Ken asked Jeff if he had had thrown it away. Jeff replied that he "wouldn't do that" to himself. All this information was available to the personnel at the VA. Unfortunately, his sisters called their parents to let them know that they were bringing Jeff home because the VA wouldn't commit him.

Meanwhile, Kevin called around to try to get some help for Jeff. But as soon as he mentioned that Jeff had a drinking problem, he was told that, under the circumstances, he could not get help. Kevin and Joyce were angered for failing to find support for a young man who was clearly suicidal.

After his sisters brought him home, Jeff went to his room. Kevin stayed with him that night and talked to him. He told him that if he stopped drinking, he could get help with his PTSD. Throughout that week, all of Jeff's family stayed with him. On Friday night, Jeff watched the Red Sox game with his parents and then went to bed. Later, when Joyce went into his room, she found that he had gotten out through the window and had some friends drive him to a liquor store. Jeff's friends called Debbie to tell her that they had him in the car with them, and Debbie told them to bring him back to his parents. When Jeff got out of the car, Joyce was astonished to see that he was dressed in camouflage, something he had never done before, and that he also had his boots on, as though he were ready to go into battle. Kevin got upset and threw out the bottles Jeff had bought at the store. By then, it was midnight and Kelly and her husband arrived. Joyce was so upset that she went to sit in the car with them. Kelly said that she just didn't know what to do other than call the police. The night ended and Jeff ultimately went to bed.

The next day, Kevin bought a book on PTSD. Jeff read it and told his parents that he had a number of the psychological symptoms of that illness. With tears in his eyes, he said, "I think I am going crazy." Joyce asked him if he was ready to get some help, and he agreed. She called the VA on Tuesday and was referred to the Veteran's Center in Springfield, which was the first time she had ever heard about it. She wondered why she hadn't received that information before. Jeff got an appointment for the following Friday. Jamie, a Vietnam veteran, helped Jeff with all the paperwork. Jamie told Kevin that he would come to their house and meet with the whole family so that they could all work together.

Meanwhile, Kevin and Joyce persuaded Jeff to see a psychiatrist. Jamie called him and let him know that there was a bed available in New York, but that he would have preferred to have Jeff treated at a Vermont facility where dual diagnostics could be performed. Unfortunately, there was no bed available in Vermont. The psychiatrist replied that he should take whatever bed was available because Jeff was in such bad shape.

The following day, Kevin, Joyce, Debbie, and Jeff left to spend the weekend at Camp Sunshine, as they did every year. It's a camp for children who have life-threatening illnesses, and the family was going to be there during the oncology week. Jeff really didn't want to go, but his mother knew that he had always loved being there. She told him, "Let's just have a good time together." That day, he shaved, perhaps because he was interested in dating, since Julie had broken up with him because she had difficulty dealing with his problems. Joyce reflected that Jeff didn't have anything positive left in his life. He was no longer attending school. He didn't have a job or see the girl he loved. He had even given his mother his car because she had totaled hers.

When they arrived at the camp, Jeff saw an open bar. He had a couple drinks and went out for a walk. A few hours later, the Luceys saw two camp administrators running after Jeff because some of the girls he had approached called to tell them that he was acting weird. They brought Jeff over to Kevin and asked him to take Jeff away immediately. Kevin and Jeff arrived home at 2:30 in the morning. Jeff went into his room and stayed there most of the next day. Joyce was beside herself with worry. She was afraid Jeff was going to hang himself or overdose with alcohol. She had remained at the camp because she couldn't find the keys to Jeff's car, but she spoke to him that evening. The last words she said were, "I love you."

The following day, Joyce's father took Jeff to his appointment with the psychiatrist and then wanted to take him to McDonald's. Jeff said, "Grandpa, you don't understand. I can't go with you." When he got home, he shook his grandfather's hand, something he had never done before. Joyce later saw it as a way of saying good-bye. Monday night, Kevin had a very painful time with Jeff. He called the Veteran's Center, where someone spoke to Jeff and told his father that he was very suicidal.

That night, Jeff climbed into his father's lap, and Kevin held him for forty-five minutes. The next evening, Kevin came home to find the TV on. The basement door was open. Kevin walked downstairs, saw Jeff's platoon picture on the floor, along with photos of his sisters, and then—Jeff hanging from a beam with a garden hose. He took the hose off of him and held him. Then he folded up the rug for a pillow and laid him down. Ironically, the VA called three weeks after he died, letting them know that Jeff had an appointment.

On Jeff's tombstone, the Luceys put an epitaph from the Shinedown song he listened to so often. One year after his death, they received a letter from the Massachusetts State Police informing them that Jeff had tested in the ninety-fifth percentile and would have obtained the job he had applied for. They placed the letter on his grave.

After Jeff's tragic death, the Luceys gained an international reputation for speaking out and helping other veterans and their families. Two weeks after Jeff died, Kevin and Joyce wanted to be involved in outreach work so that other families wouldn't be without help. They contacted the Veterans Education Project, which has a program for veterans to visit schools, colleges, and universities to talk about their personal experiences. The Luceys immediately participated and met with a marine sergeant who was in Iraq at the same time as Jeff. While Joyce was telling him Jeff's story, they noticed the same behavior in this Marine as they had seen in Jeff—grinding one hand into his other and keeping a faraway gaze while they were talking.

A few days later, Kevin received a call from the executive director of the Veterans Education Project, who suggested that the Luceys attend a Veterans for Peace conference. One of the speakers specialized in PTSD. During the conference, the Luceys met Nancy Lessin and Charlie Richardson, the founders of Military Families Speak Out, who invited them to a large meeting they were heading. Nancy asked the meeting attendees to introduce themselves, and the Luceys discovered that many of the participants were Gold Star Families. When it was Joyce's turn to speak, she broke down while telling Jeff's story. It was the first time she had spoken out.

Nancy and Charlie kept in constant touch with the Luceys. Nancy asked them if they would be willing to talk to a radio station in Cambridge that was interested in their story. The Luceys met several people there: an Iraq veteran who was active in Iraq Veterans Against the War; Amy Goodman, editor of *Democracy Now!* a daily television and radio program; and Patricia Folkrod, who was making *Ground Truth*, a documentary film. When Patricia heard their story, she asked them if she could tape an interview with them, and Jeff's story became part of her film.

Their next effort was to join the Eyes Wide Open Movement sponsored by the American Friends Association, which was coming to the North Hampton and Amherst areas of Massachusetts. The members of Eyes Wide Open were creating a display of the boots of servicemen and servicewomen who had been killed in action, an exhibit that would be traveling around the country. The Luceys and their daughters donated Jeff's uniform, the placards that Debbie and Kelly had made for Jeff's wake, and a pair of Jeff's boots.

The local press became interested in the Luceys' story, and soon after Kevin and Joyce were contacted by newspapers from around the world. The first time, they were contacted by a woman who called from Japan. She was crying as she told Kevin that she heard Jeff's story on *Democracy Now!* while she was holding her baby boy on her lap. She said she was so upset by the story that she burst into tears. She works for a publisher and asked for permission to put the transcript from the program into a book they were publishing. Two months later, the Luceys received a book from Tokyo, written in Japanese with the chapter about Jeff marked up in the margin.

Then the foreign press started coming to their house: Swedish, Swiss, Russian, German, Italian, and Qatar's Al Jazeera. Once a month, journalists would spend four or five days with them. Four days after the first anniversary of Jeff's death, the Luceys were invited to Paris, where the documentary *Hidden Wounds*, which included Jeff's story, was being premiered. *Ground Truth* was shown at the Sundance Festival in Utah. *Over the Bridge*, a film whose director was a professor at the University of Notre Dame, was also widely circulated.

Patricia Folkrod asked the Luceys to accompany her to New York, where Eyes Wide Open was going to exhibit Jeff's uniform and boots in Central Park. Debbie Lucey and Nancy Lessin accompanied Joyce and Kevin. Nancy introduced them to two Gold Star Families whose children were killed in Iraq a few months before Jeff died. All of a sudden, they found themselves marching with Military Families Speak Out. While they were marching, Nancy brought over a film crew from PBS. Debbie was marching with small pictures of Jeff that she gave to people who were watching and to CNN.

About a month later, a PBS crew came and filmed Jeff's story as part of a documentary it released, "The Soldier's Heart." PBS invited the Luceys to New York City a number of times to take part in interviews.

They received yet another invitation from the Veterans Education Project to attend a community meeting where veterans from the Vietnam War were talking about their experiences. When Operation Iraqi Freedom (OIF) and Operation Enduring Freedom (OEF) began, they triggered flashbacks for these veterans. There was a question-and-answer period after the presentation, and Debbie was called to the microphone. She asked, "What happens when someone comes back with PTSD and no one wants to help?" Then she told them about Jeff.[61]

Invitations continued pouring in from all over the country and the Luceys visited forty-five states. At the same time, they were receiving telephone calls and e-mails from people whose sons and daughters, mothers or fathers, had committed suicide either in a war zone or when they returned. They tried to respond to every one of them. Once, they had a two-hour telephone call with Cheryl Softich. They maintain these contacts to relieve the pain and loneliness of families that have lost a loved one in the armed services to suicide. They are expressing the depth of compassion and understanding people develop through their grief. Those who haven't had similar experiences may have difficulty understanding such profound sorrow.

The Luceys also joined the American Foundation for Suicide Prevention, which sponsors walks and other events to both support the foundation and create awareness of suicide.

Over time, they created a healing community. In that endeavor, they have met some wonderful people whom they have helped to deal with grief in a society that they believe has become self-absorbed.

When the Luceys give interviews and presentations, they bring memorabilia of Jeff. Joyce reminds the listeners that it is not their story they are telling but their son's story, that they have become his voice. They bring his Cub Scout cap as well as his boots and his diary, photos of the Quabbin reservoir where Jeff used to go when he wanted to be alone—personal things people can relate to so that they can connect to him.

Sometimes Kevin shares a special memory of Jeff. His family volunteered at Camp Sunshine in Maine for many years. Once when Jeff came with him, he saw this little girl dancing on the stage. He jumped up and started dancing with her. The little girl died a few years later. He tells his audience that now Jeff is dancing up at the stars.

But the Luceys did more than outreach. They sued the VA for negligence, and the US government settled the case for $350,000. They are plaintiffs in a class-action lawsuit against Prudential Insurance that alleges that company cheated the families of dead soldiers out of more than $100 million in interest on their life insurance policies.[62]

The United States is just beginning to respond publicly to the suffering of returning soldiers from the Iraq war. There are legions of soldiers affected by PTSD. Yet all too often they end up taking their own lives. In 2010, a *New York Times* article revealed that the number of veterans from Iraq and Afghanistan who suffer from PTSD had reached 4,300. It took a lawsuit by the National

Veterans Legal Services Program to make it possible for returning soldiers to have access to disability benefits.[63] But given the bureaucracy, it takes years to process claims for war wounds and PTSD.

On August 2, 2009, the *New York Times* published, for the first time, a two-page spread on suicide of returning veterans and established that statistics do not convey the complete picture: "Suicide counts tend to be undercounted. Nor are there reliable figures for veterans who have left the service; the Department of Veterans Affairs can only systematically track suicides among its hospitalized patients, and it does not issue regular suicide reports."[64]

THE SUFFERING OF FAMILIES

We need to think of the parents, spouses, siblings, and children of soldiers who have committed suicide because it will affect them for the rest of their lives. Grief over the suicide of a family member lingers for a long time. Members of that family may think of themselves as failures because they could not prevent that terrible death from occurring. Even though mothers like Cheryl and parents like the Luceys have moved into the public sphere to help other veterans and prevent further suicides, their grief continues unabated. One mother had difficulty eating three years after her son's suicide, and she wound up in the hospital. Some relatives are unable to sleep, although they may wish they would be able to see their son or daughter in their dreams. For most family members, not a day goes by that they don't think of the loved one they lost. Kevin Lucey says that he thinks of Jeff ten times a day. Cheryl Softich said, "I will talk to him till the day I die and I will not let anyone forget about my son."[65]

For parents, losing a child is out of sequence. They feel that somehow they are the ones who should have died first, not their child, and they live on with a painful emptiness in their family. It is hard for them to find words that can acknowledge or express the pain they feel after a suicide.

One mother wrote, "Not one day goes by that I don't want my son back and I can't stop that—just like I can't stop the visions I have of my child all by himself sitting in his truck—his mind filled with horror, scared and alone. That is what breaks me and it hits me at night more than any other time no matter what I am doing. It's like a movie played in the background of my head and clear as day. He was alone and he was scared. I was his mom and I wasn't there."[66]

Like other mothers, Cheryl Softich's grief does not diminish as the years pass. She always takes three days off from work on the anniversary of Noah's suicide because she needs this time to mourn. She will drive by the spot where he killed himself or sit by his grave for a few hours. Often she has difficulty eating, and she is currently under the care of a psychiatrist who specializes in patients who have experienced trauma. Cheryl has the support of the Gold Star Mothers. She and Joyce Lucey stay in touch like other parents of servicemen and servicewomen who have taken their lives. They remain in contact to share their sorrow.

Joyce Lucey feels that the seven years since the suicide of her son, Jeff, have made little difference in her grief. The fact that she has a loving family with two daughters and grandchildren doesn't take away the absence that haunts her. While we live in a society that expects people to "move on and recover," that is not how families grieve over a death that could have been prevented had appropriate medical care been available to the suffering loved one. Like so many other families that have lost their children to suicide, Joyce feels that there is no closure for her.

When someone we love commits suicide, the shock, pain, and all the emotions associated with loss are heightened. They are not only more intense, but they also occur simultaneously. It seems impossible to include them in our frame of reference. The tragedy of such a death prolongs the period of shock and grief that loved ones experience afterward.

A mother or a spouse relives the pain their loved one experienced in the months before their death and in the seemingly endless minutes of dying. In their replay of events, the anguish their loved one suffered is magnified. Knowing how painful such a death can be, they can only imagine the emotional pain of those who chose such an ending as a relief.

Because suicide is so difficult to understand, family members go over and over the last moments they spent with their loved ones and examine their last conversations and final events in order to seek some sort of explanation, as if they could find a reason for what happened, some cause to blame. Behind the details that they sift like ashes after a fire is the feeling that they, as a spouse or a mother, are responsible for the suicide. They think that somehow they could have prevented it. Their imagination unfolds an endless list of "if only": if only they had been there at the time or done something that would have helped their loved one. This is one of the biggest issues suicide survivors face. Everyone has a powerful sense of responsibility to those they love, a feeling that is closely related to conscience. It is simply not possible to sidestep this process.

If it is awkward to talk about the death of a loved one, it is even more difficult to talk about the suicide of a loved one. Many relatives of such a painful death experience a deep sense of isolation when they return to their lives as parents of small children or to their careers. It is as if such a terrible tragedy can set them apart from others. Suicide survivors are also victims. Life goes on around them as if nothing had happened, but for them it will never be the same.

It is rare to find someone who is able to listen sympathetically while a loved one reveals his or her pain over a suicide. One mother found a lack of understanding in the place where she worked. A wife wished that someone would acknowledge what she was experiencing. There is already a stigma against suicide in both the military and in our society. Some religions fail to understand or accept it. The Catholic religion considers it a sin, which is the reason that Kevin Lucey left the church. A rabbi's letter to the editor in the *New York Times* on the suicide of veterans pointed out that "suicide . . . is neither heroic nor cowardly, and families in which such a death is being mourned deserve condolences without special reference to the cause of death."[67] In fact, grief often causes a survivor to question the existence of the Creator.

Family members feel that suicide remains defined by shame, and survivors feel that the silence of people not mentioning a loved one's suicide is one of the most difficult parts of their mourning. A letter or a conversation acknowledging the reality of what occurred and expressing sympathy helps them to know that they are not alone. Because there are such powerful taboos about suicide, the families of soldiers who committed suicide need our society to acknowledge the bravery and pain of their loved ones as well as their own sorrow.

Chapter 6

HEALTHCARE

WHAT WORDS CAN DO

for James Wright

As he scans the list
of battle-frayed soldiers,
the officer shrugs.
Their night sweats,
their inner numbness
are a foreign language to him.
Can no longer be deployed
is what he doesn't say.
But in a small town up North
a college president walks out
of his kingdom of books
and humming classes,
across neatly mowed lawns
and into hospital wards
where days keep collapsing
in the corridors. A former marine,
he comes with his own
memories, speaking the language
of tremors, nightmares
and invisible wounds.
He moves from one
bed to another,
holding each patient
with his words. He turns these
words into ladders
the maimed can climb up
and out into the world again.[1]

—Marguerite Guzmán Bouvard

Considering the high rate of PTSD among veterans, there is insufficient healthcare for treating them. More than 40 percent of returning soldiers from the Iraq and Afghanistan wars seen at Veterans Affairs (VA) hospitals suffer from mental-health disorders.[2] However, many of them live in rural towns, far away from veterans' hospitals. Those who live near a veterans' center, such as Amy Smee, experience a lack of psychological and physical support. She found the hospital understaffed. "I had a lot of difficulty coming back and leaving all that behind. The veterans' hospital is like McDonald's medical care. You're in and out in a few minutes."[3] She arrived with a list of questions, but the physician she saw was too busy to answer any of them. She suffers from a severe hip injury and lives with constant pain, besides having PTSD. She wasn't offered any medical or psychological help. She threw away the pain medications she was given and also decided that she didn't want to be in a group for her psychological problems where she was the only woman and the men were veterans from the Vietnam War. Three years later, she found counseling at the veterans' hospital in Reno, Nevada, and was given medication for depression. Amy is one of the thousands of veterans who require long-term care and who are either left without any or must wait years to find an appropriate response.

Like so many veterans, she has trouble sleeping and she experiences nightmares. When she and a planeload of soldiers returned from Afghanistan, they were each handed a bottle of Tylenol PM®, as if that useless gesture could have helped them with the psychological issues of returning home. In addition, giving soldiers sleeping pills or antidepressants adds pressure to the brain, which is bad for those who have sustained a brain injury.

Not only is there insufficient medical care for returning soldiers but also there are not enough psychologists to give them adequate support. Brooke Kinna, the spouse of one veteran remembers that her husband was one of the soldiers who got "stop-lossed" ("stop-loss" means keeping a soldier in combat longer than his contract stipulates). "He had already served his four years. But they told him, 'We are "stop-lossing" you. We're sending you over there no matter what. You're just out of luck.' He was supposed to be getting out of the military. When he got home after the fifteen months, they reactivated him and meant to send him to Afghanistan. He went to Columbus, Georgia, for his twenty-six-day rest. Then he went to Camp Otaberry in Indiana. That's where he met a civilian psychologist who found that he had PTSD. If it weren't for her, they would have sent him over there. She fought for him. They do send back people who have PTSD."[4]

In 2005, after the surge, our military leaders were not prepared for the epidemic of psychological problems. Before the war in Iraq, soldiers were not allowed to take medications, but by the time of the surge, more than twenty thousand troops in Iraq and Afghanistan were taking sleeping pills and anti-depression pills, even though there were no physicians to supervise them. Military leaders trust that these prescriptions are effective, but civilian psychiatrists are concerned that they may be inappropriate because those medications can have serious side effects.

A number of veterans don't want to get help at the VA. One woman's son told her, "Going back to the VA is like going to the backyard of the dog that bit him."[5] For many veterans, to go into the VA hospital, to see the wounded, to sit there and be told to fill out paperwork—fill it out again, and again—they find it easier to stay away. Patricia Alvarez Alviso, the mother of a veteran, believes that the long waits and paperwork make it more difficult for those who need help. They don't have that patience. Few soldiers have the means to pay for civilian medicine. Patricia's son has child support, his own apartment, and car payments to deal with. Besides, most soldiers earn very low pay.[6]

What is most upsetting is the reason for the ruling by the Ninth Circuit Court of Appeals on a suit by Veterans for Common Sense (VCS) and Veterans United for Truth regarding healthcare for servicemen and sevicewomen. The court declared that this was a problem for the president and Congress to solve, but since these branches of the government were unwilling to do so, the court ruled on behalf of the plaintiffs.[7]

The PBS documentary "The Soldier's Heart" reveals how difficult it is for a serviceman or servicewoman to get help. That documentary film depicts the story of a soldier who was at war, and because he felt unable to go into battle, he requested a three-day rest period. He was refused the rest and was called a coward, and the verbal attacks continued the next day. One week later, he was charged with cowardice. The military was sending a message that fear and anxiety would not be tolerated and that, if soldiers complained of mental-health problems, their leaders would blame them and their unit would have less confidence in them. The military is concerned with maintaining a ready force and doesn't seem to want to hear about PTSD. In fact, many soldiers with combat stress are redeployed, as Brooke Kinna, the wife of a soldier, noted, and this exacerbates their problems.

A member of the Department of Defense who was interviewed in "The Soldier's Heart" acknowledged that it was necessary for the military not to forget that soldiers are in harm's way a long time after they return home and that the DOD is still responsible for them. He also indicated that there were plans to set up a screening process for soldiers on their return. But he added that the DOD was not a monolith, but "a million different people, all taking two steps forward and one back at any time."[8]

The organization Veterans for Common Sense (VCS) disclosed astonishing statistics about the healthcare of service members obtained from the Department of Defense and the VA through the 2006 Freedom of Information Act. For example, in 2009, VCS revealed that every day more than 250 Iraq and Afghanistan war veterans entered the Department of Veterans Affairs hospitals and clinics and that more than 425,000 of these veterans were treated and diagnosed at VA facilities.[9] The VCS is the only nonprofit organization with a full-time Freedom of Information campaign to publish reports on veteran healthcare. It has only been able to do so after threatening litigation. The VCS continually posts updates of statistics on its website. Its work has inspired national and local media coverage about veterans' needs for better healthcare. As a result, *PBS NewsHour*, the *CBS Evening News*, and the *New York Times* have worked with VCS to produce programs and publish articles about veterans that rely upon the VCS research.

That research also assisted Harvard University professor Linda Bilmes and Columbia University professor Joseph Stiglitz in estimating the human and financial costs of caring for veterans in their book *The Three Trillion Dollar War: The Cost of the Iraq Conflict*.[10] VCS also provided the information for a *Time* magazine article that appeared on October 3, 2011, revealing that nearly three quarters of a million veterans back from Iraq and Afghanistan have sought medical care from the government and more than half of them suffer from a mental-health condition, including PTSD.[11] The magazine described the mental-health issue as "the U.S. Army's third front," and "while its combat troops fight two wars, its mental-health professionals are waging a battle to save soldiers' sanity when they come back, one that will cost billions long after combat ends in Baghdad and Kabul."[12]

It wasn't until Major Nidal Malik Hasan killed thirteen people on the base in Fort Hood, Texas, in 2009, that a higher military authority created a program to address the problems in the military system. Perhaps the reason that Hasan was hired as a psychologist was because there weren't enough physicians to help veterans. Lieutenant General Robert W. Cone, the post's commander, wrote to local advocates for disaffected soldiers, deserters, and war resisters, asking them to help him understand the gaps in the army's system for helping veterans. In the month after the shooting, Lieutenant General Cone made certain that the Pentagon would send psychologists, therapists, and chaplains to counsel soldiers and their families and deal with the post's chronically understaffed mental-health network. It created a new system for trauma counseling.[13] Making this important change is challenging for the entire army because it is short by almost one thousand behavioral-health specialists.

The military has an insufficient number of psychiatrists to handle more than half a million troops.[14] Faced with so many soldiers coming back psychologically harmed, the Pentagon now has made the diagnosis and treatment of PTSD a top priority, although care varies from base to base, with some bases providing good care and some of them woefully underequipped.

But nearly half of the cases requiring attention remain untreated because of the stigma attached to mental disorders in the military. It is very difficult for soldiers to come forward and acknowledge their problems because they still carry the values of behavior required in battle. They all need to go through a program that would help them understand that it is alright to seek help and talk among themselves about their experiences and that doing so would give them psychological support.

The quality of care for the physical health of our veterans is also very uneven. While some hospitals provide excellent care, many do not even address the problems of returning veterans. The United States is now working with Vietnam to remove some of the Agent Orange that was dumped during the Vietnam War when our military sprayed millions of gallons of toxic herbicides on trees and vegetation that provided cover for enemy forces. As a result, many of our troops developed various kinds of cancer—such as leukemia, Hodgkin's lymphoma, and melanoma—as well as diabetes and a number of other debilitating illnesses. Nevertheless, in Iraq and Afghanistan, US soldiers are also subjected to toxic exposures from burn pits. In a 2006 memorandum to the Pentagon, Air Force Lieutenant Colonel Darrin Curtis, who was responsible for assessing environmental health hazards at the Balad Air Base in Iraq, expressed his concern about these exposures. Smoke from burning plastics, foam, papers, rubber, waste, metals, chemicals, and oils were contaminating the air. Given the fact that the base had ballooned into a city of twenty-five thousand, hundreds of thousands of tons of refuse were burned daily. In 2007, Defense Department documents disclosed that dioxin levels at Balad were fifty-one times what the military considered acceptable. For people deployed at the base for over a year, cancer risks from dioxin and other volatile compounds were twice the normal rate.[15] In fact, burn pits were in use at bases throughout Iraq and Afghanistan. It took the Disabled American Veterans' advocacy and legislative initiatives and reporting by the *Army Times* to get thousands of veterans as well as active servicepersons to seek help about their exposure concerns. Amy Smee was one of these veterans tasked with burning garbage, and she felt quite ill afterward, besides suffering from intense headaches. In addition, she was diagnosed with PTSD. A number of lawsuits have been filed against Defense Department contractors by burn-pit victims and their survivors since the story was first reported in the *Army Times*.[16] But there are too many veterans who have died from brain cancer and damaged lungs and who suffer chronic pain from life-altering illnesses.[17] It often seems as if the welfare of our troops is not in the forefront of DOD planning.

Fortunately, important changes are being made in healthcare in response to the demands of so many veterans' groups. Organizations such as VCS and Veterans United for Truth, with between fifty thousand and one hundred thousand members each, actively lobby in Congress. The largest organization, IAVA (Iraq and Afghanistan Veterans of America)—along with CIAV (Coalition for Iraq and Afghanistan Veterans) and VCS—is committed to working with and on behalf of all members of the military, veterans, survivors, and providers to strengthen the existing system of healthcare and support all who have been affected by the wars.

WOMEN WARRIORS

Women veterans have the most trouble getting the medical and psychological care they need. There are 153 VA hospitals in the country, but half of them do not have gynecologists on their staff. In addition, while seeking counseling for sexual assault or harassment, these women often endure uncomfortable flirting from security guards and other veterans as they wait for treatment.[18] Some facilities have no women's restrooms next to exam rooms, so women clad in exam gowns may have to walk through public hallways if they need to leave a urine sample in the restroom.[19] On the way, they are subject to whistles and catcalls from male veterans.

PTSD has been diagnosed in soldiers who have been in combat. Women, like their male colleagues, carry weapons. They are gunners on vehicles, they take part in armed patrols on dangerous streets, and they dispose of explosives. Yet, since the Department of Defense bars women from serving in units that primarily engage in direct ground combat, it is nearly impossible for them to prove that their experiences as soldiers qualify them to be regarded as participants in combat.

Women are more than twice as likely as men to suffer PTSD.[20] Added to that, the stress from rape and sexual harassment, known in the military as MST (Military Sexual Trauma), also takes its toll on women soldiers. Many of the physicians and clinicians making assessments have no understanding of what these women have experienced. Dealing with the VA means facing a bureaucracy that requires extensive documentation. As a result, it is very difficult and it takes a very long time for women veterans to get the help that they need.

Fewer than 10 percent of all sexual assaults that occur in the military are reported.[21] Most of these are committed by peers or by service members of higher rank. Understandably, women who have been assaulted are often too intimidated to name a superior as the perpetrator because they fear being seen as disloyal. It is more than difficult for them to report what has happened to a military policeman or policewoman. One woman who heard about another servicewoman being assaulted contacted a policewoman who took down her story but wouldn't allow her to write her own statement and only allowed her to give it to her verbally. That policewoman's report stated that the woman had consensual sex.[22] The victim then reported her case to her commander, telling him that she was the third woman in the unit to have been raped that week, and he simply brushed her off. Next, she contacted a lawyer, who told her that she could do nothing for her because there was no physical evidence. A woman general stationed at Abu Ghraib admitted that women who complain about sexual assault are simply told, "There are more important problems."

In 2005, the Department of Defense created the Sexual Assault Prevention and Response Office (SAPRO) to make it easier for women to come forward. The government's statistics indicate that the number of women who experience rape in the military is double that of the civilian rate.[23] Women contacting SAPRO can make restricted and confidential reports, meaning that while they can get treatment, their assault won't be investigated.

Treatment for MST is not what it should be. The staff is often uncomfortable dealing with its victims. Since most VA hospitals are understaffed, less than 7 percent of women can be referred to a female counselor.[24] It is also extremely rare for women to be able get into an all-female therapy group.

On February 14, 2011, a federal lawsuit accused the Department of Defense of allowing a military culture that fails to prevent rape and sexual assault to continue. Further, the DOD was accused of mishandling cases that were brought to its attention, thus violating the plaintiffs' constitutional rights. The suit was brought by two men and fifteen women who were veterans and/or active-duty service members. It alleged that Defense Secretary Robert Gates, and his predecessor, Donald Rumsfeld, ran institutions in which perpetrators were promoted and where military personnel flouted the modest institutional reforms mandated by Congress. It further alleged that the two Defense secretaries failed to take reasonable steps to prevent plaintiffs from being repeatedly raped, sexually assaulted, and sexually harassed by federal military personnel.[25]

WALTER REED ARMY MEDICAL CENTER IN WASHINGTON, DC

In the past, Walter Reed Army Medical Center had a national reputation for excellent service. It maintained its high standards in surgery, and amputees received excellent care. However, the outpatient care for veterans returning from Iraq and Afghanistan has been found to be grossly inadequate by servicemen and servicewomen and their families. One woman's story about her husband's treatment at Walter Reed helps us to understand a patient and his or her family's distress. Part of Angela Buckley's experience was a very good one. She became friends with other families that were there for their loved ones. She refers to that experience as "the unique relationships you can't find in the civilian world" and she says "that all of a sudden it doesn't matter what race you are or what state you come from, you become a family."[26] They had their meals together, lived in the same building, the Malone House for outpatient families, and met in the hospital halls. They were able to talk to each other at the end of the day, share their problems, and gain mutual support.

Angela discovered that soldiers are highly stressed at Walter Reed because of the way it is run. Soldiers are each assigned a nurse case manager who takes care of their medical appointments—and is supposed to assist them—and a primary-care military physician who makes referrals. Then they are each assigned to a platoon sergeant and then to a company. She found that they were treated as if they were still on active duty and not the way wounded soldiers would expect to be treated. It's a huge place, and every doctor has a different assessment, which is very confusing for the patient's family. Because a patient like Angela's husband had so many physicians involved in his case, there was the ever-present possibility of being prescribed a dangerous combination of medications. Angela checked out every single one of them. She saw too many overmedicated patients who did not know what time or day it was. Angela was lucky to have a woman in her circle of friends who was a soldier's mother and a nurse. That nurse would do some research for her on every medication the patients were prescribed. Angela also spent a lot of time talking with younger soldiers who had no family. One of them told her about three medications that shouldn't be taken together, because it is a deadly combination, and said that three people had died from it. He urged her to check everything the doctor prescribed, to either ask him or go online, telling her, "don't ever trust them completely. We have too many people die."[27]

Family members who accompany their soldiers to the hospital were classified as nonmedical attendants. Once they were designated as such, those assignments had to be renewed every thirty days at the Casualty Affairs Office. The primary-care physician had to sign them, and the gate commander had to confirm them. The first time Angela applied for orders, she had to wait for sixty days. She was a wreck because she was afraid she was going to lose the room at Malone House where she and her daughter were staying and she couldn't afford to pay the bills for her residence there. The manager told her that she could stay and put her in touch with a major who was in charge of the orders. He straightened things out for her immediately.

Angela and her daughter spent eight and a half months at Walter Reed. Even Malone House was run like an army. Every week, there was room inspection by army personnel who would look for alcohol and drugs. One of them told her that she and her daughter were now under army regulations and that if they found wine or drugs, the two of them would be evicted from the room. Her daughter called them "the meanies." Because it was a military post, there were surveillance cameras everywhere.

Angela is a woman who speaks her mind and has become a very strong advocate for her husband's care. Peter returned from Afghanistan with traumatic brain injury, PTSD, and other physical wounds to his ears and to the nerves on his left side. He was scheduled for surgery because his eardrums were collapsing. There is a distinction at Walter Reed between active-duty soldiers or amputees, who get the best care, and the personnel from the National Guard. As Peter was with the National Guard, his nurse case manager didn't think his surgery was urgent. Angela demanded to know why his surgery was postponed and insisted that he have it as soon as possible. She argued that if his ear ruptured, the injury would affect his brain. She got the surgery scheduled immediately.

Outpatients are required to work for four hours a day. They may be assigned to reception duty desk, or some patients may be up all night taking messages from phone calls. After Angela's husband had surgery, he was told that, from then on, he had to work for four hours a day in a stock room. Angela made a ruckus to the person in charge. She told him that he needed to think of Peter's mental health and that confinement was a very bad experience for a soldier who had been in a thirty-six-ton truck that was inches away from sinking when it almost rolled over into a canal.

She even took on a congressman who was visiting Walter Reed, telling him that she was upset about the different classification of treatments. She told him, "It's just wrong. What makes you think that a National Guard soldier doesn't bleed and die like an active-duty soldier?"[28] The congressman was shocked. She suggested to him that if he really wanted to see what it was like at that hospital, he should come unannounced and mingle with the soldiers on the weekend and hear their stories. She also spoke with the right-hand man of an admiral who was the best friend of the then chairman of the Joint Chiefs of Staff, Mike Mullen. As a result, she was invited to the Pentagon. There, she explained to her hosts that when they visit the hospital, the staff only shows them the nice areas and they have very little contact with the soldiers. It's called "view time." The first stop is the area for amputees, who happen to receive the very best care.

Angela's time at the Pentagon went very well. She met the wife of a commander, who told her that she had to let people know what was going on and that information gets filtered to those who are at the top of the hierarchy. Then she spoke to the commander who was running the hospital, and he assured her that changes would be made.

But Angela felt that perhaps she went too far by disclosing the names of a physician and a case manager who were responsible for the deaths of several soldiers. This prompted an investigation to be opened at the hospital, and her husband was questioned because of e-mails criticizing their performance that originated from the Joint Chiefs of Staff and were sent to the hospital staff that was caring for her husband. Her husband was then summoned to a major's office, where he was interrogated for forty-five minutes and reprimanded for speaking with the commander. Angela's husband replied, "My wife talked to this person at a social event. I don't tell my wife who to talk to and who not to talk to." Angela told the major that she was a strong believer in pointing out what is wrong, and the major angrily responded, "I can't control you." Angela looked him in the eye and told him, "That's right because I didn't sign a contract with the military. I'm independent. Don't threaten me." The major made an official complaint to the commander who is a casualty-affairs officer, and Angela also told him what had occurred. The commander assured her that he would sort it out, and he gave the major a phone call to tell him to resolve the situation.

Angela also discovered that it was very difficult to get a diagnosis for PTSD because applicants for medical help are frequently told that they are "faking it." She regards PTSD as the signature wound of these wars. She also found out, as did Veterans for Common Sense, that the military doesn't disclose complete statistics, and that if a soldier dies, it is always recorded as, "Under Investigation." She feels that we will never be able to know the real number of deaths of soldiers in the hospital.

While Angela's husband was at Walter Reed, she met a member of the nonprofit organization called Need—which provides service dogs called "service dogs with purple hearts"—who promised her that they would give one to her husband when he returned home. Peter now has a dog that helps him go up and down stairs and can open doors. Need provides such dogs for soldiers who walk with a cane or who have balance problems, like Peter.

There are a number of charity groups founded by corporations and, especially, retired members of the military. They have organized events, such as Friday Night Dinner, for the families of wounded veterans at the hospital. One of them was founded by a retired general whose wife is very active in reaching out to families. Another was organized by a retired colonel. There was also a program at Walter Reed sponsored by a member of the Kennedy family. The woman in charge of these rehabilitation services helped Angela's daughter with her anxieties. There is counseling available to the children of outpatients. It's hard for these young people to process what they are seeing around them, such as amputees with severely swollen black legs and worse. Angela's daughter, Sophie, matured during that period and returned home with painful memories but also as a stronger and more mature young person.

Sophie wrote a very moving story about her time at Walter Reed. She was only eleven years old when she wrote it to help her classmates understand what she had experienced. It demonstrates the wisdom of an adult, as this passage shows.

> Have you ever dealt with stress that feels like five Empire State Buildings piled on top of you? I've dealt with that, but soldiers and their families at Walter Reed Army Medical Center also have. Perhaps they've even had stress numerous times. I've seen and dealt with problems that most of you haven't. I've met soldiers and their families. Soon they became my family because we help each other out in tough situations. I've even made a friend who lost two of his legs in the war and now has prosthetics. . . . Life at Walter Reed was depressing, sad, and there were tough moments for soldiers and their families. It normally was appointment after appointment all day long, but my mom and dad and I still saw our friends. We have done this for 8 or 9 months and then we came back to Massachusetts. The ride from Washington, D.C., to Massachusetts was very long and tiring for my mom because my dad couldn't drive. The reason why I am writing this is to tell about life at Walter Reed and that stress is never good for all of mankind.[29]

When Peter and his family returned home, they went to see a civilian physician at one of the Spaulding rehabilitation centers. During each visit, the physician told Angela that he could have done so much for Peter if he had been able to treat him earlier. He explained the medical issues involved in the combination of traumatic brain injury and PTSD. Angela told him that at Walter Reed, they were unable to focus on both. This method is reminiscent of what Jeffrey Lucey experienced at the VA hospital when the staff refused to treat alcohol problems and PTSD together.

In 2007, the organization Veterans of the Wars in Iraq and Afghanistan called for change at the Walter Reed Army Medical Center, claiming that staffers responsible for managing outpatients had caseloads of more than 125 patients each and that recovering soldiers faced bureaucratic delays, overworked case managers, and horrific living conditions, including inferior mattresses, and cockroach infestation.[30]

Staffers of the organization contacted members of Congress and the media, and Congress passed the Wounded Warrior Assistance Act. The bill seeks to improve access to quality care for outpatients in military healthcare facilities, to cut the bureaucratic red tape in order to provide timely and effective medical care, and to improve the transition from care in the armed services to care in the VA system.[31] Change is a slow process, and it takes years in an institution like Walter Reed, which seems as large as a city. The most significant change occurred in August 2011. The Walter Reed Army Medical Center was closed and moved to the National Naval Medical Center in Bethesda, Maryland, and a new facility in Fort Belvoir, Virginia. The refurbished Bethesda facility was renamed the Walter Reed National Military Medical Center and is run for all branches of the military.

HOME BASE AT THE MASSACHUSETTS GENERAL HOSPITAL

The care of our military personnel is complex and diverse. Because too many veterans fall through the cracks and get insufficient care, a number of private organizations were formed throughout the country to address their needs. These programs also care for those who do not have sufficient insurance coverage. Some of them also work with the VA, as does Home Base.

The Home Base Program represents a new model for helping military personnel and their families. It is a partnership between the Massachusetts General Hospital (MGH) and the Red Sox Foundation. The idea arose out of visits the Red Sox made to the Walter Reed Medical Center following the team's World Series victories in 2004 and 2007. Players, coaches, and team officials met with servicemen and servicewomen who were suffering from physical and psychological combat injuries. As a result of these visits, Tom Werner, Red Sox chairman, used his position in New England to find ways to encourage veterans who returned with PTSD or traumatic brain injury to seek the help they needed and make their homecoming less stressful.

The Red Sox Foundation met with physicians at the MGH to help develop and implement a program that would provide the support for both returning military personnel and their families. Before his death, Senator Kennedy brought together officials from the Red Sox Foundation, the MGH, the Department of Veterans Affairs, and the Department of Defense to find ways of coordinating their efforts.

Home Base has set a new precedent in helping every family member, parents of military personnel, spouses or partners, and especially children. More than thirteen thousand children in Massachusetts have a parent serving in the military, including the National Guard and Reserves. Thousands more have a parent or a sibling deployed in active duty during the past ten years.[32] Because

Massachusetts has a large number of National Guard and Reserves and there is no central base, children with a family member in the military like Sophie, Angela Buckley's daughter, or Rachel, Jennifer Baldino's daughter, may be the only child in their school with a parent in the military and thus may be invisible to their classmates and to the larger community. Many children whose parents are subject to multiple deployments experience the repeated stresses accompanying each deployment cycle and worry during the absence of their parent.

The directors of the Family Support Program, Dr. Paula Rauch and Kathy Clair-Hayes, prepare families for pre- and post-deployment as well as help mitigate some of the stresses multiple deployments entail on families. A child like Sophie Buckley knows what to worry about when a parent has had multiple deployments because she's heard what happened to some members in her father's unit. The Home Base family team also reaches out to people in the lives of children, such as school teachers, nurses, superintendents, or coaches, so they can understand what these children are experiencing. This is very important. During her eight and a half months at Walter Reed, Angela Buckley found a parochial school whose principal was the mother of a veteran and who accepted Sophie in her school without charge. That helped compensate for the lack of understanding Angela experienced in her daughter's school at home.

One of the goals of the Home Base family team is to help families communicate with their children. Some families, like Angela's, have excellent communication with their children. Other families may experience such anxiety that it may cause tension and misunderstanding, for example, in a mother's relations with her children. The ages of children are important, too, whether they are entering adolescence while a parent is deployed, or graduating from high school and making important choices. Returning soldiers expect to find their children just as they were when they left. Months after his return, Jennifer Baldino's husband was emptying the dryer and was shocked to discover a bra that belonged to his daughter because he remembered her as a little girl of twelve . Children, too, have a difficult adjustment to make when their parent returns. They see not only physical changes but also changes in their parent's moods, which can be very upsetting.[33]

A wonderful part of this program is that it is reaching out to parents of young soldiers who are in their late teens or early twenties. Clair-Hayes, one of the founders, has found that these parents are left out of the military loop, especially if the soldier's spouse is the point of contact. The program also addresses the particular stress of the soldier's siblings, who not only see their parents concern about their child in combat but also have their own worries about that brother or sister.[34]

As noted in the chapter on spouses (chapter 4), the psychological symptoms returning service personnel express can undermine relationships within the family. The Massachusetts National Guard created the Strong Bonds weekend a few years ago, providing assistance for couples experiencing stressful relations. Home Base created a family-education group that holds four sessions about operational combat stress, PTSD, traumatic brain injury, and substance abuse issues. It represents the first opportunity for families to meet other families that are having similar challenges.

The hope of the Home Base Program is to reach out to other parts of the Northeast, including Connecticut, Rhode Island, Maine, New Hampshire, and Vermont. Because practitioners need to be licensed in different areas, the first expansion will be in Western Massachusetts. The program members have been invited to Vermont to give a talk to a military community–support group that had a large unit return from Afghanistan.

One of the most innovative aspects of this program is bringing together community members to support military families. This is an important goal, given the fact that ours is a volunteer army and thus too many people are unaware of the travails of our returning service members. In early May 2011, Home Base and the Military Child Education Coalition sponsored a conference, "Living in the New Normal," that included leaders from the government, healthcare, youth organizations, education, business, and the faith community. The agenda included discussions of childcare or after-school activities, academic tutoring, transportation to after-school sports, and a community commitment to prevent homelessness among military families that are struggling to make house payments.[35] As the chapter devoted to them (chapter 4) reveals, military spouses are often multitasking between the exhausting work of child-rearing, running a household, and holding a full-time job.

An important and unique aspect of the Home Base Program is its team of veterans from the Iraq and Afghanistan wars who reach out to former active service members who have experienced deployment, combat-related stress, and traumatic brain injury, and connect them with the program's services. It includes four extraordinary veterans. The program is headed by Mary Bergner, who has served on active duty with the army for ten years. After she left the army, she then joined the National Guard and earned her commission as an officer through Officer Candidate School. She has received several awards and medals over her seventeen years of service, including the Bronze Star Combat Action Badge and the Iraqi Campaign Medal. Each one of the four members in this team has earned a number of awards for outstanding service.

Roger Knight, one of the veterans on the team, was deployed several times to countries in South America and twice to Afghanistan. During his seven years of active duty, he was twice awarded the Bronze Star for his service in combat, the Army Achievement Medal, the Afghanistan Campaign Medal, the NATO medal, and a number of other badges. In his work as a veterans outreach coordinator, he feels that he is continuing his service. While he was still in Afghanistan, he found out about the job opening through Home Base's social media. He had his first interview in Helmand Province in the Sangin Valley, Afghanistan, from a satellite phone in the middle of the night.

Roger understands the importance of veteran-to-veteran outreach. Veterans speak a common language and are able to share their experiences with each other, which is very important for them in their civilian lives. Few people in the civilian world, other than family members in close contact with relatives who have been in combat, have the necessary framework to understand a veteran's experience. While many of our veterans enroll in universities or colleges after they return, their civilian fellow students cannot always relate to them. Few inquire about what happened to them while at war. Yet veterans need appreciation and understanding.

An important aspect of veteran-to-veteran contact is that it reminds them of the camaraderie they had before they came home to face the difficult problems of returning from war. The most important task of the coordinators is to reduce the stigma attached to asking or receiving help. Roger speaks of combat stress rather than of PTSD because he feels PTSD makes that kind of stress sound abnormal. He keeps telling veterans that they were an asset to our country when they served, and they can be an asset when they return.

Roger says that the colleagues he works with feel that they are still serving. "The one thing you learn in the military is service, doing something for the greater good while you are out there. When you leave, you have that same instinct, discipline, and still have drive. This isn't just a nine-to-five job. Some of the men and women who served over there are not living the life they envision when they come back. It's not an easy task, but it's a worthy task."[37]

In the two years that the Red Sox Foundation and Massachusetts General Hospital Home Base Program has been operating, it has served 450 veterans.

What makes Roger's work so unique is his ability to respond immediately to a veteran's problems. For example, Professor Kathleen O'Neill, who teaches veterans at Bunker Hill College in Boston, is in touch with Home Base. She had a student who came to see her and told her that he had "hit bottom." She immediately called Roger Knight, who rushed to the college in ten minutes.

Roger takes these young men out to have coffee at Dunkin' Donuts and then gets them connected to the program. He is able to notice veterans experiencing problems and then get them an appointment the same day. For those veterans who don't live near Boston, he tries to get them into a program within their own community that can help them.

One of the goals of veteran outreach coordinators is to educate the community about the needs of our military personnel and to describe the signature wounds of Operation Iraqi Freedom and Operation Enduring Freedom. Coordinators like Roger have spoken to clergy, firemen, and police. They have also educated veterans' coworkers, who don't even know that a colleague has returned from military service. They have spoken to family-readiness groups of National Guard units and sponsored symposiums on PTSD and traumatic brain injury. The coordinators have also contacted congressmen, senators, and local community leaders to spread the word about the issues returning military personnel face.

Home Base is being replicated throughout the nation with funding from the Robert R. McCormick Foundation and Major League Baseball organizations. Other new initiatives include the Atlanta Braves and Emory University program in Georgia that established a public-private partnership called Brave Heart to provide care for PTSD. Similar programs are being created in Detroit, Los Angeles, and San Diego. Members of these programs have come to Boston to discuss the challenges the local program has faced and the successes it has had. Roger realizes that the most difficult issue is the number of veterans who are falling through the cracks and not getting the care they need, which is an issue he keeps speaking about to the public.

One of the most innovative aspects of the program developed by the outreach coordinators was to take veterans and their families on outings, to bring them together for an enjoyable experience. It started with a hike for veterans and then grew to a number of activities, such as community rowing, community boating, a sailing day on the Charles River, and baseball-game outings. Participants went skiing, snowboarding, and ice fishing in New Hampshire. According to Roger, "when they are skiing, the only thing that they can think about is not falling down." Home Base coordinates each one of these outings with a nonprofit organization that has a program set up to provide sports for physically wounded veterans. These events also create a dialogue between veterans, something that is very important because they are used to working as a team, and when they come home, they miss that close rapport. They start by asking each other where they served in Afghanistan or Iraq, whether in Helmand Province, Tikrit, or Kabul, and that is how they begin to share their mutual experiences. As a result, these outings have helped create a veterans network.

Thus, the Home Base Program gives veterans and their families hope. As the veteran coordinators have shown, helping each other is one of the greatest sources of happiness and contentment, no matter how difficult the job may be.

PROJECT SHARE

In 2010, an anonymous philanthropist established a charity called Project Share to help brain-injured soldiers. The program is based out of the Shepherd Center for Brain and Spinal Cord Injury in Atlanta, which is a nationally recognized hospital for head injuries.[38] The Pentagon's primary health plan for soldiers and seriously wounded veterans' hospitals, Tricare, does not cover the treatment of cognitive problems that result from accidents occurring during the war.[39] Thanks to Project Share, soldiers stay for two or three months in their own apartments and get excellent daily care that the Veterans Administration or the government is unable to provide for tens of thousands of US soldiers returning from Iraq and Afghanistan.

BURGEONING CHARITIES

Years after the wars began, charities have been created to deal with the dramatic increase in substance abuse and PTSD among returning veterans. One of these is the Veterans Healing Initiative (VHI), which was formed in 2009. It is aimed at raising funds for veterans who need treatment for these problems and at helping them heal what VHI refers to as "the war within." Its goal is to address the stress of repeated deployments with reduced time between them—higher exposures to combat trauma—and reach out to the many returning veterans who do not receive the care they need. VHI collaborates with veterans' services; private and public charities; community-based organizations; federal, state, and local agencies; and veteran drug courts to promote veteran recovery programs.[40]

The Wounded Warriors Project is a nonprofit organization that has many roles, including helping veterans deal with combat stress, appearing before the Senate and Congress in support of the Veterans Traumatic Brain Injury Rehabilitative Services Improvement Act, helping veterans find jobs, providing rehabilitative retreats—such as horseback riding, canoeing, and fishing—and more. It also created a newsroom with quick links to relevant topics concerning the project. In 2011, it received an award for being the best nonprofit health organization for veterans.[41]

CRIMINAL BEHAVIOR

Jonathan Shay, a psychiatrist who works with veterans, has found that combat service sometimes paves the way for criminal actions after soldiers return to civilian life.[42] For many of them, violence is a constant presence in their minds, which prevents them from concentrating on civilian pursuits. The skills they acquired while at war—such as the ability to respond instantly with lethal force, perpetual mobilization for danger, endurance, and stealth, among others—are irrelevant to civilian life. Some of the veterans who remain in combat mode and have committed crimes may actually feel better in prison because they feel safer with the door closed.[43]

Since the warrior class is so small, the same troops have to be sent back for tour after harrowing tour of duty. In 2008, the RAND Corporation released a study that revealed that deployments have been longer, redeployments to combat have been common, and breaks between deployments have been insufficient.[44] During the troop surge, one platoon was redeployed after barely one year, although that is not enough time, as soldiers need at least two years back home to recover. But as a general remarked, "It was a supply-and-demand problem."[45]

Our veterans' injuries are not only psychological but also moral. At Fort Carson in Colorado Springs, over the past five years, fourteen returning soldiers have been charged and convicted in thirteen murders and manslaughters. One of those who served in Baghdad during the surge had a mental breakdown, lost control, and shot one of his fellow soldiers. Another, who was a decorated veteran, was found guilty as an accessory. He was charged for putting a gun to his girlfriend's head and is now serving the second year of a ten-year prison sentence.[46] He joined the infantry when he was nineteen and excelled as a soldier even though his juvenile criminal records should have prevented him from getting into the army. The army is so desperate for soldiers that it grants waivers to people like him. In one year, his platoon faced more than 1,000 roadside bombs, captured 1,800 Iraqis, and sent 500 Iraqis to Abu Ghraib.[47] There has been an increase in the number of veterans who are facing charges of domestic violence, firearms violations, and drunken driving.

Another veteran was also nineteen when he went to Iraq. Two months after he came home, he felt paranoid and unsafe and became a cocaine addict. He needed help to get off drugs. He asked his commander for help in dealing with the symptoms of PTSD. His superior replied, "You didn't tell us the first time," and the soldier answered that he was asking now and that was all that mattered. The commander denied having any recollection that he had been asked for help, even though the soldier's medical records indicate that he did alert doctors that he was having nightmares, was feeling numb, and was worried that he might lose control and hurt someone. Shortly afterward, he was discharged from the army without a PTSD diagnosis. That meant that he was ineligible for medical care, and his commander gave him a dishonorable discharge. Since then, he has lived in a trailer park in Texas. He got in touch with another veteran who lives there and had also been discharged for the same reasons. They kept taking drugs, and one of them was jailed for beating up his wife, something he regretted deeply. He was decorated in Iraq for capturing the fifth-most-wanted man in the country, Saddam Hussein's brother.[48]

The documentary *Wartorn* retraces the story of a veteran, Lance Corporal Nathan Domingo, who attacked a Middle Eastern cab driver at gunpoint because he was having a flashback. When he returned from Iraq, Nathan was having horrible nightmares. One of his psychologists thought he was having another nightmare about the war when he attacked the cab driver and that he had automatically gone into combat mode. In his mind, he was back in Iraq, doing his job, feeling that he was still at war. Yet he was sentenced to six years in prison.

Another veteran never thought he would be sitting in a cell, charged with armed robbery. He felt that he returned from war weaker, not stronger. In the documentary *Wartorn,* General Peter Charelli estimates that nearly 30 percent of the veterans who are or have been incarcerated suffer from PTSD.[49]

The following incident illustrates how a distraught returning veteran, still feeling at war, can easily run afoul of the law.[50] One night, a young veteran marine went out drinking with his buddies. After he was thrown out of a bar, he beat up the bouncer. Soon after, there were five or six police officers after him. He jumped into his truck and pulled out at top speed, brandishing his automatic rifle, which is a felony. He drove home with the police in hot pursuit. His mother could see the flashing blue lights of the police cars spread all over her lawn and police officers with automatic rifles at the ready, surrounding the house and preparing to arrest her son, who was holed up in the house. He told his mother that he would try to slip out quietly through the back door and get picked up by one of his friends whom he had alerted. The mother waited a few minutes before walking out of the house through the front door with her hands up, yelling to the police to put their weapons down. Later on, the mother received a text message from her son, telling her that he was safe in another town but needed to get out of the state because there was a warrant pending for his arrest. The mother then hired an attorney, a former navy officer through Veterans for Peace. He managed to get her son probation and secure veterans' services counseling and anger management for him. But he was arrested a few months later and thus had two cases pending against him. Because he failed to honor his five-year probation and had a double arrest for drunk driving within ninety days, he was sent to prison. His heartbroken mother believes that he actually wanted to be jailed and was literally begging for help after all he had gone through in Iraq.

In Massachusetts, a group of people tried to create special courts for veterans, but they couldn't get the funding for it and the state was unable to provide it. One of the judges in that state became an advocate for the cause. She feels that substance abuse is a big problem for soldiers, and she believes that some courts have been successful in dealing with it. That's why she wants to see the institution of veterans' courts.

Combat during war is often immoral, although that kind of behavior is considered normal. It's the situation that is not moral. When they come home, soldiers have learned that the lines between right and wrong, between good and bad, are blurred and that that certainty eluded them during combat. They may have tried to shoot a sniper from a rooftop, only to have killed an innocent family inside the house. Or they may have observed a wire snaking up to a home that they suspected was connected to an IED and they responded, as was their duty, by killing the perpetrator, along with innocent people who were not involved. Confusion about what is taking place, aggravated by brain injury, may affect their thought process.

As with care for PTSD and mental health, it took too many years for the courts to grant the respect and accommodate the special needs that veterans deserve. In New York state, since 2008, a criminal court program has been tailored to military veterans, to provide treatment for defendants who struggle with coping with their experiences of war. The new Veterans' Court in Queens is now taking defendants whose lesser misdemeanors may have resulted from mental or substance-abuse problems arising from their military service and steering them to treatment programs. Courts use the model of long-established specialty courts, like drug-treatment and mental-health courts, that seek rehabilitation for defendants rather than imprisoning them.

The justice of the State Supreme Court in New York who heads the new court noted that what sets this court apart from others like it is the assigning of veterans to mentor the defendants. Veterans identify so much more with people who have been in the military. They can penetrate that tough exterior and tell them, "I was there, too. I experienced that, too."[51]

There are now seven Veterans' Courts: in Brooklyn and Buffalo, in Monroe and Onondaga Counties, and in the third judicial district. The crimes they adjudicate include drug offenses, theft, assault, and weapons possession. The defendants usually spend at least a year in the treatment program. For those who suffer from PTSD, the court and prosecutors consult with an expert in PTSD. The New York State Health Foundation has contributed more than $200,000 for training judges, prosecutors, and defense lawyers on veterans' issues.[52]

In Pennsylvania, veterans charged with either nonviolent crimes, substance dependency, or mental-health problems, are placed in a special docket. After an initial screening and assessment by the court, they are offered a place in a treatment program geared to veterans instead of being forced to stand trial.[53] Compliance is monitored through regularly scheduled court hearings, when participants can be sanctioned for noncompliance or rewarded for their success. Such courts also serve as an appreciation of past service and a way to reawaken the veteran's pride, discipline, and courage. The fact that veterans are in the program with each other fosters the sense of comradeship that they lost when they came home. This approach has been adopted by courts across the country, including in California, in Oklahoma, and in Wisconsin; and one was established in Leavenworth, Kansas, by a soldier lawyer.

These courts are being established at a time when the legal system is bracing for an influx of veteran defendants as soldiers return from Iraq and

Afghanistan. Judges around the country have been lenient in their sentencing of veterans, and the courts are finally acknowledging the impact that war can have on the life of a soldier, that he is depressed because he's away from his buddies in the military, that he doesn't have a job, that he doesn't know what to do, and that he then starts drinking or turns to drugs and does not receive the help he needs.

At the federal and state levels, judges are trying to work around guidelines that focus on the nature of the crime rather than on the qualities of the person who committed it. Estimates released by the Bureau of Justice Statistics in 2008 found 229,000 veterans in local, state, and federal prisons, with 400,000 on probation and 75,000 on parole.[54] A number of judges have reduced the sentences from years to months to take into consideration the veterans' mental health and their service to the country. Those judges are involved in a broader disagreement over sentencing and over rigid federal sentencing guidelines that ordinarily do not take into consideration the military-service record of the defendants in determining whether to impose sentences below the recommended range. The US Supreme Court has declared that the federal sentencing guidelines are advisory, not mandatory.

Attending to the needs of so many of our returning soldiers will occupy this country for decades to come, but we are just beginning to acknowledge them and recognize their contribution to our country.

Chapter 7

HIDDEN GRIEF

Fig. 7.1. Tim Kahlor and Laura Kahlor with their son, Ryan. *Photo ©
Mathieu Grandjean, www.mathieugrandjean.com.*

JUNDEE AMERIKI

Many the healers of the body.
Where the healers of the soul?
            —Ahmad Shauqi

At the VA hospital in Long Beach, California,
Dr. Shushruta scores open a thin layer of skin
to reveal an object raveling up through muscle.
It is a kind of weeping the body does, expelling
foreign material, sometimes years after injury.
Dr. Shushruta lifts slivers of shrapnel, bits
of coarse gravel, road debris, diamond
points of glass—the minutiae of the story
reconstructing a cold afternoon in Baghdad,
November of 2005. The body offers aged cloth
from an *abaya* dyed in blood, shards of bone.
And if he were to listen intently, he might hear
the roughened larynx of this woman calling up
through the long corridors of flesh, saying
Allah al Akbar, before releasing
her body's weapon, her dark and lasting gift
for this *jundee Ameriki*, who carries fragments
of the war inscribed in scar tissue,
a deep intractable pain, the dull grief of it
the body must learn to absorb.[1]

—Brian Turner

WHY WE GRIEVE ALONE

While we admit the reality of death and dying in our culture, we have yet to publicly acknowledge the problems of the survivors and the importance of mourning. After a death we are left with disrupted lives and months and often years of pain and suffering. We also suffer from loneliness, for in our contemporary society, we consider mourning to be morbid, something to be avoided at all costs. However, it is the denial of mourning that is unnatural and unprecedented in history.

The emotions associated with grief are very powerful and include anger, guilt, despair, and sadness. Imagine how they are heightened when society denies their very existence. Not only do we experience intense emotions when we grieve, but in addition, we are made to feel that somehow these emotions are inappropriate. Just when we are in need of social support, we find ourselves isolated, without a common ritual or even a language with which we can communicate our feelings to others.

When asked to list the major emotions we experience in our daily lives, few people would include sadness or even consider it a powerful and enduring emotion. On the contrary, sadness is often regarded as an unacceptable sign of fragility or vulnerability. Therefore, the experience of sorrow may come as a great shock to us. We have not been prepared for its intensity by our education, by social ritual, or by the stream of publications and visual media that provide us with common experiences and fill so much of our lives.

In fact there is even a new theory called "speed grieving" that claims a person can heal more quickly by simply identifying the stages of grief and giving oneself a set amount of time to recover. This view reflects how we live in the moment and have trouble facing reality.

It's as if our very consciousness of mourning has disappeared along with the rituals. In our society we don't think about loss or grief. We prepare ourselves for happiness and success, not for personal catastrophe. The freedom and optimism that pervade our culture and are so liberating are reinforced by our school curricula. However, rarely is the other side of reality acknowledged. The fact is that the future we all dream of may hold loss and illness as well as joy and achievement. If these aspects of our lives are introduced not as aberrations but as part and parcel of the normal human journey, we will not be caught off guard and bewildered when we experience sorrow. Nor will we feel as if we have somehow failed.

There are many taboos surrounding illness, and this includes post-traumatic stress disorders that are also known as combat stress. These taboos are even more strongly held in the military culture, which is hierarchic and emphasizes strength and resilience and regards emotional states as a sign of weakness.

We associate grief with loss through death, but we also experience grief as a consequence of some of the major changes and different losses in our lives. We experience the emotions and disruptions of grieving as a result of these losses just as we face the death of a loved one.

Veterans and their families experience a myriad of losses: physical and psychological injuries and changes in family relationships. One military wife gave up her full-time job to care for her husband, who returned from two tours in Iraq with a traumatic brain injury and Post-Traumatic Stress Disorder (PTSD). She has had to adjust to an entirely new relationship with her husband, who faces a number of debilitating problems such as short-term memory loss and difficulty with impulse control and anger. She feels that her biggest loss is the loss of the man she married, with whom she had a loving relationship. There is a growing community of spouses, parents, and partners who care for severely injured loved ones who return from war unable to look after themselves. These family members not only grieve over the injuries of their loved ones but also over changed relationships and overwhelming new routines. As we all do, they suffer from a complex set of emotions in such situations—guilt, anger, and profound sadness. We grieve for the person who can never be the same but is still present in our lives.

MINIMIZING THE LOSSES SERVICEMEN AND SERVICEWOMEN EXPERIENCE

The HBO documentary *Wartorn* reveals that some World War II veterans still haven't recovered from the trauma of combat and remain estranged from their families. Some family members, friends, and acquaintances expect too much from a veteran of any war. They would like them to recover quickly and revert to their previous roles and behaviors, while these good servicemen and servicewomen are still suffering from what they have seen and participated in.

Our interpretation of loss is too narrow. There are many losses that cause us to grieve that are not visible in our social perceptions or conversations. That includes the grief of losing one's buddies, the grief of events that occurred during war, of seeing death of Iraqi and Afghan children. Many service members express their sorrow in different ways, constantly watching military channels on television, thinking about their buddies and those they have lost.

Because we are so uncomfortable with sadness in our society, those who are grieving often don't have the words to express it or feel that somehow they shouldn't express it. US servicemen and servicewomen often say that they feel like a *failure*—a word that contains the meaning of sorrow.

Twenty-one-year-old Corporal Dakota Meyer was interviewed on *60 Minutes* in September 2011 as he received the Medal of Honor from President Barack Obama. But he was not pleased to receive an award. He spoke little, saying chiefly that he felt like a failure because the four marines he tried to rescue five times died.

On September 8, 2009, just before dawn, a patrol of Afghan and US forces were walking in a narrow valley toward a village to meet with elders. Corporal Meyer maintained security at a patrol rally point. The patrol was ambushed by numerous enemy fighters firing RPGs, mortars, and machine guns from a number of positions on the slopes above. Hearing on the radio that four US marines were cut off, Corporal Meyer took the initiative. With a fellow marine driving, Corporal Meyer took the exposed gunner's position in a Humvee® as they drove down the steep terrain in a daring effort to disrupt the enemy attack while local enemy fire was concentrated on their vehicle. He and his driver made three trips into the ambush area. During the first two, he and his driver evacuated two dozen Afghan soldiers, many of whom had been wounded. Despite a shrapnel wound to his arm, Corporal Meyer made two more trips into the area to recover more wounded Afghan soldiers and search for the missing US team members. Still under heavy fire, he left the vehicle on his fifth trip and went on foot to locate and recover his buddies. When he found them, he ran toward them until he threw himself down to get cover from the shooting and fell on top of one of the dead marines.[2]

Corporal Meyer said he would accept the medal in the names of his four dead "brothers," that he would rather have them alive than receive a medal. What this young man was feeling was intense grief. Receiving the Medal of Honor from President Obama did not make him feel honorable. He kept thinking of his four friends who died in battle. His grief was not a part of the interview or the many articles written about him in so many newspapers.

Amy Smee lost two soldiers that she was very close to while they were in combat together. She reflected that she was very lonely: "You lose a battle buddy and it's awful. My 'sister' died in action. My family doesn't understand that. They think, oh, you lost a friend."[3] Amy had a profound respect for her lieutenant, Laura Walker, and found her to be a very caring person. When Laura saw Amy cry over something terrible that happened, she too would start crying. Amy felt that her lieutenant was too young to die and would have become an exceptional leader. She lost two of the best soldiers in her battalion, Lieutenant Laura Walker and the chaplain sergeant who was driving her. Then when she came home, Amy lost the recruiter who was overseeing the unit when she began to serve. She regarded him as her father. He was passionate about serving and protecting the country, but he was diagnosed with a brain tumor and died before he could go overseas. Amy felt that he was the person who taught her to be a dedicated and good soldier.

What heightens Amy's grief is the lack of ceremony or ritual that she can be part of to honor the people she lost. Her family doesn't understand her loss, nor do the people she knows at work. She has nobody in her social support system whom she can talk to about this.

In addition, Amy lost close relationships that she couldn't replace when she returned. Nor does she find anyone who is interested in celebrating Veterans Day or even talking about it. She even tucked away the Bronze Star she received because her family and acquaintances were not interested. Amy's experiences that hurt so much have been marginalized and rendered invisible. She not only needs to be thanked and celebrated for her service but to be understood as well.

Return to Iraq is a healing ceremony created by a man who volunteered at Walter Reed Army Medical Center. It helps soldiers who were physically and psychologically wounded go back to Iraq and leave again with honor and salutes to be greeted when they return. It was like a homecoming for someone like Steven Cornford, who attended. He received a silver star for valor for trying to help his lieutenant, Neil, who was shot in the leg, after he himself was shot in the shoulder. He tried in vain to stem the bleeding in Neil's leg while holding his rifle. Seeing a buddy die in a unit is like losing a family member. Neil was a father figure to him. Steven came back with so much anger, felt suicidal, and had difficulty dealing with his wife. He wanted to salute when he was "medevaced" and on the operating table, but he passed out.[4] When Steven returned to Iraq, he said he could sense the presence of Neil.

Servicemen and servicewomen need ceremonies that can make their sorrow visible and help them honor their fallen comrades. While there are public funerals in the United States for veterans who died, troops face the deaths of their comrades on too many occasions while they are in combat and do not have the time to mourn or honor them. Thus, their comrades remain in their dreams and memories. Often, like Amy Smee, returning soldiers do not have anyone to share their stories and their memories with, so they remain silent.

Many veterans and their families find the holidays to be a difficult time as they live with an invisible pain while watching the people around them celebrating. If they live near a military base or are close to other military families, they are able to share their sorrow and feel whole again. For example, Angela Buckley and her family travel to Virginia for Christmas to spend time with other military families, and it is the one period of the year when she can feel pleasure and perhaps relax.[5]

ANGER AND GRIEF

As we traverse the early phases of the grieving process, shock and numbness, we experience the transformation of our lives and feelings. However, the quest for meaning is also a part of our journey through grief. As we struggle with our religious beliefs and our views of a just world, they change radically. Our belief in a benevolent Creator is often shaken as we ask ourselves, "Why did this happen to my child or my spouse; why did this happen to me? I've always been a good person." We wonder why good people are not spared physical and emotional wounds and untimely death. We question a divine plan and think, "Unjust, unfair, inexplicable," as we examine our shattered lives. We may be thrown back on ourselves and the ground under our feet may no longer seem solid. Some of us, like Cheryl Softich, find our faith a source of support and experience a deepening of our beliefs.[6] Others, like Kevin Lucey, find emptiness in religious ceremonies and withdraw from religious observances.[7] Even those who turn to their religion with a renewed understanding may feel angry with a Creator who allowed the death or maiming of a loved one. Death causes us to examine not only our own lives but also our place in the universe.

Kevin Lucey is angry with God for allowing his son to suffer so much, and with the government for not providing for veterans.[8] Anger and grief are intertwined. It is an integral part of the grieving process. Soldiers with combat stress feel anger because they are numb and need to turn off their emotions in order to continue serving. Shock that causes us to become numb is part of the first reaction to grief because it allows us time before we can feel its full force that tears us apart inside. So many servicemen and servicewomen return with profound anger. Like Tim Kahlor's son, Ryan, and many others, they express this by constantly pounding a fist against a wall. How can a veteran process the grief of losing his buddies, of seeing so much death and carnage in a society that doesn't want to hear any bad news and rarely reaches out to those who feel a deep sorrow?

Anger, guilt, and sorrow are unpredictable and do not necessarily occur in sequence. Everyone can feel very vulnerable because of the intensity and unpredictability of these feelings. It is difficult to explain how a person feels, that the meaning he or she had held about life is no longer there. When he or she returns home, a serviceman or servicewoman can rage against witnessing death and especially the lack of understanding about the horrors they have witnessed and been a part of. Denying these manifestations of mourning can push people into extreme forms of behavior, such as turning to alcohol or drugs.

THE GRIEF OF RETURNING WITH MENTAL AND PHYSICAL DISABILITIES

When we see a person struggling with physical disabilities, we rarely think of the sorrow he or she experiences by coming home from combat a changed person. A service member who can no longer walk or who has lost his or her memory can no longer make family decisions or do the chores he or she once did to keep the household running feels the loss every minute of the day. Nor can returning soldiers re-create the intimate relations they had with family members before they were deployed. When Angela Buckley's husband, Peter, received from a society called Needs a service dog that helped him go up the stairs and move throughout the house, it was the first time she saw him smile.[9]

Imagine being a serviceman or servicewoman who was physically fit, walking, running, and carrying sixty-pound packs as well as armor, and then suddenly being unable to move or able to move only with great difficulty. Imagine the pain of these people watching others go through their days with great ease and taking their health for granted while they lost their status among family and friends. Peter Buckley's parents have expressed little interest or care about his condition, which adds to his sorrow and feeling of loneliness.[10]

Many of the women veterans who are homeless because they cannot reintegrate into society grieve about no longer being a mother or a wife, of having changed so much they have to adapt to a new way of being. They have lost their self-esteem and their former roles and images. Male veterans who are unable to cope with their return and are homeless because they can't find jobs or reintegrate feel as if they are in another planet, discarded.

We don't like to talk about psychological, physical, or emotional wounds, even though sharing our stories is very healing. Sharing is not complaining. We need to learn how to listen and how to move beyond our own lives and concerns that are so much less demanding than those of our wounded veterans.

Again, in a society that has adopted the new concept of "speed grieving," it is important to remember that the sorrow over a changed and damaged life lasts for years, not weeks or months.

GRIEF OF THE PARENTS

Tim Kahlor's son, Ryan, returned from combat with PTSD and a traumatic brain injury. Tim describes his life now as living on a roller coaster and being always on edge, afraid that something dreadful is going to happen.

> Dealing with a son that has PTSD is essentially grieving. It's a grief that wants you to get that person back that was there before, that person that hasn't been changed so much by the war, by everything that they have seen and that has happened to them. You know you'll never get that person back that you had, so it's like that person is gone. You have to learn to get used to this new person. Even though you have him, it feels like you've lost the person you had. You'll see glimmers of them, but they are not there anymore, so you are always grieving that loss, the innocence that person had when they left. When my son came back from his second tour, it was as if he was totally empty. It will never by the Ryan who left in 2003. When you mature, people remain the same while they grow in their experiences that are normal ones, like work, school, family members and friends. When they experience war, it is something you could never have imagined. I still can't grasp what Ryan experienced. To ever get him back is impossible. It's like veterans never come home from war and are constantly at war. They have good days and bad days, but it is like he too has been killed. When they are killed in combat, the pain for them is over. When they come home, it's like they are the walking dead. The worst part of it is always wishing you could get that person back. It's like our veterans die over and over again. It's a constant up-and-down thing. I talked to Ryan last night and he was in a good mood. He's got a girlfriend that has been great for him and he bought a used car, all these good things happening, but it can all fall down the next day. Some little thing can set him off. I always worry that my son will commit suicide.[11]

Although Tim is able to find some comfort in his private conversations with his wife, Laura, they both suffer from "permanent grieving." There are phases of grief, even though they are not necessarily sequential. But to stay trapped in a grief like Tim feels is heartbreaking and draining. In his case, people who work with him and see him as easy to be with do not understand his sadness or his rare moments of losing his temper. Tim finds his colleagues getting upset over insignificant matters. But when he gets angry, people are outraged because they want his good nature to be permanent. He reflects: "I'm not allowed to be upset because I always try to figure out a way of making things a little better, be a positive force and change things."[12]

An important phase of grief is that of disorganization, which includes the disruption of lifelong habits and patterns. Living with someone, we develop habits for the minute details of our lives. Most important, family members share each other's thoughts, feelings, and hopes. Tim and his wife found their role as parents transformed and feel powerless to reach out to Ryan, help him recover, and regain the close relationship they once had with him.

People like Tim's colleagues expect him to pull himself together and resume his normal reactions and activities. Former friends, like his neighbors, may pull away and avoid talking about his life just when he and his wife need them most.

When Tim and Laura needed to take care of themselves because of their sorrow, Tim had an additional burden besides his job. Seeking adequate help for Ryan was a long and trying journey, and Ryan did not get the healthcare he needed. Further, Tim spent a great deal of time taking part in demonstrations on behalf of soldiers and veterans, helping military family members, and now he feels "burned out."[13]

He has found that there are no rituals or services for this kind of loss, no social customs that help others respond to him. He does go to counseling, as do many family members if they have the time and money, but grieving requires years and takes a toll on our lives that few people can recognize or understand.

GRIEF OF A SPOUSE

When a veteran returns with physical and emotional wounds, there are great changes in family relationships that include loss. A spouse mourns the changes in a relationship she once had with her husband . Her love hasn't changed, but she grieves for the life she once had, the intimacy and the sharing. She may get angry at her new role, which requires caring for him or losing her job to care for him or finding that he is like one of her children, but her love prevents her from walking out on him.

Angela Buckley's husband has been on a number of tours of duty. She felt the stress and sadness of being a single parent and running the household by herself.[14] Like other spouses, she worried and grieved, especially when there were blackouts of communications and she couldn't call or e-mail her husband. During that period, no word goes out about who died or was injured because the military has a forty-eight-hour period for notifying the next of kin. During those "blackouts," everyone knows that something painful has happened.

Now that her husband has returned severely injured, she has to spend hours driving him to medical appointments every day of the week. And she is the one who takes care of the household. She feels very sad because they were very close and used to work as a team. She also feels lonely facing such a difficult situation by herself.

Angela has been caring for her husband for many years and feels exhausted. She has to deal with the bureaucracy, since her husband is still on active duty on medical hold. That means calling his platoon sergeant every day at nine o'clock, except Sunday. And she needs to telephone his nurse case manager three times a week. In addition, Angela has a lot of paperwork to do for his care, besides driving him for hundreds of miles every month.

"I feel grief for our relationship and our life. My husband can be very explosive. He used to be a big joker. That was taken away. I walk on eggshells half of the time because I can't control his anger. I can deal with physical things, but it's the unpredictable outbursts of anger that grieve me."[15]

Given the stigma attached to PTSD, it took her a long time to persuade him to see a counselor. She knows that having "behavioral-health counseling" on a person's record means the end of that person's career, and she heard such people referred to as "psychs" when she was at the Walter Reed Army Medical Center with Peter.

Angela has no one to support her or to understand the sorrow she feels at the changes in her family and her daily efforts to keep it functioning as best as possible. Some spouses cry every night after an exhausting day of caring for their returned loved ones. Others try to hide their grief from their children so their life can have a semblance of normality. What makes it even more difficult for them is that their grief and the overwhelming work of caring for their family members while working and running the household is invisible.

The children of physically and emotionally wounded veterans will mature, and many grow stronger inside in ways that will help them through life. Parents of veterans who face the same problems are able to reach out, make new friends, and engage in political and social action. However, often the spouses do not even have the time to take care of their own needs, either physically or emotionally. Perhaps remaining very busy, as they may have done while their spouse was deployed in order to deal with their loneliness, might help them over the long term.

CHILDREN OF SERVICEMEN AND SERVICEWOMEN

Nearly six in ten of the troops deployed today are married, and nearly half of them have families.[16] The children have borne the brunt of the emotional strain of their parents' deployments. Few people realize how much the children of veterans are suffering. When one of their parents is deployed, they often cry themselves to sleep. They worry constantly, "Will my daddy (or mommy) be safe? Will he (or she) come home?" As is normal for children who are struggling with fear, sadness, and uncertainty, some of them act out in school. The boys get into fights or are unable to concentrate on their studies. A girl like Sophie Buckley worries constantly that her father might die because he has been through a number of deployments and she knows a lot about military life.[17] Children worry about their safety and about death. They want their family back together and feel different from the children at school who have a normal home life they take for granted. Their classmates who do not have parents in the military are unable to understand their pain and anxiety.

Many children visit their parent at the Walter Reed Army Medical Center and see the mother or father they used to spend happy times with in a wheelchair with swollen legs and bandages around their foreheads. It's shocking and frightening for them to see so many wounded adults. These experiences change their lives. While it helps them mature more quickly, it also frightens them. The world no longer seems predictable or safe, and they worry that if one parent is so ill, will the other parent also have difficulties, and will they find themselves alone?

Children grieve when a parent returns physically and psychologically wounded. For example, an adolescent son mourns his former life with his father, who returned from the war physically diminished and who can no longer play ball with him on the weekends or be as close as they once were. He lost the father he once knew and needs to adjust to the new person he still loves.

THE HEALING POWER OF UNDERSTANDING

What helps people move through the journey of grief to a new place is the discovery of new friends while they were in the most difficult period of grief and meeting with them to share common interests, such as political action and efforts to make homecoming easier for veterans. They see their whole network of relationships in a new light. At first they may be disappointed in their old friends, but ultimately these tensions and stresses help them to make the necessary decisions in order to create a new life for themselves. It is a long process that moves in fits and starts.

Because Tim Kahlor lives and works in a culture that doesn't embrace sorrow, he finds great comfort in being with other people in Military Families Speak Out (MFSO).[18] When there is a gathering of members, he feels that there is complete understanding and that sometimes he doesn't even need to talk. He can just walk up to a member and be hugged. He is close to a woman who lives in New Jersey and whose son was in Iraq at the same time as Ryan and is now in jail. They've had the same experiences and talk to each other with ease. When there is a gathering of members, there is no need for explanations. Everyone knows exactly how they feel, and all they have to do is hold each other's hand. No matter whether their son or daughter has PTSD, has gone AWOL, or is in prison, they are able to share their feelings. That is where Tim gets the healing that he so desperately needs. It is very much like veterans talking to each other, sharing the experiences they carry within them that civilians are not concerned with, are not interested in, or simply are unable to grasp.

Giving of ourselves in different ways is a significant coping technique. It brings us new friends who can share our sorrow. It also helps us move beyond our daily life and changes our perspectives. Most important, it renews our self-esteem.

Once a year, Cheryl Softich spends a weekend with a branch of Gold Star Mothers where "we eat, cry, laugh, cry."[19] She once took with her her daughter, Sarah, who found it very helpful. Talking together and grieving together makes people like Cheryl and the Luceys feel less alone.[20] In addition, both Cheryl and the Luceys have become active on behalf of other veterans. They have come to understand that all the soldiers are their children, and they try to do all they can to help them.

It is more than difficult to reach the other side of grief. Some people, like the Luceys, have discovered new meaning in their broken lives and, over time, new perspectives that deepened their appreciation of their journey through time. The Luceys sent a moving note to their large circle of friends who have had family members deployed:

WE GIVE THANKS

For all the wonderful and beautiful souls who have joined us on our journeys as well as those who have invited us on their paths;

For the opportunities to touch the lives of so many veterans and their loves ones;

For the organizations that have supported both Jeff and our family;

For those who have kept Jeff alive by the telling and teaching of his torment and tragedy;

For our brave sons, daughters, husbands, wives, brothers, fathers, mothers, sisters, friends and neighbors who are among the ranks of our warriors, our wounded warriors of both hidden and physical wounds as well as the heavenly ranks of the fallen;

And finally, for the empty chair instead of symbolizing the loss, would celebrate the twenty-three years we had the honor and privilege of walking along with our son, sharing in the laughter, the tears and the adventures of his life. . . .

Let us all take a moment during our Thanksgiving festivities and remember all mentioned, but especially all those who have empty chairs.

Kevin & Joyce Lucey, the proud parents of Cpl. Jeffrey Michael Lucey and Debbie and Kelley, the proud sisters of Jeffrey, a 23-year-old USMC reservist forever young

Succumbed to the Hidden Wounds of PTSD
03/18/81–06/22/04

Chapter 8

BRIDGING THE CHASM

Fig. 8.1. Dr. Judith Broder, founder and chair, the
Soldiers Project. *Photo courtesy of Judith Broder, MD.*

SHABBAT PRAYER, ON THE OCCASION OF WAR

beginning with a line from Siegfried Sasson

A flare went up; the shining whiteness spread,
as though it were a match bright enough
to light the room, but not so bright it snuffed
the residue of darkness overhead.
There once was darkness signifying calm—
our candles glowed
beside the window, the nights did not explode,
or bullets ricochet, or firebombs
turn streets to ash. We drank a glass of wine.
The night served as the complement to day,
like salt or something sweet. And in this way,
we tasted syrup mixed with brine.
And, in this way, we learned a prayer
that joined the shadow with the shining flare.[1]

—Jehanne Dubrow

SOCIAL REINTEGRATION

We tend to think of change as requiring vast and important transformations. Yet we can create a discourse between the military and civilian worlds in so many small ways that are like ripples beginning on the surface of a lake that get wider as they move, for every connection we make affects family and friends and continues in ways we may never know about or see. Yet they do make a difference.

Veterans have created unusual ways of revealing their sacrifices and experiences. Veterans for Common Sense, Veterans for Peace, Military Families Speak Out, Vote Vets, and a number of other military organizations that were formed after Operation Iraqi Freedom (OIF) and Operation Enduring Freedom (OEF) have been very active in lobbying the administration for healthcare and contacting the media for recognition of their postcombat problems. They make certain that the local community is aware of the need to recognize veterans.

The Home Base Program in Massachusetts has inspired the establishment of similar practices around the country. It is very active in maintaining community relations by sponsoring conferences and getting in touch with people at the grassroots level who are in contact with veterans and their families, universities, schools, clergy, and coaches, as well as businesses.

One of the most effective ways of promoting understanding of the travails of our veterans is through art. Revealing social and political problems through theater, poetry, photography, and film has been extremely effective throughout history. Also, documentaries such as those shown on PBS, including "The Wounded Platoon," "Iraq/Vietnam," and "The Soldier's Heart," and HBO's *Wartorn*, portray powerful stories and have been widely viewed. Private filmmakers, such as Patricia Folkrod, who created the film *Ground Truth*, have had their work shown around the country and at the Sundance Festival in Utah. The documentary *Hidden Wounds* was premiered in Paris, and the film *Happy New Year*, produced by Laurel Manning, about a soldier who committed suicide, will be featured at an international film festival.

Websites where veterans write about their difficulties coming home are very popular. Two of them are sponsored by the *New York Times: Opinionater* and *At War* are blogs where soldier-authors share their moving stories. US soldiers and their families have found unusual ways of taking space in our society, of having their voices heard, of speaking together about their experiences when their lives pass unnoticed in the larger society. In a world where so many civilians are rushing through their days, assaulted by information that excludes so much of the soldiers' reality, it is always possible to create a place where theirs can unfold in new ways.

WRITING

Poetry gives an important voice to memory and culture. It is a free space where there are no rules or limits, where one's inner journey can be revealed in a way that others can share, and that can give us new ways of understanding the daily lives of our warriors. It is an important bridge between the lives of our soldiers and the world of civilians. It opens us up to what they have endured and accomplished.

Brian Turner has become an important emissary from the military to the civilian culture. His first book won a key literary award, the Beatrice Hawley award, and his second book received widespread acclaim. His work has been featured on National Public Radio, the BBC, *PBS News Hour* with Jim Lehrer, and *Weekend America*. He travels around the country, giving readings, including one at West Point. A line from one of his poems was included in the wonderful traveling exhibit Always Lost: A Meditation on War. His readings not only are helping the soldiers prepare for deployment but also are making a connection between the military and the civilian society that the policy of a volunteer army has sundered. His poems are beautifully rendered versions of the horrific experiences of war, and they help civilian society share those experiences.

What is even more striking about his work is the way the poems reveal his understanding and honor not only for his fellow soldiers in Iraq but also for the Iraqi culture and the practice of Islam. His second book *Phantom Noise*, embraces that culture. Many of the poems are prefaced with a translated quote from Iraqi poets and philosophers, and one of the most haunting poems, "Ajal," is an elegy for a child who died. He wrote it in the voice of the father of an Iraqi child. "It should not be like this Abd Allah, / many years from now, your own children /should wash your body three times /after your death. They should seal your mouth/ with cotton, reciting prayers in a wash / of light and grieving, a perfume of lemons / and jasmine on your skin."[2] Brian Turner also wrote a touching blurb on the back of a book by Iraqi poets titled *Flowers of Flame*. He has opened a dialogue not only that we need within our country but also one between the two very different cultures of the United States and Iraq.

Jehanne Dubrow, whose husband is in the navy, has written a wonderful book of poems, *Stateside*, that reveals the pain and difficulties wives experience while their husbands are serving in combat. In that book, she compares herself to Penelope waiting for the return of Odysseus, who returns as a man she barely recognizes, "I can't help asking if, when he came home / did they lie together or sleep alone?" She also writes about her loneliness in a society that does not understand the pain of separation she feels while her husband is away at war, "She's Ithaca, trapped in her own body, / an island circled by the seas." As a professor of literature, she makes certain that her students know about her situation and read poetry that focuses on war.

SPEAKING THE UNSPEAKABLE

Because veterans felt that there was not enough coverage of their experiences in the wars, Veterans for Peace created a sacred space along a beach in California. They arranged a wall of photos of all the soldiers who died and placed wooden crosses in the sand with the name of each one of them inscribed. And beside each cross they placed a pair of boots. Evenings, candles are lit near each cross and pair of boots to honor that holy ground.

It is a place where veterans can speak to each other about their experiences, where families can talk about the loss of their loved ones and can discuss what the wars have meant to them. Veterans need spaces where they can talk among themselves and be together. It is healing for them to talk about what they endured. They feel as if they are part of a family, have the same frame of reference, and can share the memories and stories they can't forget. They consider themselves as brothers and sisters.

Veterans and their families meet there to talk about what they have endured and also about the Iraqis because they discovered that for too many people in the United States, Iraqis are statistics and not families. One veteran observed that sixty Iraqis die for each American soldier.[3] Another said that there was barely one paragraph in the press about veterans as he prepared himself for another deployment. Another expressed anger at recruiters coming to schools and attempting to lure students into enlisting with the promise of all sorts of benefits. Patricia Alviso turned off television programs that included recruiters in the high-school class where she teaches. Many of the veterans who come to that sacred place to talk are against a volunteer army. They want the draft to be reestablished. One person believes, as many others do, that the media do not cover properly how soldiers are being hurt in combat.[4] Yet another tells about opening a car door and seeing a whole family dead. He believes that we killed too many Iraqis because we don't understand their language and their culture. Among the people who come to this sacred place are wives who are now widows, mothers who have lost their sons or daughters, and especially veterans who need a space to say exactly what happened in Iraq and how they feel about it. They speak about repeated flashbacks in their dreams and also their dreams about being shot at and losing friends in their unit. They also discuss the high suicide rate in Iraq, as well as how many soldiers have lost their arms, legs, and eyesight. They exchange stories about how soldiers don't feel as if they fit in our society when they return, how they are redeployed too soon and even when they are suffering from PTSD (Post-Traumatic Stress Disorder). They want people to know the trauma of the physically wounded and also of those who suffer from PTSD. One veteran admitted that he watched one of his buddies shoot himself in the foot just to get out of Iraq. This is a significant and rare place for truth, where they tell about their own suffering in Iraq and their beliefs, important matters that are not discussed in our society.[5]

Soldiers not only share experiences but also have their own language. Jehanne Dubrow, an army spouse, recounted that the words *whisky, tango, foxtrot* represent a curse.[6] And then there are the names of platoons and units: Alpha, Bravo, Delta. There is a great need for listening to a returning veteran and sharing his or her pain.

One veteran whom I interviewed came from a dysfunctional family and spent his life on the streets before enlisting. After we talked, he said that he felt inadequate because so many other soldiers were in more horrific circumstances, and he said that he saw two of his buddies blown up while he remained unharmed. I put my arms around him and held him for a few minutes. Listening, sharing, and touching are important. Here again, it happens at unexpected times.

PHOTOGRAPHY

Erin Trieb is a prize-winning and noted photojournalist whose life changed after she worked in Afghanistan with the 3rd Brigade of the 10th Mountain Division. She was involved in firefights and worried about being hurt by IEDs. But she found it even more demanding to photograph the effects of PTSD among the same soldiers after they returned to Fort Drum in upstate New York in December 2009. There, she discovered that almost every soldier she spoke to was having problems that included using drugs, binge drinking, attempting suicide, and abusing wives.

As a result, she decided she would like to be of service to them. In July 2011, she opened The Homecoming Project, a website aimed at encouraging discussion of the aftermath of the wars in Afghanistan and Iraq, at connecting soldiers to the assistance they need, and at offering opportunities for service organizations and individuals. She felt "privileged to see things behind closed doors that others don't get to see. It's a sacred exchange that comes with responsibilities."[7]

She spent the next two years documenting soldiers she had come to know in Afghanistan and focused on three of them. She not only took their photos but also listened to their stories and stepped in to offer assistance. She stayed with some of them in their homes. One of them called her from Fort Drum and told her that he had cut himself badly. Erin immediately drove from Brooklyn and accompanied him to a civilian hospital. They reconnected when he got out of the hospital and she was encouraged to see that he recovered and also reached out for help.[8]

After she learned of a specialist's suicide, she drove to Kalamazoo, Michigan, and was welcomed into the family home by his mother and listened to many stories. She found that sharing stories of loss can make a difference and that it was important to listen and empathize with soldiers and their families. Her photos are being widely exhibited, which is another moving way of connecting the military and civilian worlds.

Sergeant Stacy Pearsall was in the US Air Force as one of the few women admitted into the elite ranks of combat photographers. She is one of only two women to win the Military Photographer of the Year award from the National Press Photographers Association, and she won it twice.[9] Her photos are extremely moving, and one of them captures an extremely difficult decision that needed to be made in combat. She was aboard a cargo plane that needed to take off before sunrise to avoid enemy ground fire. The pilot was asked to delay the departure so a critically wounded soldier could be brought onboard. If he missed the flight, he would die, but including him meant risking getting shot down. The pilot got on the intercom and asked for a show of hands on who wanted to stay for the wounded soldier and who wanted to leave. Everybody raised his or her hands to stay. This story was captured in a stunning frame of soldiers carrying a stretcher into the plane against the sunrise, as shown at the beginning of chapter 1. Stacy said "he survived because everybody sacrificed their lives—or put their lives in danger for him. And I think that that's a real representation about what it's like to be in this fraternity we call the military."[10]

Stacy was hurt three times by IEDs. She didn't seek help for three years because she didn't want to seem weak, but after she eventually saw a physician, she was discharged. Because of her wounds, she wasn't able to carry equipment anymore. Yet she and her husband, a retired Air Force combat photographer, have opened a studio in Charleston, South Carolina. While she was at the VA hospital getting medical care, she met so many wonderful veterans there from World War II, Vietnam, Korea, OIF, and OEF that she began bringing her camera and taking portraits. Eighty-eight of the three hundred portraits she took are hanging in the hallway of the Robert H. Johnson VA Medical Center in Charleston. Stacy's photographs were on exhibit at the Montclair Art Museum in 2011. She was motivated to show the public what our soldiers have experienced, as she rightly feels that we are not acknowledging the sacrifices they have made. Stacy's photographs will be published in 2012, thus fulfilling her hope that her photos and all that they represent can get a wider reach.

We need to give space for social memory so our society can share the experiences of its soldiers. Photographic exhibits are a powerful way of doing this. They help us understand the suffering and courage of our soldiers.

THEATER OF WAR

There is a very unusual event that is occurring all over the country. It brings together the military and civilian worlds and helps our soldiers toward social reintegration. The Theater of War is an innovative project that presents readings of ancient Greek plays—Sophocles's *Ajax* and *Philoctetes*—as a catalyst for dialogue about the challenges faced by service members, veterans, their families, their caregivers, and their communities. The performances are followed by a town hall–style discussion facilitated with the help of military community members. It's a wonderful opportunity for civilians to hear the veterans' reactions and to enter into the conversation. The fact that a series of Greek plays by Sophocles can draw audiences from Richmond, Virginia, and the Oregon Shakespeare Festival, to the American Repertory Theater in Cambridge, Massachusetts, and small towns across the country is a public way of giving veterans an important place to vent their feelings.

Theater of War has delivered over 125 performances at more than 50 military sites and theaters throughout the United States. They have been attended by over 25,000 service members and veterans of every rank, their family members, as well as caregivers and the community.

Ancient Greek drama was a ritual, a form of storytelling and communal therapy to help veterans reintegrate into civilian society. Sophocles himself was a general. The audiences for whom these plays were performed were comprised of citizen-soldiers, and the performers were veterans. *Ajax* was produced in 460–440 BCE. In this play, Sophocles makes a hero out of a suicide. In the Theater of War production, Ajax kills himself on stage rather than off stage as in ancient tragedy. He also displays moments of madness, and in a soliloquy, he experiences a crisis in his understanding of the moral basis on which he lives that develops into pity for human suffering. In *Philoctetes*, Sophocles creates a hero out of a deserted and lonely disabled veteran.[11] The plays are complex, as are the relations between actors and the gods, but one of the primary themes is honor.

The productions that take place around the country include professional actors and military personnel. After a play performance, there is a lively panel discussion between service members and civilians, a very moving dialogue. We live in a society that is rushing from one event to another without stopping to reflect. We need to have a conversation with our returning veterans, but to have them tell us what they want to share, not to ask them questions.

Many soldiers spoke out after a performance of *Ajax* in the American Repertory Theater in Cambridge in 2010. Some mentioned that when they go into places like Dunkin' Donuts, they see people turning away from them. These soldiers think that because such people believe that war is wrong, they blame the soldiers for it. Veterans said that people should understand the soldiers' desire to go to war and what their values are. And when someone wishes to say "thank you" to veterans for their service, they should look at them straight in the eyes and shake their hands. Touch is important, and looking at a person signifies sincerity.

THE SOLDIERS PROJECT

Dr. Judith Broder is a psychiatrist who was planning to retire when she saw a play in 2004, *The Sandstorm: Stories from the Front*. It was written by Sean Huze, a then active-duty marine. It is comprised of ten confessional monologues by marines who have served in Iraq. She was stunned by their accounts and the pleasure they felt in revenge killing for someone who had been wounded or killed. They revealed that because of what they had seen, had done, and hadn't managed to accomplish, they felt as if they were no longer fit for ordinary society. In the play, a sergeant who is loved by his men acts as part parent, brother, and counselor to the others who share their insights and perceptions. A lance corporal is a young man trying to come to terms with the death of young children in a war zone. A corporal terrorizes an Iraqi man and eats his lunch while watching the man slowly die in the desert heat. In an ironic moment, a PFC (Private First Class) attempts to bring a foot back to its owner after a harrowing military skirmish. One marine gives a touching account of losing his best friend in the war. The play is deeply disturbing but is traveling across the country, giving audiences insightful and compelling views of the wars too few people are aware of. It is a continuation of Sophocles.

At the end of the play, the people around Dr. Broder asked her if she had a child in the service. She replied, "No, but all of these men are my brothers and sons," a remark she made spontaneously without thinking and that led her to begin a complex and far-reaching program for veterans, their families, and the community. What moved her to start her free program for traumatized soldiers was that each one said that they were burying their pain silently because they didn't want to upset their loved ones with these horrors.[12]

The very next morning, Dr. Broder developed a plan for the Soldiers Project to provide free, confidential, unlimited psychotherapy to anyone who had served or who was going to serve in Iraq and Afghanistan, as well as to their families. She also wanted to provide special training to the therapists who would be willing to provide this treatment and to support them because she knew that they would be as upset as she was after she saw the play. She knew that anyone exposed to such wrenching stories was going to need backing.

Dr. Broder was also determined to educate civilian communities regardless of their political views about the traumas of war. She felt that too many people fail to identify with what these young men and woman are experiencing during the wars. She often heard, "Well, they chose to do this."[13] She was morally outraged and felt personally wounded by what she heard about our volunteer army. She was also upset that many returning veterans are unable to find employment.

Dr. Broder is a member of a psychoanalytic institute that has a project called the Ernest S. Lawrence Trauma Center. Since she was working on one of its projects, she proposed the Soldiers Project, and the center endorsed it readily because it is dedicated to bringing the members' knowledge to the community's grass roots. The project now is a separate nonprofit and has become a nationwide organization.

The Soldiers Project began in Southern California with eight volunteers. In the first two years, Dr. Broder spoke at hundreds of venues, spreading the word about the project and educating the public. By then the project included dedicated volunteers who provided treatment and also made liaisons with the military, the VA, and with anyone who was trying to help veterans and their families.

The Department of Veterans Affairs was the first place where Dr. Broder made contacts. She was told that the VA was not attending to veterans who had psychological problems. Being a grassroots person, Dr. Broder made presentations to the local VA, and it was enthusiastic about the project and became one of its most important referrals. The Soldiers Project has established good connections with the VA so that when a veteran with a traumatic brain injury contacts the project, he or she can be admitted into the system without having to negotiate with its bureaucracy.

The project's mental-health professionals offer free psychotherapy to any military service member who has served in Iraq or Afghanistan. It also offers free therapy to their loved ones, boyfriends, girlfriends, spouses, children, parents, and grandparents. There are no fees and there is no limit to the number of sessions provided. Individuals, couples, and families may attend sessions. The psychologists who work in the project see service members prior to, during, and following return from deployment and keep in touch via phone or the Internet as needed.

As of 2011, there were nine locations throughout the country, including Boston, Chicago, New York, and more that can be contacted toll-free. They are staffed by four hundred volunteer clinicians. The project is being funded by grants as well as by private donations. It received two prestigious prizes that provided enough for it to function for several years. In 2009, Dr. Broder was awarded the Purpose Prize for people who have helped humanity when they were over sixty years old. That gave the project a great deal of publicity. In 2010, she was awarded the James Irvine Foundation Leadership Award for a project that will improve society.

Dr. Broder has created yet another program, Adopt a College, funded by the James Irvine Foundation. Project volunteers work closely with a college's administration and faculty to help veterans succeed. This includes creating "vet-friendly" campuses where volunteer mental-health workers educate staff and faculty on the psychological issues of returning troops and provide referrals for the Soldiers Project. "War is not over when it fades from news coverage or when troops return home. In many homes and in many soldiers' minds, it rages on. The least we can do is fight for them—for their mental well-being, their education, and the opportunity to not just return home but to normalcy and a better life."[14] This is a very useful project because of the gap of understanding existing between the veteran students and students who know very little about the toll of combat or even about the war. This is why veteran students tend to socialize only among themselves.

A major part of the Soldiers Project is involving civilians because of the divide in our society between military and civilian cultures. This includes seminars and yearly conferences. The project runs seminars on PTSD, traumatic brain injury, reintegration, and family life. The seminars are taught by experts in the fields of domestic violence, PTSD, suicide, and military culture, providing education not only to veterans' families but also to civilian society. Dr. Broder has found that these seminars have created a caring community for veterans.

Dr. Broder is determined to get communities involved, and she accomplishes this by inviting community members to the conferences she periodically holds. She is upset when she finds that people do not want to hear soldiers' stories or learn about the pain we cause people. "These soldiers are trying to do the right thing. We don't want to know that wanting to do the right thing leads to traumatic brain injury and death. We would rather close our eyes and say that we are protecting freedom."[15] Part of her vision is "to bring across the point that we are all in this together."[16] These conferences create opportunities for the civilian and military communities to interact with each other in a number of ways.

The first annual conference took place in 2008 in Los Angeles. It included panel discussions; workshops on the treatment of mind, body, and spirit; spiritual issues; addictive behavior; and more. The keynote speakers included Congressman Bob Filner of the 51st congressional district. He chairs the Committee on Veterans Affairs. He has worked continuously to ensure that GI benefits keep up with inflation and to obtain more mental healthcare for veterans. There were a number of highly qualified speakers, such as Jonathan Shay, MD, a psychiatrist at the Department of Veterans Affairs (DVA) outpatient clinic and author of a number of books about combat trauma. This all-day conference was open to the public and it covered the many issues veterans and their families face.

Dr. Broder also included a performance of *The Sandstorm* by Sean Huze in one of her conferences. The latest conference, which took place in April 2011, had the motto "Women and War: Hidden Strengths, Hidden Wounds." It included the play *Into the Fire: Voices of Veterans and Their Families.* Just as important were two panel discussions in which marines from the Female Engagement Team shared their stories about reaching out to Afghani women. Partners, mothers, daughters, and caregivers also spoke out. Again, speakers included nationally known writers such as Sara Neeson, the Academy Award–nominated filmmaker of the documentary *Poster Girl.* Dr. Broder is now planning a conference on suicide.

At a time when so many people in the country feel powerless and angry because of social and economic conditions, Dr. Broder has shown the tremendous difference that can be made by one very caring person who has contacted people eager to donate their time and talents throughout the country.

GIVE AN HOUR

Barbara Van Dahlen is a clinical psychologist who has been practicing for nineteen years in the diagnosis and treatment of children. She has spent her career coordinating with and interacting within large systems, including school districts and mental-health clinics. Concerned about the mental-health implications of the wars in Iraq and Afghanistan, Dr. Van Dahlen founded Give an Hour in 2005. The organization created a network of mental-health professionals who are providing free services to US troops, veterans, their loved ones, and their communities. Currently, the network has more than 5,200 providers.

Dr. Van Dahlen is a whirlwind of activity and has reached out to co-operate with over seventy national associations, such as the American Psychiatric Foundation, the American Red Cross, Blue Star Military Families, Disabled American Veterans, Gold Star Mothers/Gold Star Wives, National Military Families Association, Operation Homefront, Vets 4 Vets, the National Veterans Legal Services Program, and many more. This cooperation has been helpful in linking the military and civilian cultures. She is also in touch with a number of veterans' organizations such as Veterans for Common Sense and Student Veterans of America, an organization that works to make changes that help veterans feel more comfortable on campuses.

Her work has received wide attention. She has been interviewed by the *New York Times*, the *Wall Street Journal*, NPR, *Good Morning America*, NBC *Nightly News*, and military media outlets such as *Stars & Stripes*. Dr. Van Dahlen has testified on Capitol Hill on the VA and access to care. She has also participated in discussions at the Pentagon, the VA, the White House, and Congress. She is working with governors and state directors of Veterans Affairs on initiatives to address important issues at the local level. As if her day were longer than twenty-four hours, she also writes a monthly column for Veterans Advantage, an organization that connects veterans with low-cost assistance.

In 2009, she started a new national initiative, the Community Blueprint Network. It exists on the website Points of Light, an organization that harnesses volunteers in communities and solves social issues. Give An Hour received a large grant from the Bristol-Meyers Squibb Foundation and from Walmart to help finance the program. Dr. Van Dahlen's purpose is "to wrap the communities around those who serve and their families."[17] There are five areas that the organization tries to cover locally: behavioral health, employment, education, homelessness, and legal issues. One area, called Smart Funders, helps engage a philanthropic organization for these purposes. What the organization describes as preventive areas are family strength, reintegration, and volunteerism. Dr. Van Dahlen looks for community leaders, such as mayors or business leaders, to sponsor programs for veterans. She has also provided mental-health training about military issues to homeless shelters and established legal and financial assistance for veterans. Give an Hour works with Habitat for Humanity to help with employment opportunities, volunteer opportunities, and affordable housing. Dr. Van Dahlen has found that communities will naturally be interested and have organizations that concentrate on a few problems.

Give an Hour has been involved for almost a year in two communities, Fayetteville, North Carolina, and Richmond, Virginia. It is also taking shape in other communities around the country. In one community, the organization is going to create a military culture night so that children can learn about that culture. Dr. Van Dahlen is determined to close the gap between the civilian and military communities. Her goal is to provide opportunities to help soldiers "instead of saying we support our troops and applaud them at sporting events."[18]

Despite the large outreach of Give an Hour's Community Blueprint Network, Dr. Van Dahlen has only twelve people on her staff, but half of them are connected to the military. She feels that tapping people's skills and directing them to a worthy cause is rewarding work. She also draws upon the military culture's pride in serving their country and their communities. Thus she encourages the many who receive her organization's services to give back in a number of ways, such as driving other veterans to the VA. "Service is a huge part of healing and our philosophy. Many of them are not ready to go to a civilian job, so making sure that there are opportunities for them to volunteer in meaningful ways in their communities is really critical."[19]

ALWAYS LOST: A MEDITATION ON WAR

The most powerful reminders about war can happen in small places. Always Lost: A Meditation on War has taken on the significance of the Vietnam War Memorial, where soldiers, as well as their families and civilians, can come to talk and share their emotions. It was designed and conceived by three professors at a college in a small town in Nevada.

In fall 2008, sociology professor Don Carlson was stopped in his tracks by the *New York Times*'s Rosters of the Dead. "Four thousand faces of American military who had perished in the Iraq War stared at me," he said, "and I realized that this war has been perhaps one of the most impersonal wars ever fought."[20]

He approached Professor Marilee Swirczek with an idea, a collaboration between his sociology class, which would research and quantify the impersonal demographics of the Iraq War, and her creative writing class, which would personalize the war through poems, prose, and images. Retired Marine Major and English instructor Kevin Burns selected the name for the exhibit from an observation by the writer Gertrude Stein: "War is never fatal but always lost."[21]

Kevin Burns referred to the wars in Iraq and Afghanistan as the "2 percent war," because only 2 percent of our population know about it or even think about it. He and Marilee Swirczek decided to work on this exhibit as a class project. Because he took her creative writing class for ten years, they remained in close contact. They decided not to use a textbook for a semester but instead work on the theme of war and conflict in a civilized society and contemplate the human cost. The design and establishment of the exhibit took two semesters. They have been working on it for three years, and their efforts are ongoing. They also wanted a way to connect the wars in Iraq and Afghanistan to previous wars, to every conflict that occurred in history. Therefore, they selected dozens of meditations and philosophic statements from different countries. One by Plato, "Only the dead have seen the end of war,"[22] became their mantra. The meditations include observations by generals, veterans, and writers about the nature of warfare. The professors were involved with their students as they prepared the exhibit in a communal contemplation of war and conflict in a society we regard as civilized. The meditations played a large part in making the students think about war in a global sense.[23]

Professor Swirczek asked her students to go to the wall, look at all of the faces, chose one, and write either an elegiac poem or an essay for that person. Because the purpose of the exhibit was to involve the community in the costs of war, the poetry was a way of engaging the people who came to the exhibit.

The exhibit Always Lost: A Meditation on War is a place for veterans and their families to visit and connect with the names. Professor Swirczek sees this exhibit as a place not only for grieving family members but also for everyone in our society to look into their eyes. She regards it as a work in progress as long as our soldiers will be at war and die.[24]

The heart of Always Lost is the "Wall of the Dead," which is made up of individual photographs of the more than 6,200 US military war casualties in

Iraq and Afghanistan since September 11, 2001—sadly, the roster of the dead in Iraq and Afghanistan continues to grow

What began as a consideration of the effects of a distant war on the US population evolved into a powerful meditation on the personal effects of war on the whole community. The images and texts create a sacred space in which to contemplate the personal costs of the Iraq and Afghanistan wars, while participating in a powerful communal experience about this war and other wars in general. The catalog of this exhibit includes meditations by philosophers and writers on the costs of war, Iraq war photos, and stories of veterans who are students at Western Nevada College.

There was a wall set aside for photos of Noah Charles Pierce and for his poems. Professor Swirczek's class created a series of poems and prose pieces, many of them written by returning veterans who were also students at Western Nevada College, where this extraordinary exhibit took place.

A moving part of the exhibit is the following article.

"ESSAY: SEEKING ANSWERS TO THE WHY OF WAR"

—by Robert L. Cutts

I see dead people.

Not so strange, really. I'm a journalist. And for part of my life I was a war reporter. But what is spooky at times is the words that linger on, in the air, on the paper.

"My time is getting short, Mom, pray for me."

"Every time I read about another boy killed I relive my sorrow. But he believed so in what we are doing there."

"They haven't completed the mission, and they have to."

"Was it right? Was it wrong? I don't know. My anger destined me to hell. So many dead. So many killed."

What's scary to me is that the first two entries and the last two were written 40 years—seven American wars—apart.

The first were contents of a 1969 Memorial Day front-page story for the *Miami Herald.* It was by a Vietnam reporter colleague and friend who himself very nearly became one of those dead people.

The second two, I saw on a recent front page of a local paper—the words of one of our neighbors who lost her own son in Iraq—and on the walls at Western Nevada College, at the Always Lost exhibit now in the main gallery, where 4,139 more fallen Americans gaze back at me from the bloody shadows of Babylonia.

One was Noah Pierce, a soldier.

He didn't die from a bullet or bomb. He died from the inside out.

After two tours in Iraq filled his nightmares with enough dead people to explode, he came home and killed himself.

For us.

So that we, our children, lovers, parents, friends, did not have to join the 41 hundreds on the wall next to him.

Cheryl and Tom Softich did know this body, Noah Pierce. They are his mother and stepfather.

WNC took up an informal collection to help them travel here to Carson, so they could explain all that is in his eyes, and read again his oath of honor:

"So when you talk to me I may not seem to pay attention

I may forget to laugh at a joke

Remember freedom isn't free

I would do it all over for you."

Whether you were "over there," whether you wonder if you should be, or pay for those who are, or honor them, or don't think of them much at all because by the grace of God you don't know any of them, you lost more than a soldier when Noah was buried, fellow citizens.

You lost a poet, and a witness. Theresa Breeden's words, on the wall near Noah, spell out our loss in letters like tears:

"as though a forest's thin memory could reinvent the ashes."

We'll never know all that Noah's agony, and his love, would drive him to say. But we still hear his question in the wind—the question from the silent ranks of tens of thousands of servicewomen and men already prostrate in their sacrifice—and we must answer all of them.

Go to that good wall, read his words of American anguish—

"I don't want to die

I don't want to live

But should be dead

I'm already in hell."

—and answer them: After seven wars, and whatever those wars took from us or won for us, why are they all there?

Robert Cutts is a former journalism instructor at Western Nevada College and this piece is part of the exhibit.

As another part of the exhibit, Kevin Burns organized the display of photographs, spent endless hours finding them, and wrote an important piece that is part of the exhibit. He recounts the inspiration for his work on a wall in his photo display titled *Those Eyes.*

Over six thousand pairs of eyes, at last count, stare at me. I don't need their photos anymore to see their eyes. I see them in my sleep. They stare at me from television screens and car windshields and windows. They bore into me from walls. I am obsessed with their photos. I scan the Internet until 3:00 a.m., looking for photos to match a name. They have to be on the wall. Intellectually, I know we have to go to production, but I want—no, I need—just another and another.

We started downloading photos of the Iraq/Afghanistan war dead in February 2009. A work-study student at WNC was tasked with the mission. As the days turned into weeks, I talked with Marilee about the process of downloading the photos of our war dead, one by one. She started feeling depressed and having difficulty sleeping. I joined her in downloading the photos and immediately felt the same emotions. The sites from which we downloaded the photos often showed more than the standard boot camp graduation photo. They showed our dead service members playing Little League baseball, graduating from high school, getting married or holding their newborn children. They showed them embracing wives and husbands, girlfriends and boyfriends and partners. They showed our dead service members in their homes celebrating holidays. They were often smiling in the photos. Knowing that they will not smile again is difficult to comprehend.

Time became an issue. Students from Professor Swirczek's creative writing class volunteered to download photos. Additional students from WNC's Graphic Arts Department formatted the photos for printing. After over one thousand hours of research, downloading, and formatting, it was time to go to production.

Warriors do not line up on the parade deck, dress-right-dress, and die in an orderly fashion. War is chaos. To put organization and structure to their sacrifice seems obscene, so the faces of our fallen warriors are not in any alphabetical or chronological order.

We continue to search for photos as we are still engaged in combat. I will keep searching the Internet. I will find each one. I will look each of them in the eyes and tell them I am so proud of them. And I will thank them. I hope to God it was worth their sacrifice.

I urge all who view these men and women to gaze into their eyes and thank them, for they will be Always Lost to us.

—Kevin P. Burns
Major, USMC (RET.)
1978–1993
Operation Desert Shield/Storm

The exhibit began traveling around the country. The organizers were invited by Senator Reid and a congressman from Nevada to present the exhibit in Washington, DC. It received a $100,000 grant from the Carson Nugget Foundation as part of its Community First initiative, to fund the remounting and packing of the photos and literary works. It also has gained the support of the Nevada Arts Council, a division of the Department of Cultural Affairs and the National Endowment for the Arts; Nevada Humanities, and other organizations. The exhibit has attracted the attention of colleges, universities, and veterans' organizations and is scheduled at venues across the country through mid-2013. It will also be shown at the National Museum of American History, which is part of the Smithsonian. The gift also established a veterans' scholarship fund. Like Dr. Judith Broder's Soldiers Project, this important reflection shows that a college in a small town can have a lasting impact around the country that will act as a memorial for years after the wars in Iraq and Afghanistan have ended.

The exhibit has a guestbook that received countless pages of comments, many of them from military families. Because of the meditations, guestbook comments came from Korean, World War II, and Vietnam veterans. One Vietnam veteran wrote where he served, the dates, and but one word on the guestbook, *FINALLY*. Sometimes Professor Swirczek receives e-mails about the exhibit. One in particular moved her deeply.

> My family and I went to the exhibit tonight. It was very powerful and might possibly be a tool for me to move past the numbness I still experience since coming home. I know it might be strange to share that but I thought you might appreciate knowing that it certainly had an impact on me. I found one of my friend's faces but am still searching for the other ones. Maybe I'll locate them before the exhibit leaves. Thank you for bringing the exhibit to UW Washington County, it's so easy for those who haven't served to wander about everyday life forgetting all that's been sacrificed for our way of life.[25]

Professor Swirczek, Kevin Burns, and a poet who spent two and a half years helping with the exhibit were in a town in Wisconsin where the exhibit was installed. At the reception, they were surrounded by mothers, fathers, siblings, uncles, and aunts who thanked them. Many of them just wanted to know that their child was remembered. A mother with her son's dog tags around her neck and a photo came up to Marilee and told her son's story. Her son was nineteen years old when he died two years earlier. His unit was in a firefight in eastern Afghanistan, and he was shot through the head but lived. He was sent to Germany for medical attention, and the family flew to be there with him and to say good-bye to him before he died. He never regained consciousness. He had donated his organs, so he saved three other people.

Again and again, the organizers of the exhibit learned how important it was for the visitors to have other people acknowledge that their son or daughter lived. A lieutenant colonel complained about the lack of attention to the wars we are waging. He said, "All that was on the news was the royal wedding, and the numbers were just scrolled at the bottom of the screen, eight American troops and one civilian killed in Afghanistan, and that was it." Yet another visitor interviewed on CNN complained, "America is war weary. We don't want to hear about it."

A Vietnam veteran who also wanted to be remembered came to the gallery. He took his driver's license and veteran identification card, got a tack, and jammed it into a wall in the gallery. He also wrote a few lines with some imagery and tacked that up as well. The organizers were deeply touched by this gesture but, unfortunately, a janitor mistakenly removed those items.

The exhibit not only serves the need for veterans and their families to connect with the photos but for all members of our society to look into their eyes and recognize the sacrifice of our soldiers. It has generated an overwhelming response and has evolved into a powerful meditation on the effects of war on each one of us. It has become an accessible space in which to contemplate the personal costs and collective sacrifice of these particular conflicts.

Professor Swirczek made clear that she didn't have a political point to make. "What is most rewarding for us is the response from veterans—from World War II to Iraq and Afghanistan—who thank us for honoring those who return from war, and those who do not."[26]

EPILOGUE

Fig. E.1. Kevin Burns and the Wall of the Dead.
Photo courtesy of Marilee Swirczek.

The United States withdrew from Iraq at the end of December 2011. It has projected a withdrawal from Afghanistan that not all policymakers agree on but is supposedly expected for 2014 or beyond. But it will take decades for US troops and their families to cope with the wars' signature wounds, traumatic brain injuries from the blasts of IEDS (improvised explosive devices), EFPS (explosively formed penetrators), and HBIEDs (houseborne IEDs). These wars are not conventional wars. The explosive devices were concealed in trash and under bushes, buried in roads, and set off remotely using cell phones by insurgents who were watching out of sight, behind bushes or across the street in the cities. Further, the insurgents came from many countries. In Iraq, Iranian fighters poured across the border. In Afghanistan, fighters from Chechnya, Turkey, Uzbekistan, Pakistan, and Saudi Arabia took part in the war. The border between Afghanistan and Pakistan is just as porous as the border in Iraq. The insurgents who crossed into

Afghanistan were numerous—the Haqqanis, the Taliban, al Qaeda, and Lashkar-e-Taiba (the Army of the Pure).

Some soldiers feel that their time in Iraq has made a difference, that Iraqis now have more freedom and they are proud to have been part of that effort. Others have a different view, but all veterans want to be recognized for their service. In Afghanistan, US and NATO servicemen and servicewomen trained Afghan soldiers and police who were illiterate and unreliable. US troops have built roads and schools and treated wounded Afghanis in their hospitals. They not only fought a war but also sought to rebuild a country. US soldiers gave their lives in significant ways.

Veterans of both wars are proud of their service, but they have complex feelings about their time in combat. For example, some felt that there were not enough troops and that the military was using the wrong strategy. But they all see their deployments as defining times in their lives that have transformed them. Unfortunately, veterans of both Operation Iraqi Freedom (OIF) and Operation Enduring Freedom (OEF) find their homecoming difficult. Too many people are uninformed about the wars, and there is a deep disconnect between soldiers' experiences and life in the civilian world. As one veteran said, "There is a long way from Anbar, Iraq, to Southern New Jersey, where people are focused on their own lives." Another remarked that he felt as alien in his hometown as he was in Iraq.[1]

The United States has moved on to challenges such as the economy and a presidential campaign, with the wars at the bottom of concerns about jobs, debt, taxes, and healthcare. Given the fact that our army is a volunteer army and that only 1 percent of Americans over eighteen served in Afghanistan and Iraq, there is little dialogue between society and the military.

There is a lack of understanding not only of the soldiers who served in these wars but also of the toll their service has taken on their families. Families are caring for wounded servicemen and servicewomen, both parents and spouses. Some spouses have given up their jobs to care for their veterans and live on small disability payments, a burden they will face for the rest of their lives. There are not only the physical wounds of war but also the emotional and psychological effects of so many years in combat. Some of the troops will receive the care they need and recover, while too many commit suicide or carry these traumas with them for years to come. Meanwhile, this nation is in the midst of plans for cutting the Pentagon's budget, in particular, military personnel benefits and salaries, including scaling back its healthcare, Tricare, and the retirement system for veterans.

We live in a society where too many people are focused on the present and feel uncomfortable with physical and emotional pain. If we want to honor and thank our troops, we should remember what they have accomplished and what they are still experiencing. Living in the present, civilians have the luxury of managing their memories. We all have both good and difficult memories, but we are able to turn them off if we wish. Servicemen and servicewomen do not have that option. Many of them suffer from PTSD (Post-Traumatic Stress Disorder) or MST (Military Sexual Trauma), and as a lieutenant colonel said, "they wake up with the ghosts of the dead."[2] They have served our country with their lives and need to be remembered, not just on Veterans Day but every day.

NOTES

INTRODUCTION

1. Rick Maze, "18 Veterans Commit Suicide Each Day," *Army Times*, April 22, 2010.

CHAPTER 1: THE WARS IN IRAQ AND AFGHANISTAN

1. Brian Turner, *Here, Bullet* (London: Bloodaxe Books, 2007), p. 9.

2. Rod Powers, "The Cost of War," US Military, About.com, September 7, 2008, http://usmilitary.about.com/od/terrorism/a/iraqdeath1000.htm (accessed May 1, 2012).

3. Anna Berlinrut, interview with the author, August 7, 2011.

4. Tim Arango, "Iraq's Prime Minister Gains More Power after Political Crisis," *New York Times*, February 27, 2012.

5. Mark Danner, *Stripping Bare the Body: Politics, Violence, War* (New York: Nation Books, 2009), p. 388.

6. Larry C. Johnson, "The Arrogance and Hubris of Jerry Bremer," *No Quarter* (blog), http://www.noquarterusa.net/blog/125/the-arrogance-and-hubris-of-jerry-bremer/ (accessed 04/14/12).

7. Shannon P. Meehan, *Beyond Duty: Life on the Frontline in Iraq* (Malden, MA: Polity Press, 2009), p. 24.

8. Ibid., p. 36.

9. Dexter Filkins, *The Forever War* (New York: Vintage Books, 2009), p. 116.

10. Ibid., p. 117.

11. "The Soldier's Heart," *Frontline*, PBS, March 1, 2005.

12. Anonymous veteran, interview with the author, November 2010.

13. Walter Pincus, "Iraqi Security Forces Facing Serious Problems, U.S. Oversight Official Reports." *Washington Post,* January 30, 2011.

14. Filkins, *Forever War*, p. 121.

15. Ibid., p. 122

16. "Soldier's Heart," *Frontline*.

17. Anonymous mother of a deceased soldier, interview with the author.

18. Anonymous veterans, interviews with the author.

19. Anonymous veteran, interview with the author.

20. Ahmed Rashid, *Taliban: Militant Islam, Oil and Fundamentalism in Central Asia* (New Haven, CT: Yale University Press, 2010), p. 13.

21. Ibid., pp. 43–45.

22. Thomas Barfield, *Afghanistan: A Cultural and Political History* (Princeton, NJ: Princeton University Press, 2010), pp. 255–57.

23. Toni Johnson and Lauren Vriens, "Islam: Governing under Sharia," Council on Foreign Relations, November 2010, http://www.cfr.org/religion/islam-governing -under-sharia/p8034 (accessed May 1, 2012).

24. Seth G. Jones, *In the Graveyard of Empires: America's War in Afghanistan* (New York: W. W. Norton, 2010), pp. 91–93.

25. Ibid., pp. 91–95.

26. Ahmed Rashid, *Descent into Chaos* (New York: Penguin Books, 2009), p. 177.

27. Jones, *In the Graveyard of Empires*, p. 128.

28. Ahmed Rashid, *Taliban: Militant Islam, Oil and Fundamentalism in Central Asia*, 2nd ed. (New Haven, CT: Yale University Press, 2010), pp. 217–25.

29. Institute for the Study of War, "Haqqani Network," http://www.understand-ingwar.org/themenode/haqqani-network (accessed July 12, 2011).

30. Gail Carlotta, "Old-Line Taliban Commander Is Face of Rising Afghan Threat," *New York Times,* June 17, 2008.

31. Rashid, *Taliban*, p. 227.

32. Jones, *In the Graveyard of Empires*, pp. 148–50.

33. Ibid., pp. 141–42.

34. Rashid, *Descent into Chaos*, pp. 90–95.

35. Rashid, *Taliban*, pp. 230–33.

36. David Ignatius, "An Afghan Test for the Obama Doctrine," *Washington Post*, October 8, 2009.

37. Anonymous veterans, interviews with the author.

38. Jennifer Baldino, interview with the author, May 5, 2011.

39. Terri Tanielian, Lisa H. Jaycox, "Invisible Wounds of War," RAND Corporation Monograph, January 2008; Anonymous war veterans and their spouses, interviews with the author, 2010–2011.

40. "Life and Death Decisions Weigh on Junior Officers," *New York Times*, December 21, 2010.

41. "Humvee with Chimney for Safety Draws Military's Interest," *New York Times,* July 23, 2011.

42. Malalai Joya with Darrick O'Keefe, *A Woman among Warlords* (New York: Scribner, 2009), p. 126.

43. Joya and O'Keefe, *Woman among Warlords*.

44. "Afghan Anger over 'Rigged' Parliamentary Vote," BBC News, South Asia Report, November 10, 2010.

45. Ahmed Rashid, "The Way out of Afghanistan," *New York Review of Books*, January 2011, pp. 25–27.

46. Ibid.

47. Alissa J. Rubin, "Taliban Extend Reach to North, Where Armed Groups Reign," *New York Times*, December 15, 2010.

48. Carlotta Gall and Ruhullah Khapalwak, "NATO Push Deals Taliban a Setback in Kandahar," *New York Times*, December 16, 2010.

49. Rod Nordland, "Some Police Recruits Impose 'Islamic Tax' on Afghans," *New York Times*, June 12, 2011.

50. Ibid.

51. Ibid.

52. Rashid, *Taliban*, pp. 236–37.

53. "Lashkar-e-Taiba," Times Topics, *New York Times*, April 3, 2012, http://topics .nytimes.com/top/reference/timestopics/organizations/l/lashkaretaiba/index.html (accessed April 14, 2012).

54. Jones, *In the Graveyard of Empires*, pp. 224–26, 286.

55. Jayshree Bajoria and Eben Kaplan, "The ISI and Terrorism: Behind the Accusations," *Backgrounder*, Council on Foreign Relations, May 4, 2011, http:// www.cfr.org/pakistan/isi-terrorism-behind-accusations/p11644 (accessed April 14, 2012).

56. Joshua Hammer, "Prisoner of the Taliban," *New York Review of Books*, March 10, 2011, pp. 12–14.

57. "Ashfaq Parvez Kayani," Times Topics, *New York Times*, December 22, 2011, http://topics.nytimes.com/top/reference/timestopics/people/k/ashfaq_parvez_kay ani/index.html (accessed April 15, 2012).

58. "A Rivalry That Threatens the World," *Economist*, May 19, 2011, http:// www.economist.com/node/18712274 (accessed April 15, 2012).

59. Rashid, *Descent into Chaos*, pp. 402–409; Saeed Shah, "Pakistan Flood Response Prompts Rising Anti-government Resentment," *Guardian*, August 13, 2010.

60. Mian Ridge, "Bin Laden Killing Deepens Indian Distrust of Pakistan," *Christian Science Monitor*, May 6, 2011.

61. Jane Perlez, "Pakistan Pulls Closer to a Reluctant China," Asia Pacific, *New York Times*, October 6, 2011, http://www.nytimes.com/2011/10/07/world/asia/pakistan-pulls-closer-to-a-reluctant-china.html?_r=1&scp=2&sq=pakistan %20and%20china&st=cse (accessed April 15, 2012); M. K. Bhadrakumar, "Pakistan, Iran Become 'Natural Allies,'" Asia Times, July 19, 2011, http://www.atimes .com/atimes/ south_asia/mg19df02.html (accessed April 15, 2012).

62. Salman Massod and David E. Sanger, "Militants Attack Pakistani Naval Base in Karachi," Asia Pacific, *New York Times*, May 22, 2011, http://www.nytimes.com/2011/05/23/world/asia/23pakistan.html?scp=1&sq=Pakistan%20naval%20base %20attacked&st=cse, (accessed April 15, 2012).

63. "Pakistan Suicide Bomber Attacks Islamabad Bank," BBC News, South East Asia, June 13, 2011, http://www.bbc.co.uk/news/world-south-asia-13748838 (accessed April 15, 2012).

64. "Ashfaq Parvez Kayani," Times Topics, *New York Times*, December 22, 2011, http://topics.nytimes.com/top/reference/timestopics/people/k/ashfaq_parvez_kayani/index.html (accessed April 15, 2012).

65. Jane Perlez and Ismail Khan, "Pakistan Tells U.S. It Must Sharply Cut C.I.A. Activities," Asia Pacific, *New York Times*, April 11, 2011, http://www.nytimes.com 2011/04/12/world/asia/12pakistan.html?scp=3&sq=ISI%20want%20to%20end%20drone%20attacks&st=cse (accessed April 15, 2012).

66. Jane Perlez, "Pakistani Army Chief Faces Calls to Take Harder Line against U.S.," *International Herald Tribune*, June 16, 2011.

67. Eric Schmitt and Mark Mazetti, "Obama Adviser Outlines Plans to Defeat Al Qaeda," World, *New York Times*, June 29, 2011, http://www.nytimes.com/2011/06/30/world/30terror.html?scp=9&sq=mullah%20omar%20hiding%20in%20pakistan&st=cse (accessed April 15, 2012).

68. Eric Schmitt and Jane Perlez, "U.S. Is Deferring Millions in Pakistani Military Aid," Asia Pacific, *New York Times*, July 9, 2011, http://www.nytimes.com/2011/07/10/world/asia/10intel.html?scp=2&sq=US%20cuts%20military%20aid%20to%20Pakistan&st=cse (accessed April 15, 2012).

69. Jane Perlez and Eric Schmitt, "Pakistan's Spies Tied to Slaying of a Journalist," *New York Times*, July 5, 2011.

70. C. J. Chives, "In Eastern Afghanistan: At War with the Taliban's Shadowy Rule," *New York Times*, February 7, 2011.

71. Greg Mortenson, *Stones into Schools* (New York: Viking, 2009).

72. David Rhode and Kristen Mulvihill, *A Rope and a Prayer: A Kidnapping from Two Sides* (New York: Viking, 2010), p. 223.

73. Graham Bowley and Declan Walsh, "Afghan Officials Consider Own Talks with Taliban," Asia Pacific, *New York Times*, January 30, 2012, http://www.nytimes.com/2012/01/31/world/asia/afghan-officials-consider-separate-talks-with-taliban.html?scp=1&sq=karzai%20opens%20negotiations%20with%20taliban&st=cse (accessed April 15, 2012).

74. Anonymous veterans, interviews with the author.

75. Ray Rivera, Alissa J. Rubin, Thom Shanker, "Deadliest Day of Afghan War for U.S. Forces," *New York Times*, August 7, 2011.

76. "Drawdown in Iraq," Opinion Pages, *New York Times*, January 13, 2011, http://www.nytimes.com/2011/07/14/opinion/14thurs2.html (accessed April 15, 2012).

77. Steven Lee Myers, Thom Shanker, and Jack Healy, "Politics in Iraq Casts Doubt on a U.S. Presence after 2011," Middle East, *New York Times*, December 10,

2010, http://www.nytimes.com/2010/12/19/world/middleeast/19iraq.html?page wanted=all (accessed April 16, 2012).

78. Phil Sands, "Iraqis Demand End to 'Occupation,'" *National*, July 14, 2008, http://www.thenational.ae/news/world/middle-east/iraqis-demand-end-to-occupation (accessed April 16, 2012).

79. Tim Arango, "Spike in U.S. Deaths in Iraq Raises Worries," *New York Times Global Edition, Middle East*, June 26, 2011, http://www.nytimes.com/2011/06/27/world/middleeast/27iraq.html?_r=1&scp=1&sq=june%202011%20bloodiest%20m onth%20in%20Iraq&st=cse (accessed April 16, 2012).

80. Michael S. Schmidt, "Threat Resurges in Deadliest Day of Year for Iraq," *New York Times*, August 16, 2011.

81. Quil Lawrence, "Afghan Assembly To Discuss U.S. Relations, " *All Things Considered*, NPR, November 15, 2011.

82. *New York Times*, October 23, 2011, http://www.nytimes.com/2011/ 10/23/world/middleeast/us-scales-back-diplomacy-in-iraq-amid-fiscal-and-security -concerns.html?scp=1&sq=%22U.S.+scales+back+diplomacy%22&st=nyt (accessed September 10, 2011).

83. "Names of the Dead," *New York Times*, October 22, 2011.

84. Alissa J. Rubin, "Attack at Kabul Hotel Deflates Security Hopes in Afghanistan," *New York Times*, June 29, 2011.

85. Ibid.

86. "Maulana Fazlullah," Times Topics, *New York Times*, July 8, 2009, http:// topics.nytimes.com/top/reference/timestopics/people/f/maulana_fazlullah/index .html?scp=1&sq=taliban%20beheadings&st=cse (accessed April 16, 2012).

87. Alissa J. Rubin, "Attack on Helicopter in Afghanistan Adds to Signs of an Unstable Region," *New York Times*, August 8, 2011.

88. Alissa J. Rubin, "Brawl Erupts During Impeachment Talks in Afghan Parliament," *New York Times*, July 6, 2011.

89. Ahmed Rashid, "The Afghan Enforcer I Knew," *International Herald Tribune*, July 14, 2011.

90. Talimoor Shah and Alissa. J. Rubin, "Suicide Bomber Sent by Taliban Assassinates Kandahar's Mayor," *New York Times*, July 28, 2011.

91. "Ghuam Haider Hamidi," Obituary, *Economist*, August 6–12, 2011, p. 36.

92. Alissa J. Rubin, "Blast Kills Chief of Peace Council in Afghanistan," *New York Times*, September 21, 2011.

93. Margaret Warner, "Mike Mullen Criticizes Pakistan as a Difficult Ally," *PBS NewsHour*, September 26, 2011.

94. C. J. Chivers, "In Dust and Danger, Bloodying an Afghan Foe," *New York Times*, October 3, 2011.

95. Carlotta Gall, "Pakistani Military Still Cultivates Militant Groups, a Former

Fighter Says," Asia Pacific, *New York Times,* July 3, 2011, http://www.nytimes.com/2011/07/04/world/asia/04pakistan.html?scp=5&sq=Pakistan%20military%20involvement%20in%20Afghanistan&st=cse (accessed April 16, 2012).

96. C. J. Chivers, "Tensions Flare as G.I.'s Take Fire out of Pakistan," *New York Times,* October 17, 2011.

97. Aryn Baker, "The Unwinnable War," *Time,* October 24, 2011.

98. Brian Steller, "Afghan War Just a Slice of Coverage," *New York Times,* January 20, 2010.

99. Cameron Baker, interview with the author, May 25, 2010.

100. Meehan, *Beyond Duty,* p. 132.

101. James Dao and Andrew W. Lehren, "In Accelerating Pace of War, American Deaths Surpass 1,000," *New York Times,* May 19, 2010.

102. Elisabeth Bumiller, "U.S. Lifts Photo Ban on Military Coffins," *New York Times,* December 7, 2009, http://www.nytimes.com/2009/02/27/world/americas/27iht-photos.1.20479953.html (accessed April 16, 2012).

103. David Finkel, *The Good Soldiers* (Picador, New York, 2009), p. 141.

104. Judith Butler, *Frames of War: When Is Life Grievable?* (London, New York: Verso, 2010), pp. 64–70.

CHAPTER 2: HOMECOMING AND PARALLEL LIVES

1. Brian Turner, *Here, Bullet* (London: Bloodaxe Books, 2007).

2. Anonymous veteran, interview with author, June 2010.

3. Shannon Meehan, *Beyond Duty: Life on the Frontline in Iraq* (Malden, MA: Polity Press, 2009).

4. Anonymous veteran, interview with author, June 2010.

5. Amy Smee, interview with the author, December 2009.

6. Jonathan Shay, *Odysseus in America: Combat Trauma and the Trials of Homecoming* (New York: Scribner, 2002), p. 35.

7. "The Wounded Platoon," *Frontline,* PBS, May 18, 2010.

8. Ibid.

9. Ibid.

10. "The Soldier's Heart," *Frontline,* PBS, February 2009.

11. Jim Dooley, Vietnam veteran and counselor on ibid.

12. Dave Grossman with Loren W. Christensen, *On Combat: the Psychology and Physiology of Deadly Conflict in War and Peace* (China: Warrior Science Publications, 2008).

13. Ibid.

14. Anonymous veteran, interview with the author, 2010.

15. Anonymous lieutenant colonel, interview with the author, 2010.

16. Lisa W. Foderaro, "From Battlefield to Ivy League, on the G.I. Bill," *New York Times*, January 9, 2010, http://www.nytimes.com/2010/01/09/nyregion/09gis.html?_r=1&page wanted=all (accessed April 18, 2012).

17. Heather Demoines, interview with the author, 2010.

18. Ibid., May 2009.

19. Amy Smee, interview with author, May 2009.

20. Cameron Baker, interview with author, March 2010.

21. Ibid.

22. "Invisible Wounds of War," RAND Corporation, Center for Military Health Policy Research, March 24, 2009.

23. Ibid.

24. Heather Demoines, interview with author, May 2009.

25. "Taking Off the Armor," *At War* (blog), *New York Times*, http://atwar.blogs .nytimes.com/2011/01/11/taking-off-the-armor/ (accessed November 12, 2011).

26. Anonymous veteran, interview with the author, June 2010.

27. "Taking Off the Armor."

28. Vladislav Tamarov, *Afghanistan: Soviet Vietnam* (San Francisco, CA: Mercury House, 1992).

29. "The Wounded Platoon," *Frontline*, PBS, May 18, 2010.

30. *OEF/OIF Veterans' Statistics, Department of Veterans Affairs*, VA pamphlet, http://www.bamc.amedd.army.mil/wtb/docs/va-pamphlet.pdf (accessed April 2010).

31. Jean Twenge, *Generation Me: Why Today's Young Americans Are More Confident, Assertive, Entitled and More Miserable Than Ever Before* (New York: Free Press, 2007).

32. Tim McGirk, "The War Comes Home," *Time International*, December 7, 2009.

33. Anonymous lieutenant colonel, interview with author, April 2011.

34. Elisabeth Bumiller, "Gates Fears Wider Gap between Country and Military," *New York Times*, September 9, 2010.

35. Shay, *Odysseus in America.*

36. Anonymous warrior, *Bulldog Blog*, July 5, 2010, http://www.notalone .com?warrior-blog (accessed April 11, 2011).

37. Ibid. (accessed April 25, 2009).

38. Ibid.

39. Gloria Hillard, "Female Veterans Struggle to Stay off the Streets," NPR, August 11, 2010.

40. Jan Goodwin, "Women's VA Heath Care Falls Short," *Good Housekeeping*, http://www.goodhousekeeping.com/health/womens-health/va-healthcare-falls-short (accessed March 25, 2010).

41. Hillard, "Female Veterans Struggle to Stay off the Streets."

42. Tom Wilborn, "Women Veterans Focus on Heath Care Service," *Disabled American Veterans Magazine*, November/December 2010, p. 5.

43. Hillard, "Female Veterans Struggle to Stay off the Streets."

44. "Homeless Veterans Stand Down," *60 Minutes*, October, 17, 2010, http://www.cbsnews.com/video/watch/?id=6966795n&tag=mncol;lst;2, (accessed April 19, 2012).

45. Elisabeth Bumiller, "Gates Fears Wider Gap between Country and Military," *New York Times*, September 9, 2010.

46. Brian Mann, "Military Moms Face Tough Choices," NPR, May 26, 2008.

47. Demoines, interview.

48. Ibid.

49. Damien Cave, "Women With Post-Traumatic Stress Tend to Seek Isolation," *New York Times*, November 1, 2009.

50. Ibid.

51. Anonymous mother, interview with the author, May 2010.

52. Ibid.

53. James Gandolfini (executive producer) and Jon Alpert and Ellen Goosenberg Kent (directors), *Wartorn 1861–2010* (2011) HBO documentary.

54. Tim Kahlor, interview with the author, May 2011.

55. Ibid.

56. Ibid.

57. Ibid.

58. Ibid.

59. Ibid.

60. Ibid.

61. Ibid.

62. Ibid.

63. Ibid.

64. Nancy Lessin, interview with the author, May 2010.

65. Military Family Speak Out, http://www.mfso.org/ (accessed May, 2011).

CHAPTER 3: MOTHERS OF SERVICEMEN AND SERVICEWOMEN

1. Brian Turner, *Here, Bullet* (London: Bloodaxe Books, 2007).

2. Sara Ruddick, *Maternal Thinking: Toward a Politics of Peace* (New York: Random House, 1990).

3. Patricia Hohl, interview with the author, December 2010.

4. Ibid.

5. Ibid.

6. Ibid.

7. Ibid.

8. Ibid.

9. Cheryl Softich, interview with the author, April 2009.

10. Ibid.

11. Marguerite Bouvard, *Women Reshaping Human Rights: How Extraordinary Women Are Changing the World* (Lanham, MD: Rowman and Littlefield, 1996).

12. Softich, interview.

13. Sara Rich, interview with the author, January 2011.

14. Ibid.

15. Sara Corbett, "The Women's War," *New York Times Magazine*, March 18, 2007, pp. 14–17.

16. Ibid., p. 16.

17. Rich, interview.

18. Jan Goodwin, "Women's VA Heath Care Falls Short," http://www.goodhousekeeping.com/health/womens-health/va-healthcare-falls-short (accessed March 25, 2010).

19. Corbett, "Women's War," p. 17.

20. Rich, interview.

21. Ibid.

22. Anna Berlinrut, interview with the author, November 2011.

23. Ibid.

24. Adele Kubein, interview with the author, November 2011.

25. Ibid.

26. "Women Should Be Allowed in Combat Units," Coalition for Iraq+ Afghanistan Veterans, January 2011, http://coalitionforveterans.org/2011/01/report-women-should-be-allowed-in-combat-units/ (accessed April 20, 2012).

27. Kubein, interview.

28. Ibid.

29. Eligibility rules for VA healthcare benefits have changed, and National Guard members called to active duty may now qualify for healthcare and enroll within five years of the date separated from military service.

30. Kubein, interview.

31. Ibid.

32. Ibid.

33. Anonymous grandmother, interview with the author, December 2010.

34. Ibid.

35. Patricia Alviso, interview with the author, May 2011.

36. Ibid.

37. Marguerite Bouvard, *Revolutionizing Motherhood: The Mothers of the Plaza de Mayo* (Lanham, MD: Rowman & Littlefield, 1994) and Bouvard, *Women Reshaping Human Rights*.

CHAPTER 4: SPOUSES AND CHILDREN OF SERVICEMEN AND SERVICEWOMEN

1. Jehanne Dubrow, *Stateside* (Evanston, IL: Northwestern University Press, 2010).

2. Alyssa J. Mansfield et al., "Deployment and the Use of Mental Health Services among U.S. Army Wives," *New England Journal of Medicine* (January 14, 2010): 101.

3. Ibid., p. 108.

4. Joseph Shapiro, "Army Wives Battle with Their Own Mental Health," NPR, January 19, 2010.

5. Michael Winerip, "Joy and Anticipation for Soldiers' Return Home," *New York Times,* May 10, 2009.

6. Ibid.

7. Adam Wojack, "The Impact of Another Soldier's Death," *At War* (blog), May 24, 2010, http://atwar.blogs.nytimes.com/2010/05/24/the-impact-of-another-soldiers -death (accessed May 9, 2012).

8. Brooke Kinna, interview with the author, May 2010.

9. Anthony Shadid, "The Long, Long Shadow of Early Missteps in Iraq," Week in Review, *New York Times*, February 20, 2010, http://www.nytimes.com/2010/02/21/ weekinreview/21shadid.html?pagewanted=all (accessed April 23, 2012).

10. Jehanne Dubrow, interview with the author, October 2009.

11. Ibid.

12. Jennifer Baldino, interview with the author, May 5, 2011.

13. Ibid.

14. Ibid.

15. Ibid.

16. Ibid.

17. Leah Curran, interview with the author, March 8, 2011.

18. John H. Krystal et al., "Adjunctive Risperidone Treatment for Antidepressant-Resistant Symptoms of Chronic Military Service–Related PTSD: A Randomized Trial," *Journal of the American Medical Association* (2011), http://jama.ama-assn.org/search?full text=anti-psychotic+drugs+for+PTSD&submit=yes&x=12&y=7 (accessed April 24, 2012).

19. Benedict Carey, "Anti-psychotic Use Is Questioned for Combat Stress," *New York Times*, August 3, 2011.

20. Leah Curran, interview.

21. Angela Buckley, interview with the author, May 10, 2011.

22. Ibid.

23. Ivy Brashear, "Caregivers of Wounded Soldiers Find Their Lives Are Also Changed; Getting Compensation," *Kentucky Health News*, September 28, 2011, http://

kyhealthnews.blogspot.com/2011/09/caregivers-of-wounded-soldiers-find.html (accessed April 24, 2012).

24. "Looking After the Veteran, Back Home and Damaged," *New York Times*, September 28, 2011.

25. Sacha Pfeiffer, "For Military Kids, Massachusetts Can Be a Lonely Place," WBUR Radio, May 30, 2011.

26. Buckley, interview.

27. Gail L. Zellman et al., "Options for Improving the Military Child Care System," RAND Corporation, 2008, http://www.rand.org/pubs/occasional_papers/2008/RAND_OP217.pdf (accessed April 24, 2012).

CHAPTER 5: THE HIGH RATE OF SUICIDES

1. Marguerite Guzmán Bouvard, "Specialist Noah Charles Pierce," *Magnolia* 2 (2012).

2. Brett Coughlin, "Veterans Committees to Look at Suicides," *Politico*, http://www.politico.com/news/stories/0511/55605.html (accessed May 10, 2012).

3. Bruce Shapiro, "Casualties of War," *Nation*, January 28, 2008, pp. 7–9. Reprinted in "Always Lost: Meditation on War," Western Nevada College, Carson City, NV, 2009.

4. Ibid.

5. Ibid.

6. "VA Confirms 18 Vets Commit Suicide Every Day," *Public Record*, April 22, 2008, http://pubrecord.org/nation/322/va-confirms-18-vets-commit-suicide-every-day/ (accessed April 26, 2012); Aaron Glantz, "Suicides Highlight Failures of Veterans' Support System," *New York Times*, March 12, 2012, http://www.nytime s.com/2012/03/25/us/recent-california-suicides-highlight-failures-of-veterans-support-system.html?_r =1&pagewanted=all (accessed April 26, 2012); Brian Maxwell, "1 Suicide Every 36 Hours," *Iraq and Afghanistan Veterans of America Blog*, September 15, 2010, http://iava .org/blog/1-suicide-every-36-hours (accessed April 26, 2012).

7. Anonymous member of Veterans for Common Sense, interview with the author, August 2011.

8. Shannon P. Meehan, "Distant Wars, Constant Ghosts," *Opinionator* (blog), *New York Times*, February 22, 2010, http://opinionator.blogs.nytimes.com/2010/02/22/distant-wars-constant-ghosts/ (accessed September 20, 2011).

9. Nassir Ghaemi, "The Bell Tolls: Military Suicide in Iraq; Why Are Soldiers Killing Themselves?" *Mood Swings* (blog), February 13, 2009, http://www.psychology today.com/blog/mood-swings/200902/the-bell-tolls-military-suicide-in-iraq (accessed March 9, 2009).

10. "The Other Enemy," Editorial, *International Herald Tribune*, July 24, 2010.

11. Coughlin, "Veterans Committees to Look at Suicides."

12. Brett Coughlin, "Senators Urge White House to Send Suicide Condolences," *Politico*, May 26, 2011, http://www.politico.com/news/stories/0511/55747.html #ixzz1tD2I7JKl (accessed April 26, 2012).

13. Amy Goodman, "Soldier Suicides and the Politics of Presidential Condolences," *TruthDig Report*, July 12, 2011, http://www.truthdig.com/report/item/soldier _suicides_and_the_politics_of_presidential_condolences_20110712/ (accessed April 26, 2012).

14. Bob Herbert, "War's Psychic Toll," *New York Times*, May 18, 2009, http://www.nytimes.com/2009/05/19/opinion/19herbert.html (accessed April 26, 2012).

15. Robert Gebbia, "Military Suicide—The War within Our Ranks," appearance before the Senate Armed Services Committee, June 28, 2010, *The Hill*, http://the hill.com/opinion/op-ed/106033-military-suicide-the-war-within-our-ranks (accessed 04/27/12).

16. Ibid.

17. "Suicide Rate among Young Women Veterans More Than Twice That of Civilians," December 1, 2010, *ScienceDaily*, http://www.sciencedaily.com/releases/ 2010/12/101201162113.htm (accessed April 27, 2012).

18. James Dao and Dan Frosch, "Feeling Warehoused in Army Trauma Units," *New York Times*, April 24, 2010, http://www.nytimes.com/2010/04/25/health/25warrior .html (accessed March 23, 2011).

19. Ibid.

20. Ibid.

21. Dao and Frosch, "Feeling Warehoused in Army Trauma Care Units."

22. Jan Goodwin, "Women's VA Health Care Falls Short," *Good Housekeeping*, http://www.goodhousekeeping.com/health/womens-health/va-healthcare-falls-short?click=main_sr (accessed April 27, 2012).

23. "More Excuses and Delays From the V.A.," Editorial, *New York Times*, August 21, 2011, http://www.nytimes.com/2011/08/22/opinion/more-excuses-and-delays-from-the-va.html (accessed April 27, 2012).

24. Coughlin, "Veterans Committees to Look at Suicides."

25. "More Excuses and Delays from the V.A."

26. Robert L. Hanafin, "Military Spouse and Family Suicide Attempts Need Attention," *Veterans Today*, January 14, 2010, p. 5, http://www.veteranstoday.com/ 2010/01/14/military-spouse-and-family-suicide-attempts-need-attention/ (accessed April 27, 2012).

27. Alyssa J. Mansfield, Jay S. Kaufman, Stephen W. Marshall, Bradley N. Gaynes, Joseph P. Morrissey, and Charles C. Engel, "Deployment and the Use of Mental Health

Services among U.S. Army Wives," *New England Journal of Medicine* (2010): 101–105, http://www.nejm.org/doi/full/10.1056/NEJMoa0900177 (accessed April 26, 2012).

28. "Some Seek Mental Health Checks for Spouses of Multiple Deployed Soldiers," *Stars and Stripes,* July 5, 2009.

29. "War's Silent Stress: The Family at Home," *Virginian Pilot,* August 9, 2009.

30. Stacy Bannerman, "Multiple Deployments May Raise Risk of Military Spouse Suicide," *Truthout,* October 24, 2009, http://archive.truthout.org/1024092 (accessed April 27, 2012).

31. Alison Buckholtz, "War, Wives and a Near Suicide," *At War* (blog), April 25, 2011, http://atwar.blogs.nytmes.com/2011/04/25/war-wives-and-a-near-suicide (accessed September, 2011).

32. Ibid.

33. David Finkel, *The Good Soldiers* (New York: Farrar, Straus and Giroux), pp. 133–35.

34. James Dao, "Grieving Families Feel Slighted as Military Suicides Fall Short of Full Honors," *New York Times,* November, 26, 2009.

35. Maggie Fox, "Military Suicide Prevention Efforts Fail," *Reuters,* September 23, 2010, http://www.reuters.com/article/2010/09/23/us-suicide-military-usa-idUS TRE68M5G720100923 (accessed April 26, 2012).

36. James C. McKinley Jr., "Despite Army's New Efforts, Suicides Continue at Grim Pace," *New York Times,* October 11, 2010.

37. Greg Jaffe, "Honoring the Service of Soldiers Who Commit Suicide," *Washington Post,* July 18, 2010, http://www.washingtonpost.com/wp-dyn/content/article/2010/07/17/AR2010071702692.html (accessed April 27, 2012).

38. Mark Russell, "Questions Raised about Rising Suicide Rates in the U.S. Military," *Newservice,* November 2, 2011.

39. "Soldier Suicide Attempts Skyrocket," CBS News, January 30, 2008, http://www.cbsnews.com/stories/2008/01/30/eveningnews/main3772831.shtml?tag =mncol;lst;1 (accessed April 27, 2012); "With Military Suicides on the Rise, Parents of Two Soldiers Who Took Their Own Lives Say Obama's Words Ring Hollow," *Democracy Now!* August 6, 2010, http://www.democracynow.org/2010/8/6/with_military _suicides_on_the_rise (accessed April 27, 2012).

40. Goodwin, "Soldier Suicides"; Dao, "Grieving Families Feel Slight."

41. Brian Turner, *Here, Bullet* (Farmington, ME: Alice James Books, 2005), p. 20.

42. James Gandolfini (executive producer) and Jon Alpert and Ellen Goosenberg Kent (directors), *Wartorn 1861–2010* (2011) HBO documentary.

43. James Schugel, "Death after War: A Minnesota Soldier's Story," CBS Minnesota, May 4, 2011, http://minnesota.cbslocal.com/2011/05/04/death-after-war-a -minnesot-soldiers-story/ (accessed April 27, 2012).

44. Ibid.

45. Jim Dooley (Vietnam veteran and counselor), "The Soldier's Heart," *Frontline*, PBS, February 2009.

46. Cheryl Softich, interview with the author, April 2009.

47. Dooley, "Soldier's Heart."

48. Ibid.

49. Schugel, "Death after War."

50. Cheryl Softich with Marguerite Guzmán Bouvard, *The Short and Noble Life of Specialist Noah Charles Pierce* (Waban, MA: In Publications, 2010), p. 31.

51. Cheryl Softich, interview with the author, August 2011.

52. Brooke Kinna, interview with the author, May 2010.

53. Ibid.

54. Joyce Lucey, interview with the author, May 9, 2011.

55. Irene Sege, "Something Happened to Jeff: Jeff Lucey Returned from Iraq a Changed Man and Then He Killed Himself," *Boston Globe*, March 1, 2005.

56. Christopher Buchanan, "A Reporter's Journey: In the Tragic Story of Marine Lance Cpl. Jeff Lucey and His Ordeal in Iraq, What Really Happened?" *Frontline*, PBS, March 1, 2005, http://www.pbs.org/wgbh/pages/frontline/shows/heart/lucey (accessed September, 2011).

57. "Soldier's Heart," *Frontline*.

58. Kevin C. Lucey, interview with the author, May 2011.

59. Ibid.

60. Ibid.

61. Ibid.

62. "With Military Suicides on the Rise," *Democracy Now!*

63. Coughlin, "Veterans Committees to Look at Suicides."

64. Erica Goodie, "After Combat, Victims of an Inner War," *New York Times*, August 1, 2009, http://www.nytimes.com/2009/08/02/us/02suicide.html?_r=1&pagewanted =all (accessed April 27, 2012).

65. Cheryl Softich, interview with the author, February 2010.

66. Private letter from interviewee to the author, November 2010.

67. (Rabbi) Rav A. Soloff, "What to Say after a Soldier's Suicide," letter to the editor, *New York Times*, December 20, 2009.

CHAPTER 6: HEALTHCARE

1. Marguerite Guzmán Bouvard, *The Unpredictability of Light* (Cleveland, OH: Word Press, 2009), pp. 35–36.

2. Steven Reinberg, "Many Veterans Need Mental Health Care," *U.S. News and World Report*, July 6, 2011, pp. 11–13.

3. Amy Smee, interview with the author, April 2009.

4. Brook Kinna, interview with the author, May 2010.

5. Anonymous mother of a soldier, interview with the author, April 2010.

6. Patricia Alvarez Alviso, interview with the author, May 2011.

7. Aaron Glantz, "Suicides Highlight Failures of Veterans' Support System—VCS Lawsuit Discussed," *Veterans for Common Sense*, March 24, 2012, http://veterans for-commonsense.org/2012/03/24/suicides-highlight-failures-of-veterans-support -system-vcs-lawsuit-discussed/ (accessed April 27, 2012).

8. PBS, *Frontline*, "The Soldier's Heart," February 2005.

9. Paul Sullivan and Lauren Hohle, "More Than 425,000 Iraq and Afghanistan War Veterans Treated by VA—More Than 250 New Patients Every Day," *Veterans Today*, September 18, 2009, http://www.veteranstoday.com/2009/09/16/more-than-425-000-iraq-and-afghanistan-war-veterans-treated-by-va-more-than-250-new-patients-every-day/ (accessed April 27, 2012).

10. Linda Bilmes and Joseph Stiglitz, *The Three Trillion Dollar War: The Cost of the Iraq Conflict* (New York: W. W. Norton, 2008).

11. VCS Releases, "Iraq and Afghanistan War Impact Report," January 12, 2012, http://veteransforcommonsense.org/wp-content/uploads/2012/01/VCS_IAIR _JAN_2012.pdf (accessed April 27, 2012).

12. Ibid.

13. James Dao, "At Fort Hood, Reaching Out to Soldiers at Risk," *New York Times*, December 24, 2009, http://www.nytimes.com/2009/12/24/us/24hood-001.html ?pagewanted=all (accessed April 27, 2012).

14. Tim McGirk, "How One Army Town Copes with PTSD," *Time*, November 30, 2009, http://www.time.com/time/magazine/article/0,9171,1940694,00.html (accessed April 27, 2012).

15. "Burn Pits, " *Disabled American Veterans Magazine*, November/December 2010, pp. 14–18

16. Ibid.

17. Ibid.

18. Jan Goodwin, "Women's VA Health Care Falls Short: Female Vets Find the VA Health-care System Lacks the Resources and Initiative to Care for Women Returning from Duty," http://www.goodhousekeeping.com/health/va-healthcare-falls-short-4 (accessed February 24, 2011).

19. Jane Goodwin, "Women's VA Health Care Falls Short," *Good Housekeeping*, http://www.goodhousekeeping.com/health/womens-health/va-healthcare-falls-short?click=main_sr (accessed April 27, 2012).

20. Ibid.

21. Ibid.

22. Ibid.

23. Ibid.

24. Ibid.

25. Ashley Parker, "Lawsuit Says Military Is Rife with Sexual Abuse," *New York Times*, February 15, 2011, http://www.nytimes.com/2011/02/16/us/16military.html (accessed April 27, 2012).

26. Angela Buckley, interview with author, May and August 2011.

27. Ibid.

28. Ibid.

29. Sophie Buckley, letter to author, received November 1, 2011.

30. Michelle McCarthy, "Inadequate Care at Walter Reed," Iraq and Afghanistan Veterans of America, February 20, 2007, http://iava.org/print/3380 (accessed August 16, 2011).

31. Michelle McCarthy, "Walter Reed Fiasco Results in Positive Changes," March 30, 2007, Iraq and Afghanistan Veterans of America, http://iava.org/press-room/press-releases/walter-reed-fiasco-results-positive-changes (accessed April 27, 2012).

32. Public Relations, Massachusetts Child Psychiatry Access Project, July 14, 2011.

33. Ibid.

34. Kathy Clair-Hayes, interview with the author, November 2011.

35. Patricia Shinseki and Paula Rauch, "Serve Those Who Serve Us," *Boston Herald*, April 30, 2011.

36. Roger A. Knight IV, interview with the author, August 2011.

37. Ibid.

38. Christian Miller and Daniel Zwerdling, "Philanthropist, Not Pentagon, Bankrolls Promising TBI Therapy," *Stars and Stripes*, December 21, 2010, http://www.stripes.com/philanthropist-not-pentagon-bankrolls-promising-tbi-therapy-1.129456 (accessed April 27, 2012).

39. T. Christian Miller, Daniel Zwerdling, Susanne Reber, and Robin Fields, "Brain Wars: How the Military Is Failing Its Wounded," Dart Center for Journalism & Trauma, April 15, 2011, http://dartcenter.org/content/pentagon-told-congress-it%E2%80%99s-studying-brain-damage-therapy (accessed April 27, 2012).

40. Veterans Healing Initiative, http://www.vetshealing.org (accessed January 9, 2011).

41. Wounded Warrior Project, http://www.woundedwarriorproject.org (accessed June 2, 2011).

42. Jonathan Shay, *Odysseus in America: Combat Trauma and the Trials of Homecoming* (New York: Scribner, 2002), p. 31.

43. Ibid., p. 27.

44. Terri Tanielan, *RAND Review* 32, no. 2 (Summer 2008), http://www.rand.org/pubs/corporate_pubs/CP22-2008-08.html (accessed April 27, 2012).

45. "The Wounded Platoon," *Frontline*, PBS, May 18, 2010.

46. Ibid.

47. Ibid.

48. Ibid.

49. James Gandolfini (executive producer) and Jon Alpert and Ellen Goosenberg Kent (directors), *Wartorn 1861–2010* (2011) HBO documentary.

50. Anonymous mother of a soldier, interview with the author, May 2011.

51. Ronald D. Castille, "A Special Court for Veterans," Opinion Pages, *New York Times*, November 10, 2010, http://www.nytimes.com/2010/11/11/opinion/11 castille.html (accessed April 27, 2012).

52. Ibid.

53. Ibid.

54. John Schwartz, "Defendants Fresh from War Find Service Counts in Court," *New York Times*, March 15, 2010, http://www.nytimes.com/2010/03/16/us/16soldiers .html (accessed April 27, 2012).

CHAPTER 7: HIDDEN GRIEF

1. Brian Turner, *Here, Bullet* (London: Bloodaxe Books, 2007).

2. Andrew Malcom, "America's Newest Hero, Sgt. Dakota Meyer," *Los Angeles Times*, October 1, 2011, pp. 1–8.

3. Amy Smee, interview with the author, December 2011.

4. "Operation Proper Exit," *60 Minutes*, CBS News, November 6, 2011.

5. Angela Buckley, interview with the author, November 2011.

6. Cheryl Softich, interview with the author, May 2011.

7. Kevin Lucey, interview with the aurhor, May 2011.

8. Ibid.

9. Buckley, interview with the author, November 2011.

10. Ibid.

11. Timothy B. Kahlor, interview with the author, December 2011.

12. Ibid.

13. Ibid.

14. Angela Buckley, interview with the author, November 2011.

15. Ibid.

16. James Dao and Carrin Einhorm, "Families Bear the Brunt of Deployment Strains," *New York Times*, December 31, 2010.

17. Angela Buckley, interview with the author, November 2011.

18. Timothy B. Kahlor, interview with the author, December 2011.

19. Cheryl Softich, interview with the author, August 2011.

20. Ibid.

CHAPTER 8: BRIDGING THE CHASM

1. Jehanne Dubrow, *Stateside* (Evanston, IL: Northwestern University Press, 2010), p. 58.

2. Brian Turner, *Phantom Noise* (Farmington, ME: Alice James Books, 2010), p. 78.

3. Peter Dudar and Sally Marr (producers), *Arlington West* (Santa Monica, CA: Laughing Tears Productions, 2007), http://www.arlingtonwestfilm.com/.

4. Ibid.

5. Ibid.

6. Ibid.

7. James Estrin, "Home from Afghanistan to New Battles," *Lens* (blog), June 7, 2011, http://lens.blogs.nytimes.com/2011/06/07/home-from-afghanistan-to-new -battles/ (accessed July 11, 2011).

8. Ibid.

9. "A Life under Fire: Combat Photographer Captures, Carries Wounds of War," *PBS NewsHour*, October 27, 2011.

10. Ibid.

11. David Grene and Richmond Lattimore, eds., *Sophocles II* (Chicago, IL: University of Chicago Press, 1969).

12. Judith Broder, interview with the author, July 25, 2011.

13. Ibid.

14. Mike Tighe, "When Troops Come Home: Helping Them Shift from Combat to College," *Newsmax Independent American*, September 4, 2011, http://www.newsmax .com/US/Combat-college-troops-veterans/2011/09/04/id/ 409723 (accessed April 28, 2012).

15. Broder, interview.

16. Ibid.

17. Barbara Van Dahlen, interview with the author, November 7, 2011.

18. Ibid.

19. Ibid.

20. "Always Lost: A Meditation on War," Western Nevada College, May 28– August 14, 2009, http://www.wnc.edu/always_lost/ (accessed April 28, 2012).

21. Ibid.

22. Ibid.

23. Marilee Swirczek, interview with the author, June 2011.

24. Ibid.

25. Ibid.

26. Ibid.

EPILOGUE

1. Marilee Swirczek, interview with the author, June 2011.
2. Anonymous lieutenant colonel, interview with the author, April 2010.

BIBLIOGRAPHY

BOOKS AND ARTICLES

Baker, Aryn. "The Unwinnable War." *Time*, October 24, 2011.

Barfield, Thomas. *Afghanistan: A Cultural and Political History*. Princeton, NJ: Princeton University Press, 2010.

Bouvard, Marguerite Guzmán. *The Path through Grief: A Compassionate Guide*. Amherst, NY: Prometheus Books, 1998.

———. *Revolutionizing Motherhood: The Mothers of the Plaza De Mayo*. New York: Rowman & Littlefield, 1994.

———. *Women Reshaping Human Rights: How Extraordinary Activists Are Changing the World*. New York: Rowman & Littlefield, 1996.

"Burn Pits." *Disabled American Veterans Magazine*, November/December 2010, pp. 10–14.

Butler, Judith. *Frames of War: When Is Life Grievable?* New York: Verso, 2010.

Corbett, Sarah. "The Women's War." *New York Times Magazine*, 2007, pp. 14–17.

Danner, Mark. *Stripping Bare the Body: Politics, Violence, War*. New York: Nation Books, 2009.

Dubrow, Jehanne. *Stateside*. Evanston, IL: Northwestern University Press, 2009.

Filkins, Dexter. *The Forever War*. New York: Vintage Books, 2008.

Finkel, David. *The Good Soldiers*. New York: Farrar, Strauss & Giroux, 2009.

Franklin, E. "The Emerging Needs of Veterans: A Call to Action for the Social Work Profession." *Health & Social Work* (2009): 34.

Goodwin, Jan. "Women's VA Health Care Falls Short." *Good Housekeeping*, January 2011.

Grossman, David, with Lorin W. Christensen. *On Combat: The Psychology and Physiology of Deadly Conflict in War and Peace*. China: Warrior Science Publications, 2008.

Hamilton, S., S. Nelson Goff, J. R. Crow, and A. M. J. Reisbig. "Primary Trauma of Female Partners in a Military Sample: Individual Symptoms and Relationship Satisfaction." *American Journal of Family Therapy* (2009): 336–46.

Hammer, Joshua. "Prisoner of the Taliban." *New York Review of Books*, 2011, pp. 24–26.

Hanafin, Robert. "Military Spouse and Family Suicide Attempts Need Attention," *Veterans Today*, January 14, 2010.

Jones, Seth G. *In The Graveyard of Empires: America's War in Afghanistan*. New York: W. W. Norton, 2010.

Joya, Malalai. *A Woman among Warlords: The Extraordinary Story of an Afghan Who Dared to Raise Her Voice.* New York: Scribner, 2009.

Mansfield, Alyssa J., Jay S. Kaufman, Stephen W. Marshall, Bradley N. Gaynes, Joseph P. Morrissey, and Charles C. Engel. "Deployment and the Use of Mental Health Services among U.S. Army Wives." *New England Journal of Medicine* (2010): 101–105.

McGirk, T. "The War Comes Home." *Time International* (Atlantic Edition), 2009, pp. 163–67.

Meehan P. Shannon. *Beyond Duty: Life on the Frontline in Iraq.* Malden, MA: Polity Press, 2009.

Mortenson, Greg. *Stones into Schools.* New York: Viking, 2009.

Obituary. "Ghuam Haider Hamidi." *Economist,* 2011, p. 36.

Rashid, Ahmed. *Taliban: Militant Islam, Oil and Fundamentalism in Central Asia.* New Haven, CT: Yale University Press, 2010.

———. "The Way Out of Afghanistan." *New York Review of Books,* January 13, 2011, pp. 41–44.

Ray, S. L., and M. Vanstone. "The Impact of PTSD on Veterans' Family Relationships: An Interpretative Phenomenological Inquiry." *International Journal of Nursing Studies* (2009): 838–47.

Reinberg Steven. "Many Veterans Need Mental Health Care." *U. S. News and World Report,* July 6, 2011, pp. 11–13.

Rhode, David, and Kristin Mulvihill. *A Rope and a Prayer: A Kidnapping from Two Sides.* New York: Viking, 2009.

Shapiro, Bruce. "Casualties of War." *Nation,* January 10, 2008, pp. 7–9.

Shay, Jonathan. *Odysseus in America: Combat Trauma and the Trials of Homecoming.* New York: Scribner, 2002.

Softich, Cheryl, with Marguerite Guzmán Bouvard. *The Short and Noble Life of Noah Charles Pierce.* Waban, MA: In Publications, 2010.

Tamarov, Vladislav. *Afghanistan: Soviet Vietnam.* San Francisco, CA: Mercury House, 1992.

Thompson, Mark. "The Other 1%." *Time,* November 21, 2011, pp. 1–9.

Turner, Brian. *Here, Bullet.* London: Blooodaxe Books, 2005.

———. *Phantom Noise.* Farmington, ME: Alice James Books, 2010.

Twenge, Jean. *Generation Me: Why Today's Young Americans Are More Confident, Assertive, Entitled and More Miserable Than Ever Before.* New York: Free Press, 2007.

Wilborn, Thom. "Women Veterans Focus on Health Care, Service." *Disabled American Veterans Magazine,* November/December 2010, p. 5.

Zellman, Gail L., et al. "Options for Improving the Military Child Care System." Report prepared for the Office of the Secretary of Defense, RAND Corporation, 2008.

INTERVIEWS WITH THE AUTHOR

Anonymous grandmother, March 2009.
Anonymous lieutenant colonel, 2010.
Anonymous member of Veterans for Common Sense, August 2011.
Anonymous mother of veterans, April 2011.
Anonymous veteran, November 2011.
Anonymous veteran.
Patricia Alvarez Alviso, May 2011.
Cameron Baker, May 2010.
Jennifer Baldino, May 2011.
Anna Berlinrut, November 2011.
Judith Broder, July 2011.
Angela Buckley, May 2011, August 2011, November 2011.
Kathy Clair-Hayes, November 2011.
Leah Curran, March 2011.
Heather Demoines, June 2009.
Jehanne Dubrow, October 2009.
Patricia Hohl, December 2010.
Timothy B. Kahlor, May 2011, December 2011.
Brooke Kinna, May 2010.
Roger A. Knight IV, August 2011.
Adele Kubein, November 2011.
Nancy Lessin, May 2010.
Joyce and Kevin C. Lucey, May 2011.
Sara Rich, January 2011.
Amy Smee (in frequent contact).
Cheryl Softich (in frequent contact).
Marilee Swirczek (in frequent contact).
Barbara Van Dahlen, November 2011.

INDEX

Abbotabad, 34

Abu Ghraib, 44, 55, 63, 159, 172

Achilles, 58

Adopt a College, 201

Agent Orange, 157

Ajax (Sophocles), 198–99

Al Jazeera, 147

Al-Maliki, Nour Kamel, 18

al Qaeda, 20, 25–26, 28, 30, 33–35, 39,
    43–44, 212, 218
  in Iraq, 20
  in Mesopotamia, 39

al-Sadr, 20, 22, 38, 45

Alviso, Patricia Alvarez, 96, 155, 195,
    223, 229, 237

Always Lost: A Meditation on War
    (traveling art exhibit), 194, 204–206,
    208, 225, 232

American Friends Association, 146

American Psychiatric Foundation, 203

American Red Cross, 203

American Repertory Theater, 198–99

Amos, Marine Gen. James F., 127

AMVETS Club, 139

Anbar, 50, 212

Arbekais, 32

Armed Forces Health Surveillance
    Center, 103

Atlanta Braves, 169

At War (blog), 56, 193, 221, 224, 227

Aurakzai, Gen. Ali Muhammad Jan, 33

Baath Party, 19

Baghdad, 19

Baker, Cameron, 47, 52–57, 61, 220, 221,
    237

Balad Air Base, 157–158

Balboa Naval Hospital, 67

Baldino, Jennifer, 106, 110, 166, 216, 224,
    237

Baluchistan, 26

Barno, Lt. Gen. David, 28

Bean, Sgt. Coleman, 126

Beatrice Hawley award, 193

Bergner, Mary, 167

Berlinrut, Anna, 89, 216, 223, 237

Biden, Vice President Joseph, 29, 69

Bilmes, Prof. Linda, 156, 229

Blue Star Military Families. *See* BSMF.

Boxer, Sen. Barbara, 66, 68

Brave Heart, 169

Bremer, L. Paul, 19, 108, 215

Bristol-Meyers Squibb Foundation, 203

Broder, Dr. Judith, 191, 199–202, 209,
    232, 237

Bronze Star, 168, 182

BSMF (Blue Star Military Families), 203

Buckley, Angela, 101, 103, 121, 132, 160,
    162–64, 166, 182, 184, 186–87, 188,
    224, 225, 230–31, 237

Buckley, Sophie, 121, 166, 188, 230

Bunker Hill College, 169

Bureau of Justice Statistics, 175

burn pits, 157–58

Burns, Kevin, 205, 207, 209, 211

Bush, President George W., 18, 25–26,
    28, 33, 45, 91, 96–97, 105, 108–109

Camp Otaberry, 154

Carlson, Prof. Don, 204

Carson Nugget Foundation, 209

Casualty Affairs Office, 161

Central Intelligence Agency. *See* CIA.
Chandler, Air Force Gen. Carrol H., 127
Charbaran Valley, 43
Chechnya, 27, 211
Chiarelli, Army Gen. Peter W., 127
CIA (Central Intelligence Agency), 34, 41
CIAV (Coalition for Iraq and Afghanistan Veterans), 158
Clair-Hayes, Kathy, 166, 230, 237
Clinton, Sec. of State Hillary, 29, 68
Coalition for Iraq and Afghanistan Veterans. *See* CIAV
Community Blueprint, 203, 204
Community First, 209
Cone, Lt. Gen. Robert W., 157
Cornford, Steven, 182
Crawford, Texas, 96
Curran, Leah, 115, 224, 237
Curtis, Col. Darrin, 157
Cutts, Robert L., 206, 207

Dari, 27, 28
de-Baathification policy, 38
Democracy Now! (radio program), 146–47, 227–28
Demoines, Heather, 52, 55–56, 62–63, 221–22, 237
Der Spiegel (newspaper), 90
Dirty War (Argentina), 84
Disabled American Veterans, 158, 203, 221, 229, 235, 236
Diyala, 20
Domingo, Lance Corp. Nathan, 172
Dubai, 27
Dubrow, Jehanne, 102, 106, 109, 192, 194, 196, 224, 232, 235, 237

EFPs. *See* explosively formed penetrators

Eikenberry, Gen. Karl, 28
embedded news reporters, 45
Emory University, 169
Ensler, Eve, 89
explosively formed penetrators (EFPs), 23, 50, 128, 211
Eyes Wide Open Movement, 146–47

Fallujah, 19, 70, 89–90
Family Readiness Group, 115
FATA. *See* Federally Administered Tribal Areas
Fedayeen Saddam, 19
Federally Administered Tribal Areas (FATA), 26
Feinstein, Sen. Diane, 66
Female Engagement Team, 202
Filner, Rep. Bob, 202
Finkel, David, 202
1st Armored Division, 67
Flowers of Flame (book by Iraqi poets), 194
Folkrod, Patricia, 146–47, 193
Fort Benning, 21
Fort Bragg, 130
Fort Carson, 128, 171
Fort Dix, 111
Fort Drum, 116, 196
Fort Hood, 130, 132, 156, 229
Fort Irwin, 67, 88
Fort Lewis, 87
Fort Sill, 21
Fort Stewart, 80
Foundation for Suicide Prevention, 148
Freedom of Information Act, 156
Frontline (television documentary program), 51, 136, 215, 220, 221, 228, 229, 230, 236

Gates, Sec. of Defense Robert M., 21, 29, 30, 62, 160, 221, 222

Ghaemi, Dr. Nassir, 125, 225
Gold Star Families Speak Out (GSFSO), 70
Gold Star Mothers Speak Out (GSMSO), 75
Gold Star Wives, 203
Goodman, Amy, 146, 226
Greenert, Navy Adm., 127
Green Zone, 23, 102, 124
Grossman, Lt. Col. Dave, 52, 230, 235
Ground Truth (documentary), 146–47, 193
GSFO. *See* Gold Star Families Speak Out
GSMO. *See* Gold Star Mothers Speak Out

Habitat for Humanity, 204
Hamidi, Ghulam Haider, 41–42, 219, 236
Hanbali school, 25
Happy New Year (film), 193
Haqqani, Jalaluddin, 33
Haqqani, Ynuis Khais, 26
Haqqani, 26, 33, 41–43, 216
Hasan, Major Nidal Malik, 156
Hazaras, 31
HBIEDs (house-borne IEDs), 23, 211
Helmand, 37, 90, 168, 170
Herbert, Bob, 126, 226
Hidden Wounds (documentary), 147, 190, 193, 202
Hikmetyar, Gulbuddin, 31
Hohl, Alexander, 18
Hohl, Patricia, 76, 222, 237
Holt, Rep. Rush, 126
Holyoke Community College, 140
Home Base, 8, 165–70, 192
Homecoming Project, 196
house-borne IEDs. *See* HBIEDs
Hurt Locker (film), 58

Hussein, Saddam, 18–20, 22, 39, 131, 172
Huze, Sean, 199, 202

IAVA (Iraq and Afghanistan Veterans of America), 158
IEDs (improvised explosive devices), 21, 23, 28–31, 35–37, 43, 45, 50, 54–56, 63–64, 67, 89, 116, 128, 136, 173, 196–97, 211
Iliad (Homer), 58
improvised explosive devices. *See* IEDs
Individual Ready Reserve *See* IRR
Inter-Services Intelligence. *See* ISI
Into the Fire: Voices of Veterans and Their Families (Robert Puett), 202
Iraq and Afghanistan Veterans of America. *See* IAVA
IRR (Individual Ready Reserve), 91–92, 125
ISI (Inter-Services Intelligence), 26–27, 33–35, 42, 217, 218
Islamabad, 34, 218

JAM (Jaysh-al-Mahdi), 19–20, 36
James Irvine Foundation, 201
Jaysh-al-Mahdi. *See* JAM
JCS (Joint Chiefs of Staff), 36, 40, 42, 130, 162–63
Joint Chiefs of Staff. *See* JCS
Jones, Rep. Walter, 127
Joya, Malalai, 31, 216, 236

Kabul, 24–25, 27–28, 30, 36, 40–41, 43, 90, 156, 170, 219
Kahlor, Ryan, 65–69, 183, 185
Kahlor, Timothy B., 65–68, 177, 183, 185–86, 189, 222, 231, 237
Kandahar, 26–27, 41–42, 56, 217, 219
Karbala, 86
Karzai, Ahmid Wali, 41–42

Karzai, President Hamid, 26, 28, 30, 37, 41, 45
Kashmir, 33
Kayani, Gen. Ashfaq, 33–34, 217–18
Keene, Ret. Gen. Jack, 42
Keesling, Chance, 133
Kennedy, Sen. Ted, 163, 165
Kinna, Brooke, 107–109, 154–55, 224, 228–29, 237
Kirghiz, 27
Knight, Roger, 168–69
Kubein, Adele, 92, 223, 237
Kunduz, 32
Kunduz City, 32
Kurds, 18
Kuwait, 80, 85, 113

Laden, Osama bin, 25, 27, 34–35, 42–43, 217
Lashkar-e-Taiba, 33, 43, 212, 217
Lee, Rep. Barbara, 127
Lehrer, Jim, 193
Lessin, Nancy, 69, 146–47, 222, 237
Little League, 208
Logar, 40
Lucey, Debbie, 147
Lucey, Jeff, 8, 164, 228
Lucey, Joyce, 190, 228
Lucey, Kelley, 190
Lucey, Kevin, 149, 151, 183, 228, 231, 237
Luceys, 141, 143, 145–49, 189

madrassas, 24, 27
Malone House, 160–61
MANPADS (man-portable air defense systems), 26
Man-portable air defense systems. See MANPADS
Massachusetts National Guard, 11, 111, 167

Mazar-e-Sharif, 25
McCain, Sen. John, 98
meal ready to eat. See MREs
Meehan, Shannon, 19, 22, 44, 125, 215, 220, 225, 236
Meyer, Corp. Dakota, 180, 231
MFSO (Military Families Speak Out), 11, 69–70, 75, 94, 96, 102, 127, 146–47, 189, 192
milblogging.com, 104
Military Child Education Coalition, 167
Military Families Speak Out. See MFSO
Military Photographer of the Year Award, 197
Military Sexual Trauma. See MST
Military Spouses for Change, 130
Miller, Pfc. Bruce, 133–34.
milspouse.com, 104
Milspouse Mutterings (blog), 131
Mohammed (Prophet), 24
Montclair Art Museum, 197
Montgomery, Staff Sgt. Thad, 132
Mortenson, Greg, 36, 218, 236
Mothers of East Los Angeles, 84, 99
Mothers of the Plaza de Mayo, 2, 84, 99, 223
MREs (meal ready to eat), 89, 107
MST (military sexual trauma), 159, 213
Mujahideen, 24, 32
Mujahadin-e Khaliq (MEK), 20
Mullen, Deborah, 130
Mullen, Ret. Adm. Mike, 36, 40, 42–43, 130, 162, 219
Muqtada al-Sadr, 38
Murray, Sen. Patty, 87
Musharraf, President Pervez, 25

Najibullah, President Mohammad, 24
National Military Families Association, 203

National Museum of American History, 209

National Press Photographers Association, 197

National Veterans Legal Services, 203

NATO (North Atlantic Treaty Organization), 40–41, 168, 212, 217

Navy SEAL, 40, 43

Needs, 184

New York State Health Foundation, 174

New York State Supreme Court, 174

nonmedical attendants, 161

Noor, Gen. Atta Muhammad, 31

North Atlantic Treaty Organization. *See* NATO

Northern Alliance, 25–26

Not Alone (blog), 60

Obama, Michelle, 68

Obama, President Barack, 28–29, 33–35, 37, 39, 40, 77, 91, 96, 126, 180–81, 216, 218, 227

Odysseus, 57, 194, 220–21, 230, 236

OEF (Operation Enduring Freedom), 15, 17, 25, 149, 167, 192, 212

OIF (Operation Iraqi Freedom), 15, 17, 147, 169, 192, 212

Omar, Mullah Muhammad, 27, 33, 35

101st Airborne Division, 26

O'Neill, Prof. Kathleen, 11, 169

Operation Enduring Freedom. *See* OEF

Operation Homefront, 203

Operation House Call, 70

Operation Iraqi Freedom. *See* OIF

Operation Purple, 122

Opinionater (blog), 193

Oxfam, 32

Paktika, 43

Palin, Gov. Sarah, 69, 98

Pasha, Lt. Gen. Ahmed Shuha, 34

Pashto, 27–28

Pashtuns, 24, 26, 31–32

Patriot missiles, 21

Paul, Rep. Ron, 127

PBS NewsHour (television program), 156, 219, 232

Pearsall, Sgt. Stacy, 15, 197

Pelosi, Rep. Nancy, 98

Persian Gulf, 27, 35

Petraeus, Gen. David, 32, 37, 40

Phantom Noise (Brian Turner), 194, 232, 236

Philoctetes (Sophocles), 198

Picard, Carissa, 130

Pierce, Noah Charles, 7, 18, 82, 123, 134, 206–207, 225, 228, 236

Pierce, Noah Charles (AMVETS post), 139

Points of Light (website), 203

Politico, 126, 225, 226

post-traumatic stress disorder. *See* PTSD

PTSD (post-traumatic stress disorder), 51–53, 55, 57, 61, 63–65, 67, 70–71, 78, 82–83, 86–89, 91, 93, 99, 103–104, 109, 112, 115, 117, 119, 125–26, 132, 134, 136, 139, 141–44, 146–49, 154–59, 161, 163–65, 167–70, 172, 174, 180, 185, 187, 189–90, 195–96, 201, 213, 224, 229, 236

Purpose Prize, 201

Quetta, 27

Rabbani, Burhanuddin, 24, 42

RAND Corporation, 55, 122, 136, 171, 216, 221, 225, 230, 236

Rashid, Ahmed, 26, 41, 216–17, 219, 236

Rauch, Dr. Paula, 166, 230

Red Sox, 144, 165

Red Sox Foundation, 165, 168
Reinhardt, Judge Stephen Roy, 129
Return to Iraq, 182
Rich, Sara, 73, 84–89, 223, 237
Richardson, Charlie, 69, 146
Richardson, Rep. Laura, 98
Robert H. Johnson VA Medical Center, 197
Robert R. McCormick Foundation, 169
Rocket-propelled grenade. See RPGs
RPGs (Rocket-propelled grenade), 16, 23, 26, 37, 41, 128, 181
Ruddick, Sarah, 76, 78, 222
Rumsfeld, Sec. of Defense Donald, 160

Sadr City, 19, 22, 54–55
Sakharov Prize, 31
Sanchez, Loretta, 97
San Diego, 62, 67, 98, 169
Sandstorm: Stories from the Front, The (Sean Huze)
Sangin Valley, 168
SAPRO (Sexual Assault Prevention and Response Office), 159
Saudi Arabia, 25, 27, 30, 43, 211
Schwarzenegger, Gov. Arnold, 98
Schweinfurt, Germany, 130
Senft, Staff Sgt. David, 132
Sexual Assault Prevention and Response Office. See SAPRO
Sharia law, 24, 31, 216
Shay, Dr. Jonathan, 60, 171, 202, 220, 221, 230, 236
Sheehan, Cindy, 96–97
Shepherd Center for Brain and Spinal Cord Injury, 170
Shiites, 39, 54, 108
Shinedown
    "45" (song), 142, 143, 146
Shura, 43

Smart Funders, 204
Smee, Amy, 5, 50, 53, 62, 154, 158, 181–82, 220, 221, 228, 231, 237
Smithsonian Institution, 209
Softich, Cheryl, 79–83, 123, 126–27, 134–39, 148–50, 183, 189, 207, 223, 228, 231, 236, 237
"Soldier's Heart, The," 147, 155–56, 193, 215, 220, 228, 229
Sophocles, 198–99, 232
Spaulding Centers, 164
Special Operations Forces, 19, 26, 38
Special Republican Guard, 19
spousebuzz.com, 104
Stand Down, 62, 222
Stein, Gertrude, 205
Stiglitz, Prof. Joseph, 156, 229
stop loss, 57, 154
Strong Bonds weekend, 114, 167
Sunna, 24
Sunnis, 18
Swirczek, Prof. Marilee, 11, 205–206, 208–11, 232, 233, 237

Tajikistan, 27, 30
Tajiks, 31
Takhar, 32, 40
Taliban, 27–37, 40–43, 212, 216, 217, 218, 219, 235, 236
Taliban Movement of Pakistan, 33
Tangi Valley, 45
TBI (traumatic brain injury), 55, 67, 99, 103, 116, 127, 161, 164–65, 167, 169, 180, 185, 200, 201, 202, 230
10th Mountain Division, 26, 196
Theater of War, 198
Third Platoon, 506th Infantry Division, First Battalion, Charlie Company, 51
Those Eyes (photo display), 207

traumatic brain injury. *See* TBI
Tricare, 116, 170, 213
Trieb, Erin, 196
Trudeau, Gary, 89
Turkomen, 27
Turner, Brian, 17, 19, 49, 57, 74, 133–34, 178, 193–94, 215, 220, 222, 227, 231, 232, 236

Unlikely Wife (blog), 131
US Court of Appeals for the Ninth Circuit, 129, 155
US Supreme Court, 175
Uzbekistan, 27, 211
Uzbeks, 24–25, 27

VA (Dept. of Veteran Affairs), 48, 86, 88, 93, 115–16, 120, 126, 129, 133, 136, 141–45, 148, 154–56, 158–60, 164–65, 178, 197, 200, 203, 204, 221, 223, 225, 226, 229, 235
Van Dahlen, Dr. Barbara, 203, 204, 232, 237
VCS (Veterans for Common Sense), 70, 127, 129, 155–56, 163, 192, 203, 225, 229, 237
Veterans Advantage, 203
Veterans Affairs, Department of. *See* VA
Veterans' Court, 174, 231

Veterans Education Project, 146–47
Veterans for Common Sense. *See* VCS
Veterans for Peace, 70, 84, 146, 173, 192, 194
Veterans Healing Initiative. *See* VHI
Veterans Initiative, 62
Veterans United for Truth, 129, 155, 158
Vets 4 Vets, 203
VHI (Veterans Healing Initiative), 170, 230
view time, 162

Walmart, 53, 203
Walter Reed Army Medical Center, 8, 118–21, 160–66, 182, 187–88, 230
Wardak, 40, 45
Warrior Transition Battalions, 128
Wartorn 1861–2010 (documentary), 83, 139, 172, 180, 193, 222, 227, 231
Waziristan, 30
Weekend America, 193
West Point, 194
Whiteside, Lt. Elizabeth, 132
WikiLeaks, 30
Wounded Platoon, The (documentary), 193, 220, 221, 230
Wounded Warrior Project, 120, 230
Wounded Warriors, 171